DATE			

Balance and Refinement

Balance and Refinement
Beyond coherence methods of
moral inquiry

Michael R. DePaul

London and New York

First published 1993
by Routledge
11 New Fetter Lane, London EC4P 4EE

Simultaneously published in the USA and Canada
by Routledge
29 West 35th Street, New York, NY 10001

© 1993 Michael R. DePaul

Typeset by Computerset, Harmondsworth, Middlesex
Printed in Great Britain by TJ Press (Padstow) Ltd, Padstow,
Cornwall

British Library Cataloguing in Publication Data
A catalogue record for this book is available from the British
Library.

Library of Congress Cataloging in Publication Data
DePaul, Michael R. (Michael Raymond),
    Balance and refinement : beyond coherence methods of
    moral inquiry / Michael R. DePaul.
        p. cm.
    Includes bibliographical references and index.
    1. Ethics, Modern–20th century.   I. Title.
    BJ319.D47   1993
170'.42–dc20

ISBN 0-415-04220-8

To Sherrie

Contents

Preface

It is clear what one does in a preface: say something about the content of the book and what motivated you to write it, then thank all the people who helped you complete it. I am eager to do all this, and in particular, to thank the various people who helped me. But there is a problem. Perhaps I am a little quirky about this, but prefaces often seem to me to take on a sort of triumphant, self-congratulatory tone. The last thing I want to do is write a preface with such a tone. For the clearest consequence of my work on this book is that all the weaknesses in the position I want to take, and especially in my presentation of it, have come to stand out in sharp relief for me. I have not, as a result, come to doubt the position I advocate. I'm as committed to it as ever. I even continue to think that what I want to say is important. But I understand my own limitations somewhat better, and I can see their effects in this work all too clearly. So I intend no kind of self-congratulation here, unless it is for the stubbornness that was required to finish this project.

Turning now to the content of the book, I am concerned with a question that is out of fashion and, according to some, is deeply problematic. But there is no apologizing for it – I want to ask a question from a first-person, egocentric point of view! I find myself holding moral beliefs, and making all sorts of moral judgments. Particularly when combined with various epistemological, metaphysical, and quasi-scientific views I either hold, or find tempting, or find widely held among my contemporaries, these judgments begin to look rather motley, and even shabby. What am I to do about this? Since I don't think there is any difference between philosophy and carefully trying to think my way through something, I look to discussions of moral methodology to find possible answers to my question. But all the approaches I find seem to suffer from at least one of the following faults. They work with too narrow and intellectual a conception of rationality. They assume that a rational method of inquiry can, and must, guarantee us knowledge or truth. They presuppose that, being rational, moral inquiry ought to look like scientific inquiry. Or failing on one of these counts, they cast morality out from the realm of facts altogether. What I aim to do in this book is to articulate and defend an approach to answering my egocentric question. I will propose a method of moral inquiry that is *appropriately* rational, but that avoids any sort of scientism or overintellectualization, and does not exile morality from the realm of facts. Moral inquiry, as I propose to conduct it, will look rather different from the sort of philosophical inquiry to which we are accustomed. On my view, radical moral conversions are possible, and inquirers must be concerned to avoid naïveté, which results from too little experience, and corruption, which results from the wrong sort of experience. Moreover, as I conceive of rational moral inquiry, morally significant experience, both first-hand life experience, and experience with literature, theater, film, music, and art has a significant role to play.

Since my view recognizes various things that are neither philosophical nor even intellectual, in any usual sense, as playing a rationally significant role in philosophical inquiry, some of what I take to be my *real* philosophical debts are somewhat unusual. I also recognize philosophical debts of the more usual sort, but I'll begin with the unusual ones. If Aristotle is right, as I think he is, to say that one must be well brought up to engage in moral inquiry, the first of these debts I ought to acknowledge is to my parents, and then to a grandmother who lived with us. For if I have ample starting points, or find them easy to get, it is their doing. I should also mention, in this connection, my brother. As children, we argued endlessly about politics, and many other matters. All these discussions surely continue to influence my thinking in ways I could now never hope to discover.

If my upbringing had an effect on my prospects for profitably engaging in moral inquiry, then the character of my daily life must have an even more profound effect. I must, therefore, acknowledge my wife, Sherrie, and all the creatures, horses, cats, and dog, with whom we live. If we didn't all live as we do, I wouldn't think what I do. I'll mention only three features of the way we live. My philosophical outlook would be different if I did not start every day doing chores in the barn with Sherrie. It would also be different if I could not spend time watching her train wonderful horses like Max and Moritz. And the expression of my outlook in this book would surely have been different if I had not written so much of it with Merle the cat on my lap, and our yellow dog on the floor.

Moving on to the more common sort of acknowledgments, I might begin with economic matters. Work on this book was supported by the National Endowment for the Humanities, with a year-long Fellowship for University Teachers beginning in June, 1989, and by the Institute for

Scholarship in the Liberal Arts and the Jesse H. Jones Faculty Research Fund, both at the University of Notre Dame, in the Summers of 1988 and 1987, respectively.

Three journals allowed me to use portions of articles that they published. Material from "Two Conceptions of Coherence Methods in Ethics," *Mind*, 96 (October, 1987) appears in Chapter 1, Sections 6 and 7. And a great deal of the material in Chapters 4 and 5 was published in two articles, "Argument and Perception: The Role of Literature in Moral Inquiry," *Journal of Philosophy*, 85 (October, 1988) and "Naivete and Corruption in Moral Inquiry," *Philosophy and Phenomenological Research*, 48 (June, 1988).

I should begin acknowledging individuals by mentioning a few of my teachers. Some of them have surely affected the particulars of this book in various ways, especially since my dissertation is some sort of distant ancestor of it. But I would hope that their most significant influence has been on my more general philosophical approach, for in different ways, it is their philosophical style that I most admire. So let me acknowledge deep debts to R. M. Chisholm, George Pappas, William Lycan, Ken Sayre and especially Dan Brock, Phil Quinn (who I'll have to mention again below), and Ernest Sosa.

A number of philosophers read all or part of various versions of this book. I have not made it a practice to credit them in the text, but I hope they will be able to see where I have benefitted from their comments and criticisms. I'm grateful to all the following: Bob Audi, Marian David, Mic Detlefsen, Aron Edidin, Alasdair MacIntyre, Trenton Merricks, Bill Ramsey, David Solomon, Matthias Steup, Leopold Stubenberg, Mark Timmons, Bill Tolhurst, Eleonore Stump, Charles Taliaferro, and Peter Vallentyne.

A few people deserve special mention. Richard Fumerton did a terrific job reviewing the text for the press. He raised a number of tough questions, and thinking about them has helped me to understand my position better. Paul Weithman deserves special thanks for dropping his own projects and reading the typescript through just before I submitted it. Phil Quinn provided the quickest imaginable feedback, first on individual chapters, and then on the whole typescript. He always manages to raise the objections that seem most worrying from my own perspective. My deepest debts are to Al Plantinga and especially Richard Foley. Richard commented on the individual chapters as I completed drafts, and Al commented on the penultimate draft of the whole book. But I have a more general philosophical debt to them. Along with Aron Edidin, they formed the core of a working epistemology group at Notre Dame, until Aron, and then Richard, moved on to positions elsewhere. I learned more than I can say about epistemology and collegiality by taking part in the discussions of this group. Finally, I need to thank my wife once more, this time for checking my typescript for errors, making suggestions about how to say things better, and even a few philosophical comments. Mark Murphy deserves credit for constructing the index. And I should finally thank Richard Stoneman, Heather McCallum, Virginia Myers and Pauline Marsh from Routledge. They have made the final stages of my work on this book as easy as I can imagine them being.

Introduction

Nearly all of us would say that we think that certain things are good while others are not, that some actions are right and others wrong, that some people are vicious while others are virtuous. Although any very precise stand regarding the nature of the particular moral attitude[1] being reported here will be controversial, I find that, in my own case, I cannot distinguish this attitude from belief. When I read about a chemical company dumping its toxic wastes out in a pasture and think that this is wrong, it seems to me that I can identify a statement or proposition that I have in mind, or at least, that I can do so as well as I can in the case of many empirical beliefs, e.g., my belief that we do not float out into space because of gravity. My attitude of acceptance towards moral propositions feels like the attitude I take towards the other propositions I believe.[2] One significant similarity between my attitudes in the two cases emerges when I compare my moral "beliefs" with one another. What I find is that my attitude of acceptance is stronger towards some moral propositions than towards others, just as, e.g., my beliefs about what is on my desk are stronger than are my beliefs about what is in my attic.[3] Finally, my moral "beliefs" do not stand alone, but seem to stand in logical and evidential relations both with each other and with my non-moral beliefs. At least in part as a result of these relations, it apparently makes sense to ask questions about the epistemic status of moral attitudes, just as it makes sense to ask whether other beliefs are rational, warranted, or what have you. Thus, I ask myself whether my moral "beliefs" are rational or justified, search for reasons in support of some of my moral judgments, and decide that the reasons I have for others are no good. In short, I try to do all I can to insure that my moral "beliefs" are in good epistemic order in just the way I try to keep my other beliefs tidy. It is clear that this endeavor makes perfectly good sense. For my purposes, these similarities are sufficient to justify taking the moral attitudes I have been talking about to be beliefs in the ordinary sense of the term, even though some philosophers are sure to think me naïve.

So my starting point is that we each have moral beliefs, indeed, quite a large number of moral beliefs. Simply having these beliefs is not the end of the matter. Just as it is natural to have further questions when we have beliefs about other matters, it is natural to ask further questions about the moral realm. Thus, for example, believing various apparently dissimilar actions to be wrong, I wish to find out whether these wrong actions have something else in common, or, more generally, I wonder what, if anything, makes actions wrong. Unlike the questions we ask about some other things, questions about the moral realm are often motivated by more than curiosity. For one thing, we sometimes rely upon our moral beliefs to guide our actions, and characteristically, those of our actions that we see as specially significant. And it seems plausible to suppose that knowing what makes right actions right, or good things good, will help us to tell more easily what we should do in actual practice. In addition, many of us find that our moral beliefs are not in terribly good order: There are tensions, and often conflicts among them. The situation only seems worse when we consider the connections between our moral beliefs and other beliefs we hold, e.g., beliefs in sociological or psychological explanations of our moral beliefs. To sum up, although moral beliefs are especially significant for many of us, they do not go far enough, while still managing to get into trouble going only as far as they do.

What is to be done about all this? How should one try to resolve the tensions and conflicts involving her moral beliefs? How should one go about trying to answer her questions about morality? In short, what sort of method of moral inquiry should we employ? These are the questions I am out to answer in this book.

Oddly enough, until recently, the dominant view of "analytic" philosophy has been that in trying to construct a systematic moral view,[4] we should ignore nearly all of the very moral beliefs that led us to formulate questions about morality in the first place. The most common approach has been to select some type of belief, perhaps a theory of practical reason, or maybe even some particular type of moral belief, e.g., some highly abstract, pseudo-logical principle about right and wrong, obligation, or intrinsic value, and from this basis, derive first a moral theory, and subsequently more particular moral judgments. Philosophers tyrannized over ordinary moral beliefs, holding them guilty until proven innocent. These beliefs were not taken to have any legitimate role in the effort to provide serious, systematic answers to questions about morality. The idea was to work up from the logic or meaning of moral terms (as though one would have any chance of discovering this logic or meaning while ignoring all the more particular things one believes about how to behave and what things are valuable). Or wilder still, it has been thought that a person should jettison all the things she now believes about morality and, with a clear view of the ultimate aim of morality, adopt new principles that will attain this aim much better than anything limited by the sorry hodgepodge of things she has believed about right, wrong, virtue, vice, good, bad, and so on up until now.

These strategies for moral inquiry have obvious affinities with foundationalism. They seek to justify our moral beliefs by showing that they can be grounded on a firm foundation, often a foundation that lies in some area outside of ethics. I do not believe that such foundationalist strategies have fared well. They either succeed in locating a firm foundation, only to find that it is too narrow to construct much of a moral theory on its basis, or they begin with a broad enough foundation to support an interesting moral theory, but parts of the foundation prove to be no more secure than the moral theory they are intended to support.

Fortunately, the recent trend among moral philosophers has been to respect our ordinary moral beliefs. In particular, the coherentists, e.g., advocates of the method of reflective equilibrium, argue that there is no privileged type of proposition upon which the construction of moral theories must be based, and that the theorist is entitled to allow, and indeed must allow, almost all of the moral propositions she believes a role in the process of theory construction. Thus, the inquirer should not begin, as some foundationalists would have it, by throwing out her moral beliefs, and then attempt to win back a moral theory from some secure base of operations. Rather, the inquirer must use her initial moral beliefs, along with her other beliefs, as she tries to develop a moral theory. Her task is to mold her moral, philosophical, and empirical beliefs into a coherent system. The theorist is to accomplish this task by (i) investigating the logical and evidential relations among the things she believes, and revising beliefs where the investigation uncovers a conflict, (ii) considering the various alternative moral theories that have been formulated by others as well as the philosophical arguments that have been offered regarding these theories, and (iii) attempting to formulate a systematic moral theory that nicely accounts for her moral beliefs, coheres well with her background philosophical and scientific beliefs, has independent intuitive appeal, and can stand up through the consideration of alternatives.

The growing acceptance of coherence methods has not diminished the motivation behind the foundational approaches, nor, indeed, have the foundationalists quit the field. Foundationalists desire to attain the kind of certainty, or at least confidence, for our moral beliefs that we have in other less contentious areas of inquiry. They do not see how a coherence method could possibly satisfy this desire, and have criticized coherentism accordingly. Critics demand that the reliability of the method be established, confident that this demand cannot be met. For as they see it, coherentism only systematizes, and thus adds an air of respectability to, moral prejudices that are the products of class biases or the remnants of outmoded religious superstitions and taboos.

It would seem, therefore, that we face a familiar dilemma. There are procedures we could follow in attempting to construct a moral theory that we know to be reliable, such as giving deductive arguments based on definitions of moral terms, but if we correctly follow these procedures, we will not be able to make any significant headway. On the other hand, there are procedures that will probably lead us to an interesting moral theory, e.g., the Rawlsian method of wide reflective equilibrium,[5] but the reliability of these procedures has not been, and probably cannot be, established. This dilemma is familiar not only in virtue of its similarity to the dilemma which foundered foundationalist approaches. It is familiar because it arises in connection with nearly every type of philosophical inquiry, whether it be an inquiry into morality, other evaluative realms such as epistemology and aesthetics, or such a non-evaluative area as metaphysics. Finding a satisfactory solution to the dilemma is, therefore, of the utmost importance, not only for the purposes of the moral theorist, but also so that we might have a paradigm to use in seeking ways of dealing with the similar dilemmas that arise in other areas of philosophy. So, identifying an adequate moral methodology is important not only because it is a fundamental problem in ethical theory, but because it is a particular instance of a general problem concerning philosophical method. My hope is that if I can make progress towards solving one manifestation of the problem, this will provide significant help in solving the problem as it arises elsewhere.

Philosophers currently trying to develop an adequate moral methodology have run into this dilemma largely because they have failed to appreciate fully the diversity of the concepts of epistemic evaluation we employ. One consequence of this failure is that expectations about what a method of inquiry can provide, indeed, about what we should require of any acceptable method, are impossibly high. No method within the broad coherentist camp can be shown to be reliable in the sense that everyone who employs the method will be rewarded with moral knowledge. But contrary to the suggestion of the dilemma's second horn, this fact does not entail that coherence methods are inadequate. With the possible exceptions of mathematics and logic, methods of inquiry into other areas of inquiry cannot guarantee truth and knowledge to all inquirers.

The second consequence of the failure to appreciate the diversity of epistemic concepts is a failure to appreciate the complexity of the epistemic goals we seek in moral inquiry. Given the way they focus on whether a method can guarantee truth, discussions of moral inquiry must presuppose either that the only thing we seek in moral inquiry is the truth, or that all the epistemic goals we seek in moral inquiry are somehow resolvable into truth or some sort of truth-conduciveness. But this presupposition is false. For a start, we must distinguish between *rational* belief and *warranted* belief. To say that a belief is rational is to say that the believer has done all that she can, as determined from her own point of view, to insure that the belief is true. Rationality is, therefore, a more subjective epistemological notion, its application being determined largely, if not entirely, by features *internal* to the believer. Warrant is a more objective or *external* concept, most easily identified by noting its connection with knowledge: Warrant is the positive epistemic status that plays the central part in distinguishing knowledge from mere true belief.

Even given only this rough characterization of these two concepts, it is easy enough to see that one, rationality, is strongly internalist, while the other, warrant, is not. I maintain that an important fact follows – the two can come apart. An agent can in good (epistemic) faith do all that he can see that he should to insure the (epistemic) quality of his beliefs, thereby winning for himself rational beliefs, while still failing to attain the sorts of beliefs that have what it takes epistemically for knowledge, that is, warranted beliefs. To convince ourselves of this possibility we might think of Mr Magoo.[6] He constructs a "picture" of the world around him on the basis of his visual experience. His picture is wildly mistaken, but in a way that always seems to allow for things to work out in the end. He thereby avoids any confrontation with disconfirming experience. It seems to me that Magoo's beliefs about his environment would be rational, but they would not be warranted. As I said, the two can come apart.

How is what I've said about rationality and warrant relevant to moral inquiry? The first thing to see is that we want our moral beliefs to be *both* warranted and rational. In so far as we are engaged in a philosophical inquiry we want our inquiry to proceed in a rational way and lead us to beliefs we can rationally accept. No acceptable method for such an inquiry can direct persons to go about forming or amending beliefs in ways they would consider epistemically objectionable on careful reflection. And of course we want the inquiry to yield warranted beliefs as well. True opinion about right and good might be perfectly acceptable for living, but philosophical inquiry seeks to attain moral knowledge, and this requires warrant. The second thing to note is that warrant and rationality can come apart for one engaged in moral inquiry just as they do for Mr Magoo. An inquirer can do everything that he sincerely thinks he should to insure the epistemic quality of his moral beliefs, and yet these beliefs might not only fail to be true, but they might fail to satisfy the sorts of objective, external standards that a belief must satisfy in order to have the epistemic status required for knowledge.

Given that we seek a number of distinct and independent values when we pursue moral inquiry, i.e., at least, true, rational, and warranted beliefs, the assessment of methods of inquiry cannot focus exclusively on any one of these values. For it may be that we will find a method of inquiry acceptable, even if it cannot guarantee us one of the values we seek. To be more specific, I intend to show that one method of inquiry, the *method of balance and refinement*, which is an extrapolation from traditional coherence methods, can do enough to be considered adequate, while still falling short of guaranteeing true moral beliefs, and hence, moral knowledge, to every inquirer. The first element of my strategy for defending the method of balance and refinement is an argument that this method can guarantee rational beliefs, indeed, that it is the only method of moral inquiry that can guarantee rational beliefs. However, given that rationality is a comparatively weak positive epistemological status, guaranteeing rational beliefs is not enough to establish the adequacy of a method of inquiry. For the goal of moral inquiry is rational, systematic knowledge, and while rationality may be necessary for such knowledge, it is not sufficient. A strong form of moral skepticism therefore remains a possibility. The second element of my strategy is to foreclose this possibility. However, the argument here cannot have the same structure as the argument regarding rationality, for a coherence method cannot guarantee warranted belief. The important thing to see is that this is no fault of the method. There is a tendency to think that a method of inquiry must do all the epistemological work, but this is a mistake. The method a person employs has a proper role in accounting for the epistemological status of the beliefs she eventually comes to hold, and the person has a proper role. I maintain that whether or not a person's moral beliefs are warranted is determined largely by the contribution made by the person. Therefore, the second element of my strategy involves a sort of Kantian project. I explain how it is possible that the right kind of person following a coherence method would come to hold warranted moral beliefs.

Thinking about the project of moral inquiry as a kind of game might help to clarify my strategy, in particular the relevance of establishing the mere possibility of coming to hold warranted beliefs as a result of following the method. Previous discussions have focused on the question of whether a method can guarantee truth. The presupposition behind this approach seems to be that a game is not worth playing unless there is a procedure for playing that will guarantee victory. But this presumption is certainly false. Nonetheless, unless one values the play of the game in itself, we do not think it is reasonable to play any and every game. What then do we require? One thing might be that there is a rational approach to the game; thus one might think that Blackjack and Poker are superior to betting on cutting a deck of cards. But of course, even if there were a rational strategy, we would not want to play the game if it were "fixed," i.e., if there were no way for us to win. So, we might conclude, a reasonable game to play is one where there is a rational approach to playing the game and the game is winnable, or better, that "if we play our cards right" we will win. My strategy is to show that moral inquiry is that sort of game, if we approach it with the right method. The method takes an inquirer by rational steps to a system of moral beliefs that it is rational for her to accept, and if the inquirer plays her part, her moral beliefs will be warranted, which puts her in a position to know.

The book is divided into three parts. Part I introduces the most familiar version of coherentism, i.e., Rawlsian wide reflective equilibrium. I then raise the objection to this method that is pushed by proponents of various foundational strategies: that the method cannot guarantee anything more than a systematization of our moral prejudices. I then consider and reject attempts to meet this objection "head on" by defending the credibility of either our initial considered moral judgments or the beliefs a person would come to hold as a result of following the method of reflective equilibrium. The most significant thing to emerge from my criticisms of past attempts to defend reflective equilibrium is a new and more radical version of wide reflective equilibrium, which stands midway between the method developed by Rawls and the method of balance and refinement I wish to elaborate and to defend. Parts II and III of the book carry out the two-pronged strategy I described above for establishing the adequacy of a coherence method, while at the same time describing in detail and justifying the distinctive features of the method of balance and refinement. I argue that balance and refinement is the only rational approach to moral theory construction and describe how we might plausibly account for the warrant of the moral beliefs of a person who has followed this coherence method. Crudely put, my view is that the method is acceptable because (i) it is the only *rational* game in town for the moral theorist and (ii) it is a game the theorist just might win by arriving at warranted beliefs and possibly knowledge.

Part II of the book deploys the first part of the strategy and describes in detail the method of balance and refinement, distinguishing it from the more familiar method of reflective equilibrium. I argue that while reflective equilibrium can go a considerable way towards guaranteeing that the inquirer will be taken from her initial moral beliefs by rational steps to an overall view that it is rational for her to accept, it eventually falls short. The only rational method of moral inquiry is balance and refinement. Part of the argument is fairly traditional, focusing on the type of rationality involved when a person is moved by argument from beliefs she already holds either to adopt new beliefs or to alter old beliefs. In the contemporary literature questions about the rationality of moral methodologies have focused almost exclusively upon this element of rational belief. If we were to go along considering only this element of rationality, radical wide reflective equilibrium would appear to be fully adequate. The most interesting feature of Part II is my discussion of the influence of other types of experience, in particular certain "real-life" experiences as well as experiences with literature, theater, film, music, and art, on the development and rationality of a person's moral view. I argue that these experiences must be taken into consideration in any rational method of moral inquiry, and develop the method of balance and refinement to do so.

In Part III I explain how a person who has followed the method of balance and refinement could thereby come to have warranted moral beliefs. The account is not intended to show that following the method necessarily yields either true or warranted beliefs. Rather I want to establish the *possibility* of a person's coming to have warranted moral beliefs as a result of following the method. I accomplish this end by adopting a perceptual model and arguing that other models, in particular those that take inductive, deductive, or abductive arguments as their paradigms, cannot adequately account for various features of moral inquiry, in particular, the deepening of moral understanding that can be provided by various life experiences, literature, theater, and film. In summary, then, my overall plan is to establish the credentials of a method of moral inquiry, while granting that there is no assurance that the method will reliably yield true beliefs, by showing that the method directs inquirers to revise their beliefs in rational ways and that it is possible for them to come to hold warranted beliefs as a result.

The overview I've just given of my argument is somewhat misleading. It gives the mistaken impression that my conception of moral inquiry is relatively familiar or standard, when I think that many moral philosophers will consider my conception downright bizarre! To correct this impression "up front," let me describe one extremely significant theme that runs through the book. Nearly everyone would affirm that moral inquiry (and philosophy in general) is a rational, highly intellectual activity. Of course there is a great deal of disagreement about how exactly a rational philosophical inquiry into morality should proceed as well as about which features of the inquiry account for its rationality. But in spite of all the disagreements there is a core conception that is almost universally shared. The primary element of the shared view is that the most important feature of moral inquiry (and, I would add, philosophy in general) is the examination of arguments, the investigation of the logical and evidential relationships among believed propositions. Obviously enough, the nature of the propositions that should serve as starting points for such arguments is a matter of some debate, and indeed, there is not even agreement about which propositions are qualified to play this role. Some endorse the traditional Rawlsian coherentism that allows a person to use all her moral beliefs in her theorizing, revising where contradictions or incoherencies are discovered, while others think there is an *a priori* starting point to be found in the meaning or logic of moral language, or the theory of rational decision. Still others hold that our main task is to find a place for values within the world revealed by the natural and social sciences. But in spite of the differences among them, all of these approaches share the common view that philosophical inquiry into morality is preeminently a matter of investigating the relationships among the relevant propositions, whether these relationships be deductive, inductive, abductive, or what have you.

It is doubtful anyone holds that this is all there is to moral inquiry. Inquirers must be allowed to acquire additional beliefs, with more *facts* being especially welcome, whether they are the kind we acquire from our ordinary interaction with the world or the result of some more formal scientific inquiry. I suppose that most would recognize that new moral and philosophical beliefs must be permitted as well. But it is fair to say that according to the *intellectualist* view I am trying to identify the acquisition of such beliefs is a ticklish matter. In particular, there is a strong temptation to think that the only way moral and philosophical beliefs can be added or altered legitimately is where the addition or alteration is somehow required either by beliefs that are already present or by the acquisition of new empirical information.

The method of balance and refinement I describe and defend is opposed to the intellectualist conception of moral inquiry. Of course I do not try to argue that the intellectualist conception is completely misguided – I admit that the things this conception focuses on do indeed play a significant role in moral inquiry. This is why I incorporate the element of *balance*, which is closely associated with the coherentist approach to moral inquiry, within the method I defend. But I also wish to emphasize that the picture of moral inquiry the intellectualist provides is not complete, that it leaves out several features that are necessary for an adequate method of moral inquiry. The version of coherentism I propose deviates from the intellectualist conception in both recognizing the significant role of life experiences and experiences with literature, theater, and film in moral inquiry and allowing for revisions of moral beliefs that are not required either to cohere with other standing moral, philosophical, or empirical beliefs or by the acquisition of new empirical information. This is the element of *refinement* in the method. We should not underestimate the significance of combining these features with a broadly coherentist conception of moral inquiry that allows even an important role to the elements recognized by the intellectualist. In spite of the similarity, the method of moral inquiry I defend is not correctly conceived as a minor variant of the more familiar intellectualist versions of coherentism. According to balance and refinement, philosophical inquiry into morality takes on a rather different appearance. For while there is obviously a place for argument, explanation, and theory construction, there is also a prominent place for literature, music, and art and for philosophical reflections on these. And, to the dismay of many philosophers, my conception grants a greater role to what I might as well call moral intuition or moral sense, but perhaps this will be tempered by the fact that the method also takes seriously questions regarding the development and refinement of moral sense.

Part I
Strategy

1 The method of reflective equilibrium and the no contact with reality objection

1.1 INTRODUCTION

The most widely discussed coherence method of moral inquiry is the method of wide reflective equilibrium, first described by John Rawls[1] and later elaborated by Norman Daniels.[2] The ultimate aim of this method is to bring a person's moral beliefs to a point where her considered moral judgments about particular cases and about general principles are explicated[3] by a simple and elegant moral theory that coheres with her broader philosophical outlook better than theories that capture alternative moral conceptions. As a person attempts to bring this sort of order to her moral beliefs, none of the component types[4] of belief are immune to revision. If the person's judgment regarding a particular action runs counter to what is entailed for that case by a general principle she accepts, it is an open question whether the particular judgment or the general principle should be retained. Should the person realize that a much simpler moral theory would satisfactorily explicate a set of considered judgments only slightly different from those she now accepts, this *may* lead her to alter her considered judgments, but it need not. Even if the person is confronted with a philosophical argument against a moral theory, say an argument based on her conception of a person, she will not necessarily reject the moral theory. She may just as well choose to revise her conception of a person. Thus, reflective equilibrium favors no type of belief, requiring instead that conflicts be resolved on a case-by-case basis, by appeal to such factors as the degree to which the inquirer is committed to the conflicting propositions, and the connections between these propositions and the other propositions she accepts or rejects.

Reflective equilibrium is obviously a coherence method. As such, it is subject to a familiar objection: the *no contact with reality objection*. The method obviously leads a person to the moral theory that, all things considered, seems to her to be most likely to be true, but what guarantee is there that this theory is anything more than that? What reason can be offered for thinking that the moral theory a person accepts in reflective equilibrium is true? In order to warrant our allegiance, a method for moral inquiry must bring our moral beliefs into an appropriate sort of contact with moral reality. Unfortunately, no coherence approach can insure this kind of contact between theory and reality.[5]

One might try to respond to the no contact with reality objection in either of two ways: One might respond directly, by providing a reason for thinking that the moral theory we accept in reflective equilibrium is true, or one might respond indirectly, by undermining the demand that some such reason be offered. I believe that most philosophers would consider a direct response to the no contact objection vastly more satisfying, and so would not be tempted to adopt the indirect strategy unless convinced it is the only alternative. Therefore, even though I do not think that the direct strategy can succeed, I shall begin by examining this approach to the no contact objection. I hope to show in this chapter that the direct strategy does not succeed, thereby motivating the indirect answer to the no contact objection that I shall elaborate and defend in the succeeding chapters. I shall focus upon a version of the direct response that brings important recent work on coherentism to bear in answering the no contact objection. The response is suggested by Laurence BonJour's work on coherence theories of empirical knowledge,[6] and is explicitly applied to the problem as it arises in moral methodology by Norman Daniels, as one element in his very thorough defense of reflective equilibrium.[7] The prominence of this response in the contemporary debate is not the only reason why it is important to understand its failure. For the response relies on an incorrect conception of the method of reflective equilibrium, and therefore coming to see why the direct response fails sets us on the road towards a more adequate conception of a coherence method.

The argument of this chapter is somewhat long, so it will perhaps be a good idea to provide a brief overview before diving in. We will obviously need more precise conceptions of both the no contact with reality objection and the basics of the method of wide reflective equilibrium. In the next section, I describe the method of reflective equilibrium as I believe it is ordinarily understood. Section 1.3 is devoted to what is generally taken to be the most serious objection to the method of reflective equilibrium, the objection I have called the no contact with reality objection. Our consideration of this objection will reveal that it can take two forms. A more specific version of the objection focuses on considered moral judgments, charging that unless these judgments are credible, reflective equilibrium cannot be counted on to yield a true moral theory. I shall refer to this as the *no credibility objection*. The more general version of the no contact objection is not especially concerned with considered moral judgments and the specific role they play in reflective equilibrium. The general version does not demand a defense of considered moral judgments in particular, being willing to settle for any reason for thinking that reflective equilibrium can be counted upon to bring us into contact with moral reality. I shall henceforth refer to this as the *no contact objection*. I propose to deal with these two versions of the no contact with reality objection separately, beginning with the no credibility objection.

Section 1.4 outlines what I take to be the most promising version of the direct response to the no credibility objection, due to Norman Daniels, and Section 1.5 further clarifies this response. Daniels admits that a defense of the credibility of our considered moral judgments is necessary, explains how such a defense must be constructed, and pleads that the objection is premature, since we are not far enough along towards wide reflective equilibrium for the defense to have emerged yet. I maintain that the objection and Daniels' response both fail because they are based upon an incorrect understanding of the method of reflective equilibrium, and in particular, of the role our initial considered moral judgments play. I lay the groundwork for my argument in Sections 1.6 and 1.7 by describing a conservative version of reflective equilibrium, according to which considered moral judgments play the role presupposed by the no credibility objection and Daniels' response, and a more accurate, radical conception, according to which considered moral judgments do not play such a role. In Section 1.8, I explain why the no credibility objection and Daniels' response are both inappropriate if one conceives of reflective equilibrium correctly, i.e., radically.

Unfortunately, since it makes no presuppositions about the role of considered moral judgments in reflective equilibrium, the general version of the no contact objection does apply to the radical conception of reflective equilibrium I favor. I explain how, in Section 1.9; I also explain how Daniels' sophisticated stalling tactic might be mobilized against the general no contact objection. However, as I argue in Section 1.10, this stalling tactic cannot ultimately succeed unless reflective equilibrium brings inquirers to converge upon a moral theory. But such convergence is not, after all, very likely. The prospects for a direct response to the no contact objection are, therefore, bleak, so we need to examine indirect defenses of reflective equilibrium. But that is the topic of Chapter 2.

1.2 THE METHOD OF REFLECTIVE EQUILIBRIUM

Norman Daniels has suggested that we may abstractly characterize the method of reflective equilibrium as:

> an attempt to produce coherence in an ordered triple of sets of beliefs held by a particular person, namely (a) a set of considered moral judgments, (b) a set of moral principles and (c) a set of relevant background theories.[8]

We can follow out this suggestion by specifying the particular sets of beliefs a person holds at each time as she follows the method of reflective equilibrium. This provides us with a nice way of representing a person's progress as she follows the method as well as the method's eventual goal. Accordingly, we can characterize a person's progress towards a point of wide reflective equilibrium as follows.

A person will begin the task of constructing a moral theory with a wide variety of moral beliefs. Some of these beliefs will concern the rightness or wrongness of particular actions, either actual or hypothetical, and others will concern the evaluation of persons or situations, e.g., the belief that it is good that a friend and her husband have worked out their differences and are reconciled, or the belief that Caligula was wicked. But the inquirer's moral beliefs need not all be particular. She might have beliefs about certain action types, personality traits, and kinds of things. For example, the inquirer might believe that one ought to keep one's promises, that honesty is good and goes towards making a person virtuous, and that pleasure is good. The inquirer's general moral beliefs may well be even more abstract than these examples suggest. For example, a person will most likely believe such things as that two actions sharing all their non-moral characteristics must be evaluated in the same way, and that a person can only be blamed for doing something if it was in her power to avoid doing it. The moral beliefs a person begins with, of all these various kinds and levels of generality, are called *initial moral judgments*. Let the set of these judgments be {IMJ}.

The method of reflective equilibrium recognizes that a person has little choice but to begin the process of theory construction wherever she happens to be, that is, with her initial moral judgments. But as it is usually described, the method does not allow literally all of these initial judgments to be used in the construction of a moral theory. For it is likely that some of a person's initial judgments will not have been formed in circumstances where, as Rawls puts it, "our moral capacities are most likely to be displayed without distortion."[9] Thus, the first step a person must take in following the method of reflective equilibrium is to filter her initial moral judgments, retaining only those made "in circumstances where the more common excuses and explanations for making a mistake do not obtain."[10] The judgments that survive this filtering are the person's *considered moral judgments*. We shall label the set of these judgments {CMJ$_1$}.

It may seem that the filtering process involved in a person's moving from her initial to her considered moral judgments is perfectly innocuous, but whether it actually is will depend upon how the filtering is understood. For one thing, it isn't entirely clear what the optimum circumstances for making moral judgments are. Rawls certainly tried to give uncontroversial examples of cases where a person's judgments are likely to be biased, but despite his efforts even his suggestions are questionable. For example, his claim that considered moral judgments must be made in a calm emotional state has been criticized on the grounds that our feelings of moral outrage reliably indicate egregious wrongdoings, and his claim that judgments made in circumstances where we stand to gain or lose seems to beg the question against the egoist.

There is a more fundamental problem with the conception of the filtering process. As Rawls and others describe it, the epistemic standards that considered moral judgments must meet seem to be laid down independently of any consideration of the epistemic principles accepted by the person seeking to bring her beliefs into reflective equilibrium. Rawls tells us that judgments about which we are hesitant or not confident should be ignored, as should judgments made "when we are upset or frightened, or when we stand to gain one way or the other."[11] But what if a person does not recognize these kinds of judgments as being epistemically defective? Even if the person does hold epistemic principles according to which such judgments are defective, the person might be less strongly committed to these epistemic principles than to the initial moral judgments they count against. In this case, it is arguable that the person ought to modify her epistemic principles rather than her moral judgments.

It seems then that, at least as it is usually described, reflective equilibrium sins against the spirit of coherentism by granting certain of the inquirer's epistemic beliefs a privileged status, or worse, by granting a privileged status to epistemic principles that may not even be believed by the person who must conform to them. We would do well, therefore, not to take a person's considered moral judgments to be those initial moral judgments that meet some externally imposed epistemic standard. I suggest that we instead conceive of these judgments as follows. A person is unlikely to be completely happy with all of her initial moral judgments. By this I mean that after a little reflection the person will probably grant that not all of her initial judgments were made in optimal circumstances, i.e., in circumstances she *herself* would take to be conducive to making an accurate judgment. A person must therefore begin by thinking over her initial moral judgments with an eye to eliminating those that seem to her to have obvious epistemic deficiencies. We shall take the beliefs that survive this preliminary internal audit to be the person's considered moral judgments.[12]

It might seem that there is no substantive difference between Rawls' conception of considered moral judgments and the conception just introduced, but there is. We can pinpoint the difference by asking why a person should start with her considered rather than her initial moral judgments. Two reasons have been offered. (1) According to Rawls, since a person's considered moral judgments are those formed in circumstances where the common excuses for making mistakes are absent, these judgments reliably display a person's faculty of moral judgment.[13] (2) Even though considered moral judgments are not immune to revision, they are taken to have gained something in the way of epistemic credentials as a result of surviving the filtering of initial moral judgments.[14] According to the conception of considered moral judgments I have put forth, neither of these reasons applies. Beginning with considered rather than initial moral judgments is entirely a matter of convenience. Initial judgments that do not survive the filtering process are not eliminated because they were formed in circumstances where the judge is prone to error, nor are they ignored because they do not accurately reflect the person's faculty of moral judgment. These initial judgments are eliminated because they conflict with the person's simplest, most firmly held epistemic principles.[15] Because of this conflict it is a safe bet that these judgments would be eliminated eventually, so it is convenient to drop them early on, thereby avoiding problems that might arise later on because of the influence these judgments might have had on the inquirer's moral beliefs.[16]

The inquirer's next step towards a point of reflective equilibrium would be to formulate a set of moral principles, i.e., a moral theory, that explicates her considered moral judgments. Let a person's first attempt at an explication be $\{MT_1\}$. If $\{CMJ_1\}$ and $\{MT_1\}$ do not cohere, or if $\{MT_1\}$ is not as simple and elegant as the inquirer would like, and it is safe to assume that $\{CMJ_1\}$ or $\{MT_1\}$ will fail in one of these ways, then she will have to make some adjustment if her beliefs are to cohere. So, for example, the inquirer might realize that P, a principle in $\{MT_1\}$, entails an evaluation of a certain action at odds with one of the members of $\{CMJ_1\}$, J, which is a judgment about that action. Upon a little reflection, the person might figure out a way of qualifying P so that it entails J. If we let the set of beliefs obtained by removing P from $\{MT_1\}$ and replacing it with the appropriately altered principle be $\{MT_2\}$, we can represent the person's moral beliefs after this first step with the ordered pair $<\{CMJ_1\}, \{MT_2\}>$. It is unlikely that one such change will produce a coherent system of beliefs, so the person will have to make numerous adjustments and readjustments in both her considered moral judgments and moral principles. She will therefore move through a series of pairs of sets of beliefs. When the person completes the process of mutual adjustment, so that she accepts a simple and elegant moral theory[17] that coheres with her considered moral judgments, her beliefs are said to be in *narrow reflective equilibrium*. We may let the last, coherent pair in the series be $<\{CMJ_n\}, \{MT_n\}>$.[18]

The fact that neither a person's considered moral judgments, nor her moral theory, are favored as she attempts to bring her beliefs into narrow equilibrium is sufficiently significant to warrant my calling attention to it once again. If the general principles that a person first formulates conflict with one of her considered moral judgments, say a judgment about a particular case, and this judgment is strongly held and relatively central to her belief system, then undoubtedly she will adjust the theory. However, if a person has been working at a set of principles for some time, so that these principles seem to account for a large number of her considered judgments in a nice, intuitive way, and moreover, the theory is simple and elegant and conflicts only with some more marginal considered judgments, then it is the judgments that will be revised. Cases of conflict between a provisional theory and a considered moral judgment must be resolved individually; the inquirer must choose what to revise solely on the basis of what she is most strongly committed to, on the basis of what seems to her to be most likely to be true.

In order to complete the final phase of the method, an inquirer must attempt to disrupt her state of narrow reflective equilibrium. The person is to accomplish this by considering alternatives to $\{MT_n\}$ along with philosophical arguments designed to decide among these alternative theories. Norman Daniels has suggested that we think of this process as an attempt to achieve coherence among the beliefs a person holds in narrow reflective equilibrium and the background theories she accepts.[19] The idea is that philosophical arguments bearing upon the decision among moral theories must proceed from the inquirer's broader views, e.g., philosophical or psychological beliefs regarding the nature of persons or rational decision making, or sociological views about such things as the role of morality in society. Thus, when an argument for an alternative to $\{MT_n\}$ is successful, it shows that the theory accepted in narrow equilibrium does not cohere well with the background beliefs which served as the argument's premises. Thus, letting $\{BT_1\}$ be the background theories the person accepts, a philosophical argument against $\{MT_n\}$, which the person found compelling, would serve to show that while $<\{CMJ_n\}, \{MT_n\}>$ represents a coherent system of beliefs, $<\{CMJ_n\}, \{MT_n\}, \{BT_1\}>$ does not. If philosophical arguments were always decisive, the person's considered judgments and moral theory would be coerced into coherence with her background beliefs. But such coercion is no part of the scenario envisioned by reflective equilibrium. Rather, just as narrow equilibrium is attained by mutual adjustment of considered judgments and the principles making up a moral theory, coherence among considered judgments, moral theory, and background theory is supposed to be attained by a process of mutual adjustment. Once again, no type of proposition is granted a privileged status. When an argument reveals a conflict between background philosophical beliefs and moral beliefs, it is an open question which will be revised.[20] The decision must be made on the basis of a person's degree of commitment to the propositions involved, and the logical and evidential relations among these propositions and the other propositions she accepts or rejects. If all goes well, after the person has considered the alternatives to the moral theory she accepted in narrow equilibrium and considered the relevant philosophical arguments, she will be able to attain once again a coherent system of beliefs, now including considered judgments, a moral theory that nicely accounts for these judgments, and background beliefs that support and are supported by this moral theory. Accordingly, the person will move through another series of sets of beliefs, ending up with $<\{CMJ_w\}, \{MT_w\}, \{BT_w\}>$.[21]

According to Daniels, an inquirer who has brought this sort of coherence to her beliefs has not quite reached the end state the method of reflective equilibrium seeks, i.e., a state of *wide* reflective equilibrium. For wide equilibrium Daniels requires that the inquirer's beliefs satisfy what he calls the *independence constraint*. Daniels worries that an inquirer might accept a moral theory that is merely an "accidental generalization" from her considered judgments. He wishes to insure that the inquirer's background theories provide support for her moral theory in some way that is independent of the match between considered moral judgments and moral theory. He therefore requires that "some interesting, non-trivial portion" of the considered moral judgments that constrain the inquirer's background theories be disjoint from the considered moral judgments that constrain her moral theory. This is to say that if $<\{CMJ_w\}, \{MT_w\}, \{BT_w\}>$ is to constitute a system of beliefs in wide equilibrium, there must be two proper subsets of $\{CMJ_w\}$, let them be $\{CMJ_{wm}\}$ and $\{CMJ_{wb}\}$, such that (i) $\{CMJ_{wm}\}$ constrains $\{MT_w\}$, (ii) $\{CMJ_{wb}\}$ constrains $\{BT_w\}$, and (iii) $\{CMJ_{wm}\}$ and $\{CMJ_{wb}\}$ are "to some significant degree disjoint."

In the first place, I'm not confident I really understand how Daniels' independence constraint is supposed to work. I suspect that this is because I do not know what he intends 'constrains' to signify. We certainly cannot understand constraint in terms of mere coherence, since presumably $\{CMJ_w\}$ will cohere with both $\{MT_w\}$ and $\{BT_w\}$. And it does not seem we can assume that a set of beliefs, A, constraining another set of beliefs, B, is something like a matter of B's having to entail or explicate the members of A, since if there are considered moral judgments not explicated by $\{MT_w\}$, this failure alone would show that $\{MT_w\}$ is incomplete. In this case, $\{MT_w\}$ would be unacceptable in virtue of being incomplete, not because of any violation of the independence constraint.

Secondly, it is not clear to me that the problem Daniels introduces the independence constraint to solve is a real problem. If the problem is supposed to be that the moral theory an inquirer accepts in wide reflective equilibrium might be an accidental generalization from her considered moral judgments, it seems that the problem could be solved, quite simply, by requiring that the person have made judgments about a sufficient range of hypothetical cases. Daniels also formulates the problem in terms of insuring that wide reflective equilibrium provides support for a moral theory that goes beyond what is available in narrow equilibrium. He proposes to solve the problem by guaranteeing that there will be beliefs supporting a moral theory in wide reflective equilibrium that were not involved in supporting the theory in narrow equilibrium. But why isn't the fact that wide reflective equilibrium forces a person to bring her background beliefs into the picture good enough? Daniels suggests that these might be mere reformulations of the person's considered moral judgments. But is this a possibility we must guard against? A person who explicitly cooked up all her relevant background beliefs on the basis of her considered moral judgments would not be following the method of reflective equilibrium in the first place. We need not reformulate a method of inquiry because someone making a mere pretence of following it would be involved in an objectionable procedure. Of course, it is possible, while also being incredibly unlikely, that a person's background beliefs do not conflict with what she would have accepted in narrow equilibrium, and hence, that achieving wide equilibrium would require no alterations to $\{CMJ_n\}$ or $\{MT_n\}$. And it is also possible, though again very unlikely, that a person would systematically be more strongly committed to the elements of $\{CMJ_n\}$ and $\{MT_n\}$ than to any of the elements of $\{BT_1\}$, so that achieving wide equilibrium involved a series of adjustments that moved the person from $<\{CMJ_n\}, \{MT_n\}, \{BT_1\}>$ to $<\{CMJ_n\}, \{MT_n\}, \{BT_w\}>$. However, I do not think it is appropriate to try to rule out such cases *a priori*, as Daniels seems to want to do. They are possibilities one must be willing to accept if one adopts a coherence approach to theory construction. One can take consolation in the fact that, even in these two extreme cases, a reason can be offered for preferring wide to narrow equilibrium, viz., that a person whose beliefs are only in narrow equilibrium will almost certainly have incoherent beliefs, though of course her moral beliefs will be coherent, while wide equilibrium guarantees that all of the person's beliefs, philosophical, moral, and otherwise, form a coherent whole. I shall, therefore, diverge from Daniels by ignoring his independence constraint, and take a person to have reached a point of wide reflective equilibrium when she brings her considered moral judgments and background theories to cohere with a simple and elegant moral theory.

Before moving on to consider the no contact with reality objection I would like to make two general remarks about the method of reflective equilibrium. First, the description I have offered is abstract, and quite obviously involves all sorts of simplifications and idealizations. The most obvious idealization is the state of wide reflective equilibrium itself, a state which no one could seriously hope to attain. I'll cite only one other example. I have described the method as though the order in which conflicts are considered and resolved does not effect the equilibrium state the inquirer eventually reaches, but the order in which conflicts are addressed and resolved almost certainly would matter. As we all know, idealizations can be revealing or misleading. I can only hope that the idealizations embodied in my characterization of the method of reflective equilibrium will not undermine the conclusions I draw below. Secondly, I would like to stress something that should already be clear from my description of reflective equilibrium, that is, that I take it to be a method to be followed by an individual inquirer. This understanding of the method clearly is not shared by all who have discussed reflective equilibrium. And I suppose that some may even view the egocentric perspective I adopt as, at best, quaint. But I do not see how anyone could possibly hope to understand how something like reflective equilibrium could operate for a community of inquirers without first seeing how it might work in an individual case, which would seem to be much simpler. And more importantly, the question I am concerned to answer is a question I face as an individual: How should I, a philosopher, proceed in deciding what to believe about morality?

1.3 THE NO CONTACT WITH REALITY OBJECTION

I think it is safe to say that the majority of those who have criticized the method of reflective equilibrium have employed some form of the no contact with reality objection. Some, such as R. M. Hare,[22] Peter Singer,[23] and Kai Nielsen,[24] have perhaps overemphasized the role of considered moral judgments in Rawls' method, and have therefore concentrated their attack on the epistemic credentials of these judgments in a way that suggests they understand Rawls' approach to be foundational rather than coherentist.[25] In spite of this confusion, their criticisms constitute a form of the no contact with reality objection. For the point of criticizing our considered moral judgments is clearly to challenge the assumption that the moral theory that best explicates these judgments should be thought to be true.

Other critics have kept the fact that Rawls follows a coherence method more clearly in focus. David Lyons, for example, objects to Rawls' procedure as follows:

> Suppose one assumes that there are such things as valid principles of justice which can be justified in some way; suppose one believes, moreover, that a coherence argument explicates our shared sense of justice, giving precise expression to our basic moral convictions: one may still doubt whether a coherence argument says anything about the validity of such principles. For pure coherence arguments seem to move us in a circle, between our current attitudes and the principles they supposedly manifest. We seem to be 'testing' principles by comparing them with given "data". Because the latter (our shared, considered moral judgments) are impartial, confidently made, and so on, we can, indeed, regard them as reliably reflecting our basic moral convictions. But we can still wonder whether they express any more than arbitrary commitments or sentiments that we happen now to share.[26]

Richard Brandt has provided what is perhaps an even better formulation of the no contact with reality objection. He begins by suggesting that the degree of a person's commitment to a moral judgment independent of its connections with other judgments be called its "initial credence level," and that credence levels can be represented by real numbers as subjective probabilities are in decision theory. He then characterizes the procedure for revising beliefs enjoined by the method of reflective equilibrium.

> In case of conflict between a suggested general principle and any intuitions (whether general or particular), we are to reject, amend, or add in such a way that the total resulting system of normative beliefs "saves" the total amount of initial credence (represented by the sum of the suggested fractions) better than any other system of normative beliefs. Problems arise if we try to push the numerical model too far; and some philosophers probably wish to say nothing more precise than that, in case of choice between two sets of normative beliefs, we give preference to the one which we find easier to believe as a whole.[27]

One might try to support this procedure on the ground that conflicts or inconsistencies in our moral beliefs cannot be tolerated, since these beliefs are supposed to guide action, and one following the method would be led to uncover and resolve conflicts between moral beliefs. However, as Brandt notes, there are any number of methods a person could follow that would lead her to accept a consistent set of beliefs. She could even adopt a sort of inverse method of reflective equilibrium, by, for example, revising the belief in a conflicting pair which has the higher initial credence level while retaining the belief in which she places less credence. It is possible, after all, that maximizing initial credence levels leads one into error, while minimizing them would lead one to the correct moral view.

So more must be said if the method of reflective equilibrium is to be defended. Brandt concludes:

> There is a problem here quite similar to that which faces the traditional coherence theory of justification of belief: that the theory claims that a more coherent system of beliefs is better justified than a less coherent one, but there is no reason to think that this claim is true unless some of the beliefs are initially credible – and not merely initially believed – for some reason other than their coherence, say, because they state facts of observation. In the case of normative beliefs, no reason has been offered why we should think that initial credence levels, for a person, correspond to credibilities. The fact that a person has a firm normative conviction gives that belief a status no better than fiction. Is one coherent set of fictions supposed to be better than another?[28]

It will be useful to distinguish two different objections which are suggested by Brandt's and Lyons' critical remarks. First, there is a general worry about coherence methods that goes something like this: "A method of inquiry cannot be acceptable unless it is likely to lead inquirers to accept true theories. But there is no reason for thinking that the coherent system of beliefs which a coherence method leads an inquirer to adopt will be true." Secondly, there is a more specific worry that seems to result from combining the general worry with the common conception of reflective equilibrium. According to this common conception, reflective equilibrium allows certain beliefs to guide and constrain the inquirer's attempts to formulate a moral theory. Given this conception, it seems reasonable to suppose that the question of whether the method leads to truth will turn on the status of the beliefs that play the guiding role in theory construction. So questions are raised about the credibility of our considered moral judgments and our initial credence levels. We might sum up the objection as follows: "A method of inquiry cannot be acceptable unless it is likely to lead inquirers to accept true theories. The method of reflective equilibrium will not lead inquirers to accept true theories unless the beliefs that guide and constrain theory construction, i.e., the inquirer's considered moral judgments or initial credence levels, are credible. But there is no reason to believe that these beliefs are credible." It will be convenient to deal with these two versions of the no contact with reality objection separately. I shall postpone discussion of the former, and more general, *no contact objection*, until Section 1.9. In the remainder of the present section through Section 1.8, I shall consider the latter, *no credibility objection*, along with a certain line of response to this objection.

Before we turn our attention to the response to the no credibility objection I wish to consider, we should specify more precisely what it means to say that a belief is credible.[29] In ordinary use, "credible" means reasonable or plausible, but the objection cannot be using the term in this sense. For on the one hand, if we think about the beliefs that are likely to constitute a person's considered moral judgments, for example, the belief that murder is wrong or that courage is a virtue, it would seem that these judgments are reasonable or plausible in the ordinary senses of these terms. And on the other hand, since credibility is in part a subjective notion, a matter of *appearing* acceptable, it is not clear why we should think that reflective equilibrium will lead us to true beliefs only if our considered moral judgments or initial credences are credible. Brandt's choice of "facts" of observation as an example of a type of belief that is credible and his worry that in spite of a person's conviction, her considered moral judgments might still be mere "fiction" suggest that he is thinking of credibility as a matter of having a certain connection with truth. Being credible is both more and less than being true. A belief's being credible would seem to be a matter of being trustworthy, of being a belief of a type where beliefs of that type are *generally* true. Therefore, while recognizing that reliability is a notion only somewhat more clear than credibility, I shall take it that to be credible, a belief must be reliable.[30] I shall suppose that we can understand the reliability of a particular belief in some such way as the following. A person is reliable in believing a proposition just in case she forms a true belief about the proposition in a range of possible worlds that are similar to the actual world in certain relevant respects, or perhaps, just in case the belief is produced by a mechanism that produces true beliefs within a range of possible circumstances relevantly similar to those in which the belief is actually formed. A certain type or broad class of beliefs, e.g., visual beliefs, could then be said to be reliable when most persons reliably form beliefs of this type.[31]

Interpreting credibility in this way, the objector's charge that the method of reflective equilibrium cannot be accepted unless the beliefs that guide and constrain theory construction are credible will likely seem reasonable to many, and as we will see in the next section, it seems so even to proponents of reflective equilibrium. But proponents of this method may complain that the no credibility objector has just assumed that our considered moral judgments are not credible. No credibility objectors have therefore sought to bolster this assumption. Brandt, for example, reminds us that:

> Various facts about the genesis of our moral beliefs militate against mere appeal to intuitions in ethics. Our normative beliefs are strongly affected by the particular cultural tradition which nurtured us, and would be different if we had been in a learning situation with different parents, teachers, or peers.[32]

He quotes with apparent approval Peter Singer's famous remark that we might assume

> that all the particular moral judgments we intuitively make are likely to be derived from discarded religious systems, from warped views of sex and bodily functions, or from customs necessary for the survival of the group in social and economic circumstances that now lie in the distant past.[33]

And he briefly discusses the pervasiveness and significance of moral disagreements, both between members of different cultures and between apparently sensitive, well-informed members of the same culture. Such considerations are generally taken, at the very least, to shift the burden of proof onto the shoulders of the advocates of coherence methods.

1.4 THE WIMPY RESPONSE

In essence, the no credibility objection amounts to the claims that (1) reflective equilibrium cannot be an adequate method of moral inquiry unless it is likely to lead to true theories, (2) reflective equilibrium is unlikely to lead to true theories unless our considered moral judgments are credible, or alternatively, our initial credences correspond to credibilities, and (3) the credibility of our moral beliefs has not yet been established. Most discussions of this objection have focused on (3). I think this is a mistake, and I shall ultimately want to reject (2), which will be my aim in the next few sections, and even (1), although I will not take up this assumption, which is shared by the no contact objection, until Chapter 2. But for the time being, let's view the terrain from the common vantage point and focus on (3). As I noted at the end of the last section, it is common to add to (3) various familiar reasons for being suspicious of our moral judgments, e.g., widespread disagreement about moral matters both among cultures and among even supposedly enlightened individuals within our own, so that we have a better appreciation of the obstacles facing a defender of the reliability of our moral judgments. Some may consider these obstacles so imposing that the argument for the unreliability of our moral beliefs is decisive, but I think they are more charitably taken to put the burden of proof on the shoulders of the defender of coherence methods, and, of course, to increase the weight of this burden. Viewed in this way, the no credibility objection is really more of a challenge than a completed argument against reflective equilibrium. From a coherentist perspective, we might describe the situation as follows. We know that accepting our inclination to trust our considered moral judgments is apparently in conflict with various things that we, or at least some of us, believe about our moral judgments, e.g., that others apparently do not share them or that the genesis of these judgments is suspect, because it is influenced by our learning, which is itself suspect. However, we are not yet in a position to say that we must resolve this conflict by distrusting our considered moral judgments. There may be a way of making our beliefs coherent while retaining our considered judgments, perhaps by explaining the reasons for doubting these judgments offered by the no credibility objection in a way that is consistent with the reliability of these judgments.

When construed in this very charitable way, an option for responding to the no credibility objection opens up: One could try to provide what the objector thinks is lacking, i.e., an account of considered moral judgments that shows they state facts as observations do, and hence, that they too are reliable. Unfortunately, no convincing argument for the reliability of our considered moral judgments is currently available. But perhaps this is no cause for despair. Perhaps more careful reflection on the way observation functions to justify our empirical beliefs will allow for a more subtle response to the challenge. If we look to recent work on coherence theories of empirical justification, where, as Brandt notes, something like the no credibility objection also arises, we find that Laurence BonJour has outlined an interesting line of argument that might be taken to yield such a response.

The objection the coherence theory of empirical knowledge faces is that it can allow for no *input* from the world.[34] This is comparable to the demand that some of the beliefs in the coherent system be initially credible. In attempting to defend the coherence theory of empirical knowledge against this objection, BonJour cannot simply argue for the credibility of some of our initial beliefs. For, to argue that some of our empirical beliefs, say our observations, are reliable, and to go on to suggest that they are, for this reason, credible, and that the system of beliefs that incorporates them is therefore justified, would be to come dangerously close to foundationalism and externalism,[35] positions BonJour rejects. BonJour's problem is to provide a robust account of observation, thereby providing for input from "the world," while staying within the coherentist framework – a framework where beliefs are always justified in virtue of their inferential relations with other beliefs. According to BonJour the key to solving the problem is to distinguish between two senses in which a belief can be inferential. A belief can be inferential in its origin: That is to say, the belief was formed as a result of the believer's coming to see that the propositional object of the belief stands in the right kind of logical or evidential relation to some other propositions she believes. It is clear enough that ordinary observational beliefs are not inferential in this sense; they are cognitively spontaneous. This fact is not at odds with coherentism, however. For the coherentist need not hold that all beliefs are inferential in the sense that they were *formed* as a result of a process of inference. This doctrine is contradicted empirically. In fact, it does not seem to be so much as a possibility, since the process of drawing inferences apparently must begin somewhere, and presumably with a belief. All coherentism requires is that beliefs be inferential in the sense that their epistemic status depends upon their inferential connections with other beliefs. The coherentist can allow that observational beliefs have a non-inferential origin, so long as observations are justified in virtue of inference.

According to BonJour's suggestion, the spontaneous origin of observational beliefs plays a significant role in the inference that justifies them. He notes that in a paradigm case of an observational belief, the person also believes not only that her observational belief is cognitively spontaneous, but that it is of a certain kind, say a visual belief about the color and shape of a middle-sized object, and that it was formed in certain conditions, for example, the scene was illuminated by bright sunlight, the air was clear, the object was not very distant, and nothing obstructed it. For the person to have an argument from these premises to the truth, or probable truth, of her observational belief, all she would need is a belief that her cognitively spontaneous beliefs of the kind in question formed in circumstances like those at present are very likely to be true. For this argument to justify the observational belief, its premises would have to be justified, and for a coherentist, this justification would depend in turn upon the relation of these premises to the other beliefs in the person's coherent system of beliefs.

It is important to see that on this account observations are not justified individually, in virtue of their reliability, nor are other empirical statements justified simply in virtue of their relation to observation statements. Rather, all empirical beliefs are justified in virtue of belonging to a coherent system. Two characteristics of this system that are crucial to its being coherent are the fact that it includes the beliefs necessary to construct arguments for the reliability of observations, and the fact that non-observational beliefs are appropriately related to observations. According to BonJour, a system of empirical beliefs lacking these features would simply fail to be coherent. Hence, the system would be unjustified, and in turn the beliefs that make up the system would be unjustified.

BonJour's project is significantly different from ours. While his aim is to defend a coherence *theory* of empirical justification, we are concerned with a coherence *method* of moral inquiry. Still, his account suggests a possible way of responding to the no credibility objection as it applies to the method of reflective equilibrium. The idea this response would borrow from BonJour is that an argument for the reliability of some significant subset of the beliefs included within a coherent system, the beliefs intended to provide input from the appropriate portion of reality beyond the system of beliefs, cannot be expected to precede or be independent of the rest of the system, but rather will emerge as the system of beliefs is elaborated. This response takes up a refrain similar to Wimpy's in the Popeye comics, "I will gladly pay you Tuesday for a hamburger today." The defender of reflective equilibrium who adopts the *Wimpy* response will say, "I will gladly argue that our considered moral judgments are reliable someday if I can have the use of reflective equilibrium today."

Norman Daniels[36] has presented a detailed response to the no credibility objection that takes up Wimpy's refrain. He begins by calling into question the alleged parallel between observations and considered moral judgments that no credibility objectors often take advantage of in pressing their case against moral intuitions. But he then sets these questions aside and attempts to show that it is possible to meet the no credibility objection on its own terms. This is the argument that runs parallel to BonJour's discussion. Daniels begins by admitting the basic point of the no credibility objection: that some defense of the credibility of our considered moral judgments is needed. He then argues that we should not expect to be able to offer such a defense at this time and tries to offer some hope for our prospects of eventually providing the defense these judgments need. His strategy is to admit the validity of the challenge offered by the no credibility objection, but plead that the challenge has been issued prematurely, while promising to take up the gauntlet when the time is right. In short, he offers a sophisticated version of the Wimpy response.

Daniels holds that we should not expect to be able to defend the reliability of our moral judgments at present, because our system of moral beliefs is not yet sufficiently comprehensive and coherent for it to supply us with an adequate understanding of the nature of ethical properties. Without such an understanding, that is, without a clear idea even of what moral judgments are about, it is highly unlikely that we would be able to provide an argument for the credibility of our moral judgments. However, when we draw near a point of reflective equilibrium, where our moral and philosophical beliefs are coherent and we accept a theory that explicates these beliefs, we will presumably have a sufficiently clear view of the nature of morality for it to be possible to defend the credibility of the spontaneous moral judgments with which we began. If, after following the method of reflective equilibrium through to its conclusion, we could not defend the reliability of our considered moral judgments, either because we were unable to achieve a coherent system of moral beliefs at all or because the only coherent systems we could attain did not support such a defense, then we would have reason to think that our method of inquiry was unsuitable.[37] But the fact that we cannot produce an argument for the credibility of these judgments prior to using reflective equilibrium to develop an adequate conception of the nature of morality in itself constitutes no decisive objection to that method.

In support of this position, Daniels points out that observation reports in our common-sense/scientific view once stood in a similar situation. We can now defend the credibility of such reports because we can tell a story about their reliability. But this story became available only recently, after we had progressed a considerable way towards understanding the nature of material objects and perceptual mechanisms. Our ability to argue for the credibility of observation reports appears to be an element of the coherent system of beliefs about the empirical world that we have been able to attain by following a method that is in essence the same as reflective equilibrium. If we had taken this method of inquiry to be inadequate prior to our being able to defend the reliability of our observations, as the no credibility objection suggests we should have, it is unlikely we would ever have been able to defend these judgments, and so we would not have attained the knowledge of the external world that we have.[38]

So, the no credibility objection is not conclusive until it can be shown that no theory which one might accept in reflective equilibrium can yield a defense of the credibility of moral judgment. Daniels concludes:

> the "no credibility" objection succeeds in assigning a burden of proof. *Some* answer to the question about the reliability of moral judgments must be forthcoming. But the argument is hardly a demonstration that no plausible story is possible.[39]

1.5 CONSIDERED MORAL JUDGMENTS AND CREDENCE LEVELS

Until now, I have indifferently formulated the point of the no credibility objection in two ways:

(I) Reflective equilibrium is unacceptable, unless considered moral judgments are credible.

(II) Reflective equilibrium is unacceptable, unless initial credence levels correspond to credibilities.[40]

I have not yet explained the difference between these two formulations, but the two formulations are importantly different. Depending upon which we adopt, we will be led to focus our efforts on establishing the credibility of different beliefs. I shall begin by considering (I).

The first thing to note about (I) is that the phrase 'considered moral judgments' is ambiguous. Both critics and defenders of reflective equilibrium tend to speak of considered moral judgments as though there were a single set of moral beliefs that are a particular inquirer's considered moral judgments, and sometimes as though there is a single set of beliefs that constitute *our* considered moral judgments. However, it is quite clear that different inquirers can have, and are likely to have, different considered moral judgments.[41] Moreover, the description of reflective equilibrium in Section 1.2 makes it clear that an individual's considered moral judgments change as she moves towards a point of wide reflective equilibrium. Therefore, when the no credibility objector demands to be shown that our considered moral judgments are credible, we must ask which set of considered moral judgments she has in mind.

One possibility is that the objector is thinking of the inquirer's initial set of considered moral judgments, $\{CMJ_i\}$. But it is reasonably clear that the proponent of reflective equilibrium does not, and need not, assume these judgments to be reliable. It might appear that the method of reflective equilibrium was based upon this assumption, if the method allowed only a few of the beliefs in $\{CMJ_i\}$ to be changed as the person moves towards a point of reflective equilibrium, that is, if $\{CMJ_i\}$ and $\{CMJ_w\}$ have virtually the same members. For it is not improbable that a few members of a set of highly reliable beliefs should prove to be false. For example, the memories of a normal person are highly reliable, even though some of them are false. And it seems reasonable to think that the method for uncovering the mistaken ones would involve revising those beliefs that do not cohere either with the rest of one's memory beliefs or with one's background beliefs about the past, e.g., beliefs based on the testimony of others. However, the method of wide reflective equilibrium allows for a great deal of revision to the elements of $\{CMJ_i\}$.[42] Thus, it could turn out that very few beliefs are elements of both $\{CMJ_i\}$ and $\{CMJ_w\}$, in which case, $\{CMJ_i\}$ might contain mostly false beliefs, even though $\{CMJ_w\}$ and $\{MT_w\}$ contain only true beliefs. It is not, therefore, appropriate to demand that the inquirer's initial considered moral judgments be credible.

It might then seem that we should require the elements of $\{CMJ_w\}$ to be highly reliable, for these beliefs, presumably, will not be subject to any further revisions, and, since $\{MT_w\}$ explicates these judgments, if the elements of {CMJ$_w$} are not mostly true, it is unlikely that the elements of {MT$_w$} will be true.[43] However, while it is certainly desirable that the beliefs in {CMJ$_w$} be highly reliable, as well as the beliefs in {MT$_w$} and {BT$_w$} for that matter, this requirement is out of place in the present discussion. Reflective equilibrium has been proposed as a method of moral inquiry, as a procedure the individual inquirer is advised to follow in sorting out her moral beliefs. As I distinguished the no credibility objection from the no contact objection above, it represents the concern that reflective equilibrium allows the inquirer's efforts at theory construction to be guided and constrained by beliefs that are not trustworthy. Whether or not the beliefs in {CMJ$_w$} are reliable, they are obviously not suited for the role of guide, since they only emerge as the person employs the method, indeed, at the very end of the method's employment. They are a part of the goal, or end state, the method seeks. In so far as we are concerned with the no credibility objection, we must understand considered moral judgments so that they do in fact *guide* theory construction. To function in this way, these beliefs would apparently have to be present pretty much throughout the process of following the method.[44]

We might then take the considered judgments in question to be those members of {CMJ$_1$} that survive all the way into {CMJ$_w$}, but there are several reasons for not doing so. First, not all of these beliefs will really play the same guiding role in our theorizing, and in fact, some may not play a guiding role at all. For example, there may be some elements of {CMJ$_1$} that the person is not terribly confident of at the outset, and which never figure in any of the person's decisions to revise other beliefs, but which make it into {CMJ$_w$} because they are supported and strengthened by other beliefs, perhaps elements of {MT$_w$} or {BT$_w$}. Secondly, although it is unlikely, it is possible for a person to be sufficiently unsure of the elements of {CMJ$_1$} that none of these beliefs plays a guiding role in her construction of a moral theory. Such a person might, for example, have philosophical beliefs about the meanings of moral statements that determine the theory she accepts, {MT$_w$}, and even the composition of {CMJ$_w$}.[45] In the most extreme case of this sort, the intersection of {CMJ$_1$} and {CMJ$_w$} might be empty. Thirdly, and finally, although some of a person's considered moral judgments will usually play a significant role in her construction of a moral theory, as the case just described nicely illustrates, the considered moral judgments of a person following the method of wide reflective equilibrium will not *necessarily* play a guiding role in theory construction.[46]

It is, then, strictly speaking, incorrect to interpret the no credibility objection as being directed primarily at our considered moral judgments. But if, contrary to the look of the various debates about the method of reflective equilibrium, we cannot say that our considered moral judgments guide and constrain theory construction according to this method, what *does* play this role? It would seem that the things in which we initially place a comparatively high degree of confidence, or in Brandt's terms, credence, play this role.[47] As the no credibility objector might ask, "The method of wide reflective equilibrium leads a person to accept the coherent system of moral and philosophical beliefs with the highest degree of initial commitment, but what reason is there for thinking that these beliefs are anything more than that?" This suggestion brings us to formulation (II) of the central premise of the no credibility objection.

Although Daniels frames the Wimpy response in terms of considered moral judgments, I think we can safely take him to be answering the objection as properly formulated with (II) as the key premise. For one thing, Daniels begins by cautioning against assuming that considered moral judgments must play a role in the construction and justification of moral theories roughly analogous to the role observations play in the empirical realm. These cautionary remarks indicate that he is sensitive to the considerations I've raised regarding our considered moral judgments. Secondly, it is simpler and more convenient to conduct the discussion in terms of defending our considered moral judgments rather than our degrees of commitment. And the simplified presentation generally will not involve any serious distortion, since in all but exceptional cases, some of our considered judgments will play a leading role in the construction of moral theories.

There is another point I should make about Daniels' response before criticizing it. His aim was to describe how one might respond to the no credibility objection from within the objection's own framework. We must therefore recognize that the response may rely in part upon assumptions Daniels does not share. However, (II) does not seem to be such an assumption. Daniels makes it quite clear that, at some point, the defender of reflective equilibrium must defend the beliefs that guide theorizing, i.e., the moral and philosophical judgments to which the person initially attaches a high degree of credence. One cannot go on forever as Wimpy does; at some point the tab must be paid up. It is this assumption, that the defender of reflective equilibrium must defend the beliefs that guide and constrain theory construction, that I intend to challenge first. As I have already indicated, I do not think the no credibility objection can be defeated directly. I think that a defender of reflective equilibrium, or any other coherence method, should attack the idea that acceptable methods must proceed from reliable starting points rather than try to defend the credibility of either our considered moral judgments or our initial credences.[48] As a matter of fact, if we could show that our initial credence levels were reliable, as both sides of the present debate think we must, it would count *against*, not for, the method of reflective equilibrium. For, contrary to the standard picture of the method, reflective equilibrium does not really have our *initial* credence levels guiding us all the way through to the construction of a moral theory. In order to establish this point, I shall describe two versions of the method of reflective equilibrium: a conservative version, where initial credence levels do play a guiding role, and a radical version, where they do not. The next two sections describe these two conceptions of reflective equilibrium.[49] I shall then be in a position to defend the radical conception and to show that neither the no credibility objection nor the Wimpy response apply to this interpretation of reflective equilibrium.

1.6 THE CONSERVATIVE CONCEPTION OF REFLECTIVE EQUILIBRIUM

According to the conservative conception of reflective equilibrium, a person is to achieve a coherent system of beliefs by formulating general moral principles that seem initially plausible and by investigating the logical and evidential relations among these principles, her considered moral judgments, and elements of her broader philosophical perspective. When the person uncovers a conflict[50] between two of her beliefs, she will revise the one to which she is less strongly committed. The belief to be revised may be a considered moral judgment, a philosophical principle, or an element of her moral theory. More generally, when a person discovers that some number of her moral and philosophical beliefs are in conflict, she will select, from the possible revisions that would yield a coherent system, the one that maximizes her degree of initial commitment.

One could easily take this to be a quite general description of reflective equilibrium, failing to notice the feature that is distinctive to the conservative conception, i.e., the reliance on initial credence levels. In order to emphasize the spirit of the conservative conception, allow me to oversimplify and say something that is literally false. Then I'll complicate and correct in the next few paragraphs. According to the conservative conception, in the simplest case, all the revisions necessary to attain a state of reflective equilibrium will be decided by the inquirer's initial beliefs and degrees of commitment to the propositions involved. In such cases, the person's equilibrium point is determined by her beliefs and degrees of commitment prior to philosophical reflection. The equilibrium state will simply be the union of (i) the most comprehensive conflict-free subset of her initial considered moral judgments and philosophical beliefs with (ii) a moral theory that explicates the moral judgments in this subset, which union preserves the highest total degree of initial commitment for the person.[51] On the conservative conception, the method of reflective equilibrium provides an algorithm for theory construction. The individual makes her contribution at the outset by specifying those propositions she believes and to what degree. But from this point on, anyone with the relevant cognitive capacities could do the work of determining the person's equilibrium state. The job consists of two tasks: (a) searching for conflicts among beliefs in the person's starting point and revising in a way that preserves the greatest degree of initial commitment, and (b) formulating a moral theory that "completes the curve" begun by the considered moral judgments and background philosophical beliefs that remain after these corrections.

I said that this characterization of the conservative conception is oversimplified, and hence false. The first oversimplification involves the underdetermination of theory by data. Even in the moral realm, where the "data" of considered moral judgments can include beliefs about hypothetical cases, and are supplemented with the inquirer's background beliefs, these "data" do not uniquely determine a moral theory. I do not think such underdetermination poses a serious problem for the method of reflective equilibrium, for reflective equilibrium never conceived of the moral theory as something constructed solely to "fit" considered judgments and background beliefs. It was expected all along that some revisions required for attaining reflective equilibrium would be guided by the degree of commitment the inquirer feels towards certain elements of provisional moral theories *independently* of the fit between these elements and the inquirer's considered moral judgments and background beliefs. Thus, when more than one moral theory fits the "data" of a person's considered moral judgments and background philosophical beliefs equally well, a uniquely "correct" theory can be determined, either by consulting the believer's existing degrees of commitment to the relevant theories or the "intuitive" judgments she would make about these theories upon considering them. Unfortunately, the necessary judgments will not charac-

teristically be included among the inquirer's initial degrees of commitment, for the inquirer will not, after all, have yet considered the
relevant theoretical propositions. Thus, we cannot say that the inquirer's starting point determines her equilibrium state. Putting the
point in terms of another person trying to work out an inquirer's
equilibrium point, we might say that when "completing the curve"
begun by the inquirer's considered moral judgments, the "curve fitter"
must, at crucial junctures, consult the inquirer and be guided by the
inquirer's judgments regarding various theories that might be proposed to complete the curve.

A second oversimplification results from the assumption that conflicts and inferential relations can be identified without consulting the
inquirer. For I have understood conflicts broadly, so as to include what
might be called *epistemic* as well as *logical* contradictions, and many of
the most important inferential connections are obviously epistemic
rather than logical. But the relevant epistemic principles will presumably have to be the inquirer's own, and it may be that the inquirer will
not have sufficiently well-developed epistemological views to find the
relevant principles among her beliefs. In such a case, we would
presumably need additional input from the inquirer to develop her
epistemological beliefs enough to determine the conflicts and inferential connections among her beliefs that are involved in determining her
state of reflective equilibrium.[52] The additional input from the inquirer
would come in the form of judgments regarding propositions the
inquirer had not previously considered, where these judgments will not
be determined by the inquirer's initial beliefs and degrees of commitment. Such judgments will probably have to be made about more than
epistemic principles. For unless a person begins with a very broad
range of beliefs, particularly moral, but also philosophical, some of the
propositions she has not considered are likely to be theoretically
significant. For example, a moral judgment about an unusual hypothetical situation might provide a good test for deciding between two
moral theories that agree regarding all the propositions the person
already believes. Or there might be metaphysical questions, e.g.,
about personal identity, that a person has never considered, but that
might be relevant to certain of the person's moral judgments. In such
cases, as well as in the case of epistemological principles, the person
would have to consider the relevant propositions and make judgments
about them for her equilibrium state to be decided. While it might
seem that cases of this sort occur all the time, for example, whenever a
person is convinced by a counter-example, this appearance could be
deceiving. For some might try to argue that counter-examples do not

function by eliciting new particular judgments which conflict with accepted moral principles, but by leading a person to use a more strongly held principle to decide a case about which a less strongly held, but more explicitly formulated, moral principle generates an incompatible judgment. And some might even hold that in general, when persons make judgments about propositions they have never before considered, the judgments are based on the connections between the new propositions and the beliefs they already hold.

Even after the conservative conception is complicated to take account of these two oversimplifications, it remains too simple. In particular, the conservative conception must allow an additional type of revision that is not determined by the inquirer's initial degrees of commitment. This final type of revision would, I think, be extremely rare, involving conflicts among beliefs to which the inquirer was initially equally committed. It is perhaps not so very unlikely that a person would be equally committed to conflicting propositions, but this is not enough to generate the kind of case I have in mind. For such a case, the person's commitments would have to remain equal after all the logical and evidential connections among the conflicting propositions and the person's various other beliefs were taken into account. A case of such an all-things-considered tie among conflicting propositions would almost never arise, but if it did, the person would simply have to revise at least one of her commitments in a way that is not dictated by others of her commitments.

Because cases of these two types must be allowed by the conservative conception in addition to the sort of new theoretical judgments discussed in connection with underdetermination, we cannot say that, according to this conception, a person's state of reflective equilibrium is completely determined by her starting point. The beliefs with which a person begins do, however, limit her equilibrium point considerably. On the conservative conception, initial beliefs and degrees of commitment will never be altered, unless such alteration is necessary to resolve a conflict, and the majority of these revisions will be decided quite simply in terms of the person's degrees of initial commitment to the propositions involved.[53] The only other alteration of initial beliefs will involve the addition of new beliefs where they are needed, either because the initial set does not decide among competing moral theories, or because it does not contain any propositions about some important moral or philosophical issue.

Speaking loosely, I think it is fair to say that, according to the conservative interpretation, a person's beliefs in reflective equilibrium are virtually determined by the convictions she has when she begins to reflect about morality, however well or poorly those convictions happen to be developed at that time. The conservative interpretation of reflective equilibrium is static, for it understands a person's point of reflective equilibrium as an ideal state which is virtually a function of the person's actual system of moral and philosophical beliefs at a given time. The significant point is that the only changes within this system envisioned by the conservative conception are those required to make the initial system of moral beliefs cohere, and the only additions allowed are those required to determine an outcome for the method. This version of the method of reflective equilibrium can be seen as aiming at making a person's moral convictions at a given time explicit, precise, and sufficiently comprehensive to yield a moral theory. But the method does not seek to overthrow, or go far beyond, what is implicit in the moral convictions the inquirer brings to the inquiry.[54]

1.7 THE RADICAL CONCEPTION OF REFLECTIVE EQUILIBRIUM

The radical conception of reflective equilibrium allows for, and indeed expects, revisions of beliefs and degrees of belief that go beyond what is necessary to resolve conflicts in favor of more strongly held beliefs. Both interpretations of reflective equilibrium require the inquirer to consider alternative moral conceptions, as well as philosophical arguments designed to decide among them, in order to move from narrow to wide reflective equilibrium. But only the radical understanding appreciates the full significance of this feature of the method. On the conservative interpretation, the consideration of alternative moral conceptions involves little more than having the inquirer take her own non-moral background beliefs into account and give some thought to the moral theories others have formulated and defended. The person's background beliefs provide another possible source of conflicts to be resolved, and the work of other moral theorists might contain a theory that fits better with her considered moral judgments and background beliefs than any theory she can devise on her own. Hence, according to the conservative conception, we have here only another opportunity for more of the same basic type of revision. The radical conception, on the other hand, sees the consideration of alternative moral theories as one significant point at which a person may be led to alter the structure of her moral beliefs in a way that is not determined by her previous degrees of belief in the propositions involved and the logical relations among them.

Let's consider an example of something that is not, I hope, terribly uncommon: moral conversion. The work of certain philosophers, e.g., Nietzsche or Marx, is particularly apt to cause a person to experience such a conversion. We shall take as an example a person who reads Marx for the first time and comes away from the experience a committed Marxist. How are we to think of such a shift in views within the context of reflective equilibrium? Adopting the conservative interpretation, we might suppose that the convert simply found, in Marxist principles of justice, a moral theory that explicates her considered moral judgments and that coheres well with her broader views. She simply discovers in Marx's writings a moral theory that fits her initial belief system better than any theory she was able to formulate on her own. Of course if a person adopts Marxism in this way, any appearance of the person having experienced a moral conversion will be superficial.

Conservative reflective equilibrium allows for more complex scenarios as well, where something that might aptly be called a moral conversion occurs, provided that we think of a conversion as a very great shift in moral view. For example, since Marxist theory offers an explanation of how our moral judgments are corrupted by various social and economic conditions, a person might begin by being convinced of this "socioeconomic" explanation of her moral beliefs. Movement towards a state of reflective equilibrium could then be driven by epistemological principles that the person holds constant. Moral judgments would be revised on the basis of these principles as the convert becomes aware of Marxist reasons for doubting her initial moral judgments. There are, no doubt, other scenarios compatible with the conservative interpretation of reflective equilibrium as well. The distinguishing feature of these accounts is the presence of some strongly held belief, or set of beliefs, in the convert's initial system that drives her to resolve conflicts within this system in a way that eventually leads to the acceptance of a Marxist theory in reflective equilibrium. Thus, although we find a significant alteration of moral views, perhaps even occurring over a short period of time, the alteration is continuous rather than discontinuous, in the sense that revision is driven by certain beliefs that are held constant throughout the series of revisions.

There are, however, moral conversions that cannot be understood in terms of the conservative conception of reflective equilibrium. I maintain that, when a person understands the whole Marxist perspective, she may simply find this view of the world compelling in its own right. As a consequence, she just changes her mind about various of her beliefs, now believing propositions that previously she would have considered unlikely to be true. There is no question here of the person making these alterations in order to resolve conflicts inherent in her initial system of moral, philosophical, and other background beliefs. We could even suppose that system to have been coherent and thoroughly opposed to Marxism. Thus, it would simply be false that Marxism provides the best explication of the considered moral judgments the person made prior to reading Marx, and false that Marxism coheres well with the person's initial views about the nature of persons or society. On the basis of the beliefs the person had prior to reading Marx, one would have had to expect the person to find Marxism a repugnant doctrine. Instead, we find the person making many different moral judgments – feeling as though scales have fallen from her eyes, so that she can at last see the truth about morality. Of course, the Marxist theory the person now accepts explains why she used to be committed to a system of bourgeois considered moral judgments, but unlike the case described above, this explanation was not the catalyst for the conversion. The person did not first accept this explanation of her moral judgments, because it cohered with various elements of her initial system of beliefs, and then base revisions of her considered moral judgments and moral theory on this explanation in conjunction with epistemological principles. The explanation, therefore, is supplied after the fact of the conversion. It may provide a rationalization for the change in the convert's moral views, but the important point is that it did not cause this change.

The example of a moral conversion we have been considering has two distinct features that might be taken to indicate a conversion: The convert experiences a large and relatively quick change of belief, and the change is discontinuous. The defining feature of what I refer to as a moral conversion is *discontinuous* revision of belief, not the magnitude of the revision. By a discontinuous revision, I mean, first, a revision that is not required by things that the inquirer already believes, e.g., when the revision involves the elimination of the member of a conflicting pair of beliefs to which the person is less strongly committed, and secondly, a revision that does not fit one of the paradigms allowed by the conservative conception of reflective equilibrium. Thus, as I use the term, there can be small, slow conversions, although the more striking cases, like the one I described above, involve larger and more sudden alterations in a person's moral view. So far, I have made only a psychological claim: that real moral conversions can occur. This claim is controversial, but I shall postpone a defense of it until the next section. In the remainder of this section, I wish simply to describe the radical conception of reflective equilibrium, a method that attempts to make room for moral conversions.

In a true moral conversion, changes in belief or degree of belief are not dictated by some strongly held considered moral judgment or background philosophical belief. The person simply abandons at least some of her old considered moral judgments or background philosophical beliefs, and comes to believe new things. The distinctive feature of the radical conception of reflective equilibrium is that it allows for this kind of discontinuous revision of belief, which is the distinguishing feature of a moral conversion. On the radical understanding of reflective equilibrium, an inquirer is allowed just to change her mind about something. There may be no way in which the person's new commitments are determined by the old, or any way to see them after the fact as the result of appreciating and resolving conflicts inherent in the person's considered moral judgments and philosophical views. The radical conception understands that philosophical reflection about morality, in some cases involving no more than reading the moral views of other philosophers, can sometimes lead a person to abandon her old considered moral judgments and background philosophical commitments and to adopt a largely new set of convictions. In contrast, on the conservative understanding, when a person changes her mind about a belief, it is always because she has come to see that there is a conflict among certain of her beliefs, and she changes her mind about one thing in order to continue believing something else. According to this conception, then, for the work of a moral philosopher to sway a person, the philosopher must latch onto something the person already believes quite strongly, and use this belief to force the revision of other beliefs.

The radical conception of reflective equilibrium is not static, as the conservative view is. Because the changes in a person's system of moral beliefs envisioned by this conception are neither determined nor even constrained in any straightforward way by prephilosophical moral beliefs, it is not accurate to regard reflective equilibrium, radically conceived, as a method for articulating the moral conception a person has when she undertakes the construction of a moral theory. To be sure, a point of wide reflective equilibrium remains an ideal state on the radical conception, but it is not an ideal that is determined by the system of moral beliefs a person brings to the method. I suggest that it would be more accurate to say that the ideal state aimed at by the radical conception is determined by a person's moral judgment, rather than by her antecedent beliefs. According to this interpretation, the method of reflective equilibrium goes far beyond mere algorithmic transformations on a set of beliefs. The method rather directs a person to conduct her moral inquiry in conditions that are favorable for moral judgment, conditions that will allow her the richest inputs, ample opportunity to uncover and correct incoherences in her moral judgments, the chance to interact with other judgmental faculties, and perhaps most importantly, the opportunity to mature. But this talk is very speculative and draws us away from the main line of argument.

Before returning to this main line of argument, it is perhaps worth emphasizing again the difference between the conservative and radical conceptions of reflective equilibrium. In a certain way, the conservative conception focuses on beliefs, while the radical conception focuses on inquirers. According to the conservative conception, once the inquirer's initial system of beliefs is given, the inquirer's system of beliefs in wide reflective equilibrium is very nearly determined. The inquirer is basically a container for beliefs, playing no more role in the process than a piece of paper on which the inquirer's beliefs might have been listed. The person may have played a more active role in forming these beliefs to begin with, but by the time she gets around to undertaking a philosophical inquiry into morality, there is no longer any job that the inquirer herself must perform. The individual has made her contribution to the process, and the method can take over. This is, of course, an exaggeration, but I think it is an exaggeration that truly conveys the spirit of what I call the conservative conception of reflective equilibrium, the conception which, I believe, dominates discussions of this method.[55] The radical conception of reflective equilibrium grants the inquirer a much more significant role in the process of theory construction. The method allows alterations of belief that are determined not by the relations among propositions, but by the inquirer. The inquirer is more than a satchel for holding beliefs. The inquirer plays an active role, having the freedom to react to reflection upon her own beliefs and consideration of alternative moral and philosophical conceptions in ways that are not dictated by her previous beliefs and the method of inquiry.

1.8 THE RADICAL CONCEPTION DEFENDED AND THE WIMPY RESPONSE

If we allow that people experience radical, i.e., discontinuous, changes in their moral judgments and background beliefs, and we also allow that such conversions are permitted by the method of reflective equilibrium, indeed, that the method intentionally requires the inquirer to put herself into positions where such conversions are likely to occur, as the radical conception maintains, it is difficult to see how one defends reflective equilibrium by arguing that either the inquirer's initial degrees of belief, in general, or the degrees associated with her considered moral judgments, in particular, are reliable. For the method allows these beliefs to be abandoned wholesale when large-scale moral conversions occur. While it is possible that a person whose degrees of belief are reliable might come to accept a higher proportion of truths by accepting a radically different set of propositions, the circumstances in which such a conversion would yield a favorable outcome would have to be exceedingly rare and, one suspects, rather bizarre. More importantly, when conceived radically, the method of reflective equilibrium just does not look like a method for dealing with a set of input beliefs that are already highly reliable. A method for dealing with reliable initial beliefs would presumably allow radical revision only when the inquirer had some good reason for thinking that she was in the sort of highly unusual circumstance where, although highly reliable, her initial beliefs were, as a matter of fact, mostly false. But if the person altered her moral beliefs on the basis of such a reason, no matter how large the scale of the revision, it would not count as a moral conversion: It would be a kind of revision that is compatible with the conservative conception. A method of inquiry lucky enough to have beliefs of high epistemic status as input would tend towards conservatism: It would dictate minor transformations of the input beliefs designed to refine them further. It would be wary of major alterations, since it is likely that more would be lost than gained by such changes. In short, the method would look like reflective equilibrium conservatively conceived.[56] A defense of the reliability of our initial credences, or our considered moral judgments, seems, then, as though it might be appropriate for reflective equilibrium as conservatively understood, but not if it is understood radically.

But why should we adopt the radical conception of reflective equilibrium? First, some may doubt that persons revise their beliefs in ways not dictated by other things they believe.[57] For when we change our minds about something, we are generally able to provide an account of the change along the lines suggested by the conservative conception, and many people feel foolish when they cannot. We like to think of ourselves as rational beings, and it is tempting to think that, to be rational, we must change our minds only when we have a reason for doing so, where here, we think of a reason as something else we believe. So, as I noted in the last section, my psychological claim that moral conversions can occur needs to be defended. Secondly, incorporating moral conversions into the radical method of reflective equilibrium implies a sort of positive evaluation of such conversions. This evaluation is surely controversial. Some might complain, "Even if radical conversions occur, they surely cannot be regarded as good things from a rational point of view. Moral conversions are not the sort of thing for which a method of moral inquiry must find a place – they are rather something that a method of moral inquiry ought to guard against, as the conservative conception does. In allowing for conversions, the radical conception of reflective equilibrium sanctions willy-nilly formation and revision of belief, and so is objectionable."

Let us take up the first of these objections. The question of whether persons can experience radical, discontinuous conversions is empirical. I hold that persons can experience such changes in belief on empirical grounds. I believe that I have experienced discontinuous, although not very radical, changes in belief myself. I have witnessed others experiencing radical changes. I have heard other people talk about what seemed on the face of things to be cases of radical changes in moral beliefs, and I've read descriptions of people undergoing moral conversions in numerous novels, biographies, and autobiographies.[58] There are sufficiently many examples of apparently radical conversions that those who are skeptical about them must think that the conversions we seem to have observed are only *apparently* discontinuous, that given a careful examination of the convert's belief system, we would see that there are deeply held beliefs present throughout the experience that serve to move the person to adopt a new moral outlook. I do not find this suggestion tempting in the least. Indeed, I am inclined to think that even in many of the cases where a person would describe herself as changing her mind because of certain beliefs she has had all along, the person's accepting this description is more a matter of rationalization than accurate explanation. I have no doubt that, in any case that seems to constitute a moral conversion, there is some proposition which could be used to dissolve the appearance of discontinuous revision, if only we attribute a belief in that proposition to the inquirer. But I do not think this fact constitutes a reason for attributing such a belief to the inquirer.[59] To me this looks like a case of "cooking" the data to save a theory. However, it would perhaps be best to avoid getting involved in the sort of detailed haggling over actual cases, or realistically described hypothetical cases, that would be needed to settle the issue finally. For the present, I shall simply note that my argument requires only that radical conversions *can* occur.[60] My opponent holds that such conversions cannot occur – that all conversions are of a type compatible with the conservative conception of reflective equilibrium. I would think, therefore, that the onus is upon my opponent. In the absence of an argument against the possibility of radical changes in moral belief, I am permitted to assume that such conversions can occur, and given the results of my admittedly casual observations, do occur.[61]

This brings us to the second charge against the radical conception of reflective equilibrium: that radical conversions are not the sort of rational change of belief that ought to have a place in a method of moral inquiry. I think that I can best respond to this charge by clarifying what I take myself to be claiming, and what I think is required in order to deny my claim. We have been supposing that, when a person takes up the task of constructing a moral theory, there are a great many moral and philosophical propositions the person accepts or rejects to some degree or other. It is as if the person has gone through a list of propositions, considering each in turn, and assigning a degree of commitment. It seems obvious to me that at a later time, after the person has had more experience and thought more deeply about things, the person might decide that she was mistaken about some of the assignments she made before she began to think philosophically about moral theory. And I see no reason for thinking that a person must connect any such change up with some other belief and degree of commitment on her original list. Surely, many of the moral judgments we made with absolute certainty when we were adolescents are changed in this discontinuous way – we come to look at things differently, decide that we made a mistake, and believe differently without feeling any need to justify our reevaluation on the basis of something else that we believed when we were adolescents and continue to believe. The radical conception is intended to reflect the importance of this kind of change in belief. To adopt the conservative conception and to deny the possibility of discontinuous revisions of belief is, it seems to me, to suppose that, when we begin moral inquiry, we already possess as much of the truth about morality as we ever will. The harvest is over and moral inquiry amounts to no more than separating the chaff from the wheat.

Even if one grants that radical conversions occur, and that it is proper for our method of moral inquiry to allow for such radical shifts in belief, one is likely to question my categorization of the radical method as a type of coherence method or version of wide reflective equilibrium. My characterization of radical reflective equilibrium as being more concerned with the inquirer, and granting her a more significant role in theory construction, than conservative reflective equilibrium, which focuses more on beliefs, invites one to think of moral perception, or intuition, rather than the kind of balancing of beliefs that reflective equilibrium is supposed to call to mind. As a result, the radical method may seem to be more of a form of foundationalism than coherentism. It does not really matter very much whether we think of the radical method as a version of coherentism or foundationalism, as a further development of Rawlsian reflective equilibrium or of a similar, but distinct, method. Radical reflective equilibrium is only an intermediate position encountered on the way to the *method of balance and refinement*, which I ultimately intend to describe and defend. So the important questions concern whether there are deficiencies with conservative reflective equilibrium, and whether the radical method plausibly develops reflective equilibrium in a way that avoids these deficiencies, carrying us in the direction of the method of balance and refinement. Nonetheless, it is worth pointing out that I think the radical method is a type of coherence method, as well as a close sibling of wide reflective equilibrium, in a way that balance and refinement is not. In the first place, unlike traditional sorts of foundationalist or intuitionist methods, which take certain beliefs to be unrevisable, radical reflective equilibrium does not grant any sort of proposition a privileged status. In addition, it recognizes the importance of the sorts of revisions characteristic of conservative reflective equilibrium, and incorporates all the features of that method of inquiry. It deviates from reflective equilibrium, as traditionally conceived, only in allowing initial degrees of commitment to be revised as a result of the consideration of alternative moral conceptions and philosophical arguments, where the revision is not required to resolve a conflict or to extend the inquirer's system of beliefs. This deviation can be seen as nothing more than a way of insuring that the inquirer has achieved a coherent equilibrium point that takes the most comprehensive set of alternatives into account, and is, therefore, a more stable equilibrium than that attained by the conservative method. And the deviation moves radical reflective equilibrium even farther away from foundationalist methods than the conservative conception, since it insures that the inquirer's initial beliefs and degrees of commitment are not playing a foundational role in the process of theory construction.

I have argued that neither the no credibility objection nor the Wimpy response is cogent. Both presuppose that the method of reflective equilibrium cannot be accepted, unless the beliefs that guide and constrain theory construction are reliable. But, as I have argued, if we interpret reflective equilibrium correctly, i.e., radically, no set of beliefs or assignment of credibilities serves to guide the inquirer through the process of seeking reflective equilibrium. Hence, neither the challenge to provide a defense of the beliefs that play this role nor the attempt to meet this challenge can be legitimate. But even if one accepts my arguments for this conclusion, a feeling that I have not touched the real concern about reflective equilibrium is likely to linger. A feeling that there is more to the Wimpy response than I have admitted also lingers. For it may seem that I have been unduly strict in my understanding of the no credibility objection. Whether or not the method of reflective equilibrium allows certain beliefs to guide and to constrain theory construction, opponents of the method will want some assurance that it is reliable. If certain beliefs did constrain theory acceptance, questions about the method's reliability would reduce to questions about the reliability of these beliefs. But showing that there are no such beliefs hardly chases away doubts about the reliability of the method. Thus, while I may have shown that the *no credibility objection* is based upon a mistaken presupposition, the more general *no contact objection* must still be faced. And, in spite of my contention that the Wimpy response shares this mistaken presupposition, it seemingly remains a viable option: To the challenge to defend the reliability of the final product of reflective equilibrium, the Wimpy respondent will, apparently quite reasonably, respond that this can hardly be done before we have much more of that product before us than we do at present.[62] Let us now take up these issues.

1.9 THE NO CONTACT OBJECTION AND WIMPY RESPONSE RESURRECTED

Suppose we characterize a method of inquiry, very abstractly, as a function from input beliefs onto output beliefs. We might also think of the input and output beliefs as coming in two types: *epistemic lead*, that is, false or unreliable beliefs, and *epistemic gold*, that is, true or reliable beliefs. There would then seem to be four kinds of methods:

	IN	OUT
I	Gold	Gold
	Lead	Lead
II	Gold	Gold
	Lead	Gold
III	Gold	Lead
	Lead	Gold
IV	Gold	Lead
	Lead	Lead

Using this taxonomy, we might provide a rough and ready summary of the argument to this point as follows: Both the no credibility objection and the Wimpy response assume that reflective equilibrium is a Type I or *smelter's* method. I call it a smelter's method, because the inquirer must work under the same sort of constraint as the smelter of metals – his raw materials determine the nature of his final product. If he is given something with gold in it, he can extract the gold. But if all he has to start with is lead ore, he can at best produce lead. Assuming that reflective equilibrium is a smelter's method, to determine whether it could yield epistemic gold, we need only assay the input. Thus, because our considered moral judgments constitute the distinctly moral element of the input, the debate focuses on whether or not these beliefs are initially credible. If we have the conservative conception of reflective equilibrium in mind, assuming that reflective equilibrium is a smelter's method seems a perfectly reasonable thing to do. For although conservative reflective equilibrium allows rather extensive revisions, when revisions are necessary is dictated by the logical and evidential relations among input beliefs, and what the revisions will be is virtually determined by the person's initial degrees of commitment to the input beliefs. Such revisions do not seem to be sufficiently radical, either to transmute lead into gold reliably, or to pose much danger of allowing gold to decay into lead.

I have argued that reflective equilibrium should be understood radically, so that initial beliefs and degrees of belief can be altered in ways that go beyond what is required to make the person's initial belief system coherent. Given that the radical method allows for true conversions, for breaks with a person's initial system of beliefs, it does not seem reasonable to assume that this version of reflective equilibrium is a smelter's method. Radical reflective equilibrium apparently opens up the possibility of *alchemical* methods. For a person who begins with beliefs of epistemic lead may experience a conversion that leads her to epistemic gold, i.e., to accept mostly true beliefs. In this case, reflective equilibrium would seem to be a Type II method, functioning as the philosopher's stone to turn the person's epistemic lead into gold. A fine possibility, but unfortunately, it would seem that radical reflective equilibrium is as dangerous as alchemy was thought to be. The radical revisions, that could be functioning as a philosopher's stone, could just as easily play tricks on the inquirer, by functioning as a Type III method, or turn the inquirer's beliefs to lead no matter what the quality of her initial beliefs, behaving, in this case, as a Type IV method. For there is nothing in the specification of radical reflective equilibrium which seems capable of *guaranteeing* that conversions will occur only when the input is lead, or that conversions will always yield gold as output. We might then say that radical reflective equilibrium is not aptly described as a function from input to output beliefs at all. Since the input does not determine when conversions will occur, or what the output of the conversion will be, the method can take different persons from the same inputs to different outputs.

Because the radical version of the method of reflective equilibrium allows for discontinuous revisions of initial beliefs and degrees of belief, questions about the value of the method's output do not reduce to questions about its input. So the radical method does not face the no credibility objection. But the suspicions that gave rise to that objection do not, therefore, go away. The opponent of reflective equilibrium will still want some assurance that the method is reliable, that it provides a true philosopher's stone, rather than some sort of alchemical trickery.[63] This is to say, the radical version still faces the more general no contact with reality objection, of which the no credibility objection was a specific instance. And perhaps the objection is even more forceful than it was before. We are used to thinking of methods as functions from input beliefs, or data, onto output beliefs, or theories, and to thinking of inquiry as transferring epistemic status from input to output. We therefore feel that we have a good idea of what it would take to validate a method – we seek to establish the quality of the input and to show that the method moves from input to output in ways that, at worst, do not allow for much decay of epistemic status. When we move away from this model, and give up on the idea that the output of the method will be a function of its input, we are perhaps left without any idea of how we might go about defending such a method of inquiry.

When thus faced with the no contact objection, the defender of reflective equilibrium may be tempted to resurrect the Wimpy response. She will agree that we cannot assay the quality of reflective equilibrium's final product at the present time, and that we now may not even see how we might go about defending this product. After all, we do not yet have much of that product before us. But the Wimpy respondent will argue that this shows the request for the assay to be unfairly premature, rather than that the method is unacceptable. She will admit that the method might be unacceptable for all we *now* know, but argue that its unacceptability does not follow from the absence of a defense of the method *before* the method has been tried. The unacceptability of the method will only be demonstrated if the questions about the method's output still cannot be satisfactorily answered *after* the method has been employed.

1.10 CONVERGENCE AND THE RELIABILITY OF THE OUTPUT

The Wimpy respondent admits that some argument for the credibility of the output of reflective equilibrium must eventually be provided. We have been thinking of credibility in terms of reliability, but we have not spent much time considering how the notion of reliability ought to be understood. It would seem, however, that no matter how we conceive of reliability, it is safe to assume that the relevant beliefs will, by and large, be true. This is not to say that it is impossible for most of the elements of a set of reliable beliefs to be false. For reliability, generally, is not defined as a high actual frequency of true belief, but as high frequency of true belief in some appropriately specified class of possible circumstances, situations, worlds, or what have you. As a result, we must admit the possibility of reliable but largely false beliefs. However, as I said above, we are safe in assuming that most elements of a set of reliable beliefs will be true, in the sense that, given an appropriately strong definition of reliability, it will be *extremely unlikely* that these elements are not mostly true. Thus, for example, if we are thinking of our initial considered moral judgments, no matter whether we think of reliability as a property of the individual believer, belief-forming mechanism, or type of belief, we can safely assume that if our considered moral judgments are reliable, then, at least for the most part, these judgments will be true. And if we are worried about the output of reflective equilibrium, whether we are thinking of the method itself as being reliable or of persons who have followed the method through to its conclusion as being reliable moral judges, the beliefs held by inquirers who have employed the radical version of reflective equilibrium would apparently have to be true, again, at least for the most part. It is, of course, possible for, say, a reliable mechanism to produce output beliefs that are not mostly true on a given occasion. It might, for example, be operating in an unfavorable environment. But it remains the case that if we have a set of output beliefs that are not mostly true, the presumption must be that they are unreliable in the relevant sense of reliability, be it one that applies to type of belief, judge, or belief-producing mechanism. Hence, for a version of the Wimpy response to the no contact objection to succeed, the method of reflective equilibrium must produce output beliefs that are, by and large, true. So, if these output beliefs are to have any chance of being reliable, people following the method would apparently have to converge to a substantial degree on a single system of moral beliefs. For if inquirers did not so converge, every difference of opinion would guarantee some false propositions, and enough dis-agreements would add up to unreliability. Unfortunately, I am afraid convergence is highly unlikely. To show both that the Wimpy response requires convergence, and that such convergence is unlikely, I shall backtrack a bit and begin by making the point about our initial moral judgments.

People do not agree about initial moral judgments, or even consid-ered moral judgments, to anything like the degree to which they agree about other beliefs we all assume to be reliable, e.g., our ordinary visual beliefs. Because there is such wide divergence about initial moral judgments, where by divergence I mean not only that people make different judgments, but also that many of the judgments they make are incompatible, the set of the initial moral judgments made by all inquirers will surely contain a significant proportion of false proposi-tions. If we like to think in terms of mechanisms, we would say it is unlikely that the mechanism which produced these judgments is reliable. Or perhaps we might conclude that it is unlikely there is any one mechanism that leads to these judgments in the way that there is, for example, *a* visual mechanism. However, if there is more than one mechanism, we are still left with the conclusion that the considered moral judgments of moral inquirers are not generally reliable, al-though now the explanation is that all persons do not use the same mechanism, and at least some of them use unreliable mechanisms.[64] There is, therefore, little hope that we will be able to produce an argument for the reliability of these judgments, even in the long run.

It might seem that a Wimpy respondent could retrench by claiming that people are reliable only about the moral judgments that they accept in reflective equilibrium. However, for this retrenchment to be successful, people would have to *converge* on a single system of moral beliefs, or moral theory, in reflective equilibrium. For unless there were such convergence, we could again be reasonably sure that in-quirers are not generally reliable in their moral judgments. Without substantial convergence, the set of moral beliefs held by all inquirers who have reached a state of reflective equilibrium would contain many incompatible beliefs, which would guarantee the falsity of many of these beliefs. Some, for example, Norman Daniels, might be taken to hold that convergence is not unlikely, but I do not think there is sufficient evidence to back up such optimism. Proceeding on the assumption that people have been following something very like reflective equilibrium all along, one might cite practices that were once condoned or controversial but now are agreed by nearly all persons to be immoral. Slavery provides the most commonly mentioned example.

But do such examples really provide very weighty evidence in favor of convergence? There are not all that many examples of practices we have come to agree about, and there seem to be as many practices that were evaluated with unanimity in the past, but are now controversial. Consider homosexuality. There have been times and places, e.g., ancient Athens, where homosexuality was not controversial because it was generally accepted, and other times and places where it was not controversial because generally condemned, e.g., Victorian England. And now it would seem to be a controversial matter in the United States, or perhaps I should say that it is now controversial in some places, or in some circles, while in others it is not, with these dividing between those where it is not controversial because it is agreed that nothing is wrong with homosexuality and those where it is agreed that there is. So I do not think we are justified in saying that, on balance, there is more agreement in the moral sphere now than there was in the past. Indeed, such writers as Bernard Williams[65] and Alasdair MacIntyre[66] have stressed the fact that modern ethical thinking lacks the power to generate a consensus regarding important moral issues, so they each look back to the past with their own sort of nostalgia. In any case, I think it most reasonable, for our purposes, that we hold the present state of affairs, fraught with moral disagreement at every level, accurately to indicate the promise of future agreement, at least until stronger evidence for convergence is advanced.

One familiar with Daniels' particular version of the Wimpy response might think that convergence is not necessary to defend the output of reflective equilibrium, for Daniels certainly is not so rash as to assume that convergence will occur. His discussion of convergence seems to be well balanced between optimism and pessimism. For one thing, Daniels admits that the method of reflective equilibrium might not produce convergence on a single moral outlook, where I mean by "moral outlook" to indicate the inquirer's considered moral judgments and moral theory, but instead convergence on a limited number of outlooks. I agree with Daniels: The likelihood of a limited convergence is greater than the likelihood of either convergence on a single outlook or of each person's holding a distinct outlook. However, even if people were to converge on some small number of moral outlooks, it would not be possible to show that our considered moral judgments in wide reflective equilibrium are reliable. The best case of convergence, short of convergence on a single moral outlook, would be convergence on two outlooks. But then, assuming that the theories disagree about many things, at best, roughly half the moral output of reflective equilibrium would be true, which surely is not enough to say that these beliefs are reliable.[67]

Perhaps I am being unfair. The idea is probably not that persons will converge on a few outlooks that differ in most respects, but that the outlooks converged upon will overlap to a significant degree. In this case, the area of overlap might provide a set of beliefs that can be defended as highly reliable. In this connection, Daniels points out that while there is widespread disagreement about some moral judgments, there is just as widespread, but less commonly considered, agreement about other such judgments.[68] Moreover, there might even be some reason to suspect that these judgments are credible, since some explanation of the agreement is necessary, and one possible explanation is that people judge the cases in question reliably.

I have to admit that I am not very confident about the chances for this sort of convergence on a core set of judgments. I agree with those who have claimed that the method of wide reflective equilibrium has been employed by many moral philosophers. In fact, I shall be arguing in Chapter 3 that even many of those who are opposed to this method actually employ it. I therefore think that we can take the moral outlooks that philosophers have articulated and defended as a guide to what is likely to result from following the method of reflective equilibrium. While some of the live options in ethics certainly agree about a wide range of cases, there are other theories that clearly stand apart, e.g., egoism, radical feminism, or the views of Plato, Aristotle, Marx, Kropotkin, or Nietzsche, dissenting from the contemporary mainstream about almost everything. If the survival of these outlooks indicates that they may be held by some people in wide reflective equilibrium, as I think it does, we have reason to doubt that people will converge sufficiently in reflective equilibrium to establish the reliability of the method's output. In fact, I believe we can say with some confidence that the method has been used by many thinkers for quite some time without yet producing any significant convergence. Thus, we can say that the method has been unreliable *up until now*. Perhaps this does not entail that it will never produce convergence, or never come to be reliable. However, it would seem that if those following the method of radical reflective equilibrium did, at some time in the future, converge upon a single moral view, and a true view at that, the explanation for this would apparently have to lie somewhere outside the method.

I could, of course, be wrong about the prospects for future convergence. And if inquirers employing the radical method of reflective equilibrium were one day to come to substantial agreement regarding a moral outlook in a way that allowed us to argue for the reliability of their judgments, I could hardly deny that a powerful defense of the method's adequacy would be available to us. Nonetheless, it seems clear that at the present time, from which it is at best difficult to extrapolate a curve to such future agreement, radical reflective equilibrium is in a desperate way if the only hope for defending this method depends upon inquirers reaching agreement at some time in the future. The proponent of reflective equilibrium would, therefore, do well to explore alternative strategies for answering the no contact with reality objection. For the probability that inquirers will converge just does not seem to be high enough to rest easy when the only line of defense will fail without convergence. Again, I may be mistaken about the likelihood of inquirers following the method of reflective equilibrium coming to substantial agreement about a moral outlook. And I have not really offered much of an argument for thinking that the probability of future convergence is low. But I cannot help thinking that few readers would be willing to risk much on the chance that inquirers will ever agree regarding a moral outlook, nor can I really say I consider their unwillingness unreasonable.

1.11 CONCLUSION

This chapter has attained two significant results. First, we now have a more accurate conception of the method of reflective equilibrium. In particular, we recognize that the method ought to be construed radically, in a way that allows consideration of alternative moral and philosophical conceptions to give rise to revisions of moral beliefs that are not determined by the moral and philosophical beliefs a person held when she began her philosophical inquiry into morality. Secondly, we have come to see that the predicament in which the method of reflective equilibrium finds itself is quite serious. Since the method was first proposed by Rawls, it has faced various formulations of the no contact with reality objection. From the start, everyone could agree that Rawls' method would lead inquirers to adopt the moral theory or perspective that is most coherent and, on reflection, seems most likely to be true. The question has always been, why should this count for anything? What reason is there for thinking that what seems likely to be true to me, or to us, really is likely to be true? It has been possible to hold this question off by at least tacitly accepting something like what I have here called the Wimpy response. Sure, we think, some answer must be given to these questions, but only eventually. Be patient. Wait. The answers will come in their own time. But it just isn't so! The cold fact is, there is only the slimmest chance that an answer to the questions raised by the no contact objection will ever be provided. I maintain that the method of reflective equilibrium will never yield a consensus among inquirers who employ it, and it will therefore never produce an argument for its own reliability. In point of fact, taking a reliable method to be one such that it is likely that the beliefs held by any person as a result of following the method will be true for the most part, reflective equilibrium simply is not a reliable method. I admit that the prediction which grounds this conclusion might be mistaken, but I'm also very confident no one would bet against me – unless I offered outrageously good odds.

2 A strategy for defending a method of moral inquiry

2.1 INTRODUCTION

At the end of the last chapter, we left our hero, the radical method of reflective equilibrium,[1] in a tight spot. The method was left standing naked before the demand for some reason to think that reflective equilibrium will bring inquirers into contact with moral reality. And not only did we find that *at present* there is no way of showing that a person following the method of reflective equilibrium would be led to adopt true moral beliefs, but we had to grant that it is very unlikely any such argument will be possible in the future. For any such argument would require that persons employing the radical method converge upon a single moral view in a way that seems improbable given the current level of disagreement regarding serious moral questions. Perhaps we could hang on, hoping against hope, that things will work out in the end – hoping that inquirers will one day come to agree upon a moral outlook, and agree in a way that will allow for the vindication of our hero. But this would require a martyr's faith of moral inquirers, for they would have to go on using the method of reflective equilibrium in the face of the likelihood that it will never be able to answer what seems to be the most serious challenge confronting it.

As in the old movie serials, things are not really as hopeless as they appear. A way out of danger lies in a direction we have overlooked. Our hero can reach safety by challenging the assumption that a method of moral inquiry can be adequate only if it can be shown that those who employ the method will attain the truth, or at least, that they are likely to attain the truth. If this assumption can be overturned, the possibility of defending the method opens up. To bolster our morale, prior to confronting this widely shared assumption, I might note that it holds moral methods to a standard that few, if any, methods outside of mathematics and logic can meet. For surely, we cannot say it has been *shown* even that "the scientific method" is likely to lead to the truth.

Nor has the reliability of the common-sense methods by which we form beliefs about the world around us been demonstrated. And I think we must admit that the obstacles blocking arguments for the reliability of these methods are not going to be surmounted with time. In the future, science might produce theories with greater predictive power, affording explanations of a broader range of phenomena, and perhaps even perfect consensus regarding these theories, but this would not enable us to show that the scientific method had led us to the truth. For an argument to this conclusion would have to assume that something, e.g., explanatory coherence,[2] predictive power, fruitfulness, or consensus, is truth-conducive, and no such assumption is beyond question. We should not be surprised by this result. Within their own ranges of application, the "methods" by which we form beliefs about middle-sized perceptible objects have led us to nearly perfect consensus, and have allowed for accurate prediction, and these methods have done so for thousands of years. Yet we cannot demonstrate that careful skeptical arguments are mistaken.

Although these reflections might suggest that the prospects for the method of reflective equilibrium are not absolutely hopeless, the fact that other patently acceptable methods of inquiry cannot strictly be *shown* to yield mostly true beliefs to all who employ them does not ground a defense of reflective equilibrium, at least not the defense I wish to offer. For while, e.g., the scientific method's success at yielding accurate predictions and producing consensus does not provide decisive evidence of that method's reliability, most people are inclined to think that it counts for something. And, some will surely argue, the fact that reflective equilibrium is not, and probably never will be, similarly successful not only deprives it of the weak support available to methods that are successful, but provides positive evidence against reflective equilibrium. Indeed, proponents of the no contact with reality objection might plausibly claim that their demand for a demonstration of the reliability of reflective equilibrium was grounded upon this positive reason for doubting the method's reliability, not some sort of criterion according to which it must always be possible to show that acceptable methods are reliable. Hence, it would seem that rejecting the dubious assumption that any acceptable method of inquiry must be capable of being *shown*, in some stringent sense, to be reliable is not enough. Since we have reason to doubt the reliability of reflective equilibrium, in order to defend this method, one apparently must either rebut the grounds for doubt, or undercut their relevance, by rejecting the very widely shared assumption that acceptable methods must *be* reliable. As I have indicated, I do not think we can succeed at the former.

The idea that reliability is the criterion for an acceptable moral method is not easily dismissed. On the one hand, it might seem to be supported by the thought that the point of moral theorizing is practical. Our ultimate aim is to live a good life, or to do the right thing, goals that are reasonably thought to be furthered by having an accurate picture of such a life, or true beliefs about what is right. As Aristotle said, "Then surely knowledge of this good is also of great importance for the conduct of our lives, and if, like archers, we have a target to aim at, we are more likely to hit the right mark."[3] On the other hand, even if our concern is more theoretical, so that we want moral *knowledge*, in addition to mere true belief, the reliabilist criterion apparently makes sense. For in the first place, true belief is necessary for knowledge. In addition, the dominant view among epistemologists, both past and present, is that the most significant feature distinguishing knowledge from mere true belief, commonly referred to either as justification, or warrant, or occasionally even rationality, is itself to be analyzed as some sort of connection with truth.[4]

It is not surprising that reliabilists endorse this claim. Thus, we find Alvin Goldman stating that:

> The central epistemological concepts of appraisal, I argue, invoke *true belief* as their ultimate aim. So the evaluation of epistemic procedures, methods, processes, or arrangements must appeal to truth-conduciveness, an objective standard of assessment.[5]

But contemporary foundationalists and coherentists endorse the assumption as well.[6] William Alston, from among the foundationalists, says:

> a belief's *being justified* is a favorable status vis-à-vis the basic aim of believing or, more generally, of cognition, viz., to believe truly rather than falsely. For a ground to be favorable relative to this aim it must be "truth conducive"; it must be sufficiently indicative of the truth of the belief it grounds.[7]

And one prominent contemporary coherentist, Laurence BonJour, writes:

> The basic role of justification is that of a *means* to truth, a more directly attainable mediating link between our subjective starting point and our objective goal.[8]

Fortunately I do not absolutely have to work against the weight of the dominant view regarding the connection between truth and epistemic evaluation. For, I contend, from the fact that the goal of moral inquiry is moral knowledge, it does not follow that an adequate method of moral inquiry must be reliable, even when the connection between the epistemic component of knowledge and truth avowed by the dominant view is granted. Consider an analogous case. The goal of placing a bet is to win. However, we cannot conclude that an adequate strategy or method for betting must be reliable, in the sense that following it always, or even often, yields a winning bet. If we are betting on a game of chance, the nature of the game will limit how often we could expect to win in the long run. In such a case, we might say that an adequate strategy is one that produces at least as many winning bets as any other strategy. If the odds are poor enough, we might deny that there is any adequate strategy, even though there would presumably be one or more strategies that are at least as good as any other. But whether we would conclude that there is no adequate method in such a case depends upon other factors. For one thing, whether we have a choice about playing the game is relevant. Except in bizarre hypothetical cases, it is generally up to us whether we will play a game of chance. Other activities are more frequently forced upon us. When we *must* engage in an activity directed at a certain goal, we are likely to consider strategies or methods for attaining that goal to be adequate which are not terribly likely to reach the goal in question. And even when we are not literally constrained to engage in a goal-directed activity, if the goal is sufficiently important to us, we will again consider unreliable strategies or methods adequate, provided that they are the most reliable ones available. For example, a farmer in sub-Saharan Africa might frequently lose his crop entirely, yet it may be that his farming methods are adequate. The farmer's methods may represent state of the art horticultural techniques for farming in arid subtropical conditions. If so, we might say that the farmer's problem lies with the environment in which he is forced to farm, not with his farming methods. Likewise, we might think that big cats have evolved adequate, indeed, remarkable strategies for hunting, yet as a matter of fact only a small percentage of a big cat's stalks ends in a kill.[9]

A defender of the dominant view might at this point grant that I have shown that, in general, an activity directed at a certain goal need not reliably attain that goal to be adequate, but claim that methods of inquiry, which have as they do the goal of knowledge, somehow constitute a special case. The claim would be that, because of the nature of knowledge and inquiry in particular, a method of inquiry must reliably attain the goal of knowledge if it is to be adequate. Presumably, one would defend this claim by reasoning that unreliability of a method of inquiry makes it impossible that the method *ever* attain its goal of knowledge. For knowledge requires warrant, and warrant requires a reliable connection with truth, so general unreliability entails that the method never yields warrant. Now, I do not believe that methods of inquiry constitute such a special case, and I will try to explain below, primarily in Chapter 5, how it might be possible for a generally unreliable method, like reflective equilibrium, to yield warranted beliefs. But for the time being, I'll simply avoid this argument by offering a different reason for thinking that methods of inquiry need not reliably yield true belief to be adequate. To this point in the discussion, we have considered only activities that have a unitary goal, and we have tacitly assumed that methods of moral inquiry have a unitary goal. We should need no argument to convince us that judgments of adequacy will become even more complex in cases where a method aims at diverse goals. And only a little reflection will be needed to see that moral methods actually have complex goals.

I hope that, against this backdrop, the criticisms of reflective equilibrium considered in the last chapter will now seem entirely too hasty. Indeed, I believe I can say that nearly all discussions of the adequacy of methods of moral inquiry should seem hasty, for nearly all of them presuppose that the issue turns solely upon whether such methods can guarantee us the truth. A responsible discussion of any method of moral inquiry must proceed from a more adequate conception of the goal at which the method is aimed, as well as the conditions under which the inquiry is to be conducted. In the next section, I shall attempt to develop such an adequate conception. In Section 2.3, I will attempt to characterize, in more detail, two significant epistemic elements of what I take to be the goal of moral inquiry, i.e., rationality and warrant. My efforts to specify more fully the goal of moral inquiry in Sections 2.2 and 2.3 prepare the ground for the discussion of whether the radical method of reflective equilibrium is adequate. That discussion will occupy the remainder of the book. In Section 2.5, I outline the strategy I intend to deploy in defending radical reflective equilibrium. In my opinion, the work of these three sections can proceed without challenging the dominant view of the connection between truth and epistemic evaluation, which I sketched above. Indeed, I could develop my entire defense of the radical method without challenging this view. But the fact is, I have doubts about the adequacy of the dominant view, so I shall offer arguments against it in Section 2.4. Nonetheless, I would not want my overall argument in support of reflective equilibrium to turn on my rejection of the dominant view regarding truth and epistemic evaluation. So, when describing my overall strategy for defending an approach to moral inquiry, in Section 2.5, I shall be careful to insure that this strategy remains as neutral as possible among rival accounts of crucial concepts of epistemic evaluation.

2.2 THE GOAL OF MORAL INQUIRY

I have already said something about the goal of moral inquiry. However, I have not painted a complete picture of either the goal or the conditions under which we set out to attain this goal. What I have said is that part of our aim is practical: We want the truth about what is right and good, so that we can increase our chances of doing right and attaining good. I have also noted that our aim is in part theoretical. We would not be satisfied merely with holding moral beliefs that turn out to be true. For, as J. S. Mill stressed, unless more is said about the manner in which the beliefs are held, it is possible that they reside in us as mere superstitions.[10] We want moral *knowledge*, in addition to true belief. There is very broad agreement that this is to say, at least, that we want true moral beliefs that also have a significant positive epistemic status.[11] As I noted above, beliefs having this status are variously termed warranted, justified, or rational. For clarity, let us select "warrant" to refer to the positive epistemic status, whatever it is, the possession of which distinguishes knowledge from mere true belief.[12]

Moral knowledge is not all that moral inquiry seeks. For it might be possible to come to know moral propositions in various ways, only some of which would constitute an appropriate end for a properly *philosophical* inquiry. For example, if it is possible for anyone to have moral knowledge at all, it is presumably possible for a person to come to have moral knowledge on the basis of testimony. All that would be required is that the person believe certain moral propositions, because they were asserted by an authority, or expert, who actually has moral knowledge, and whose authority the person is warranted in trusting. There is nothing wrong with such *testimonial* moral knowledge. Almost certainly, vast amounts of our knowledge, regardless of its sphere, is testimonial. In addition, the first moral knowledge each of us wins as children is testimonial. But we would surely be no more satisfied with a philosophical inquiry into morality if the only knowledge it could yield were testimonial than we would be with inquiry into planetary motion, equine physiology, or feline psychology, if these inquiries yielded only testimonial knowledge. We want to know in something like the way the expert knows.[13] We do not merely want to be able to sort true from false moral propositions; we want to know what distinguishes them. So, we should say that our goal is *fundamental, primary* moral knowledge, that is, knowledge of the ground of morality that is not based upon the moral knowledge of any other person.[14]

We seek more than even primary moral knowledge. To see this, let us begin by considering the following example from outside the moral realm.[15] I close the book I have been reading, and head out to the stable to do my chores. But I am in an odd frame of mind. The book is Descartes's *Meditations*, and I have not only been utterly convinced by his skeptical arguments for thinking that we *may* have been deceived in many of our ordinary beliefs, but have gone one better. I believe that these beliefs are, *in fact*, the result of deception. Having always thought of the world as a fouled up, uncooperative sort of place, since first reading Descartes some years ago, I have been captivated by the thought that it is even worse than I previously suspected. I have come to believe quite firmly that there is no world (as I formerly "knew" it) at all, but merely a series of illusions, constructed by an evil power, for the express purpose of deluding and tormenting me. Do not suppose that I have come to this strange belief frivolously or carelessly. I have spent a considerable amount of time examining this belief, all the evidence that seems relevant, and the arguments I am aware of that bear upon its truth. The fact is, my belief in the deceiving power has survived all the scrutiny to which I have subjected it. Indeed, under the intense light of this scrutiny, it has triumphed over the more common view of the world I once shared with, what I then took to be, others. In any case, I no longer imagine that my sense experience gives me any reason to believe that the world actually is the way it appears to be, so I strive mightily to deprive the power which I am now convinced exists of any further sport, by not forming any beliefs at all about the perceived world.

To return to my story, on the particular day in question, I leave off my customary reading of Descartes, which I do to help keep my resolve firm in the face of the strong temptation to believe things are as they seem. Then, feeling quite silly for setting out to feed the horses, even though I do not really believe they exist, I go about my business in a dreamy reverie. But suddenly, as I am distractedly leading GiGi, a spirited young filly, in from the paddock, JoJo, the cat, leaps out of the hay loft to the ground before us. GiGi is startled and rears. I am jerked off the ground, hanging onto the lead rope. Brought to my senses, quite literally, I look up at the hooves flailing in the air, and instinctively believe that a large bay horse is about to strike me. At that moment, I know many things on the basis of my sense experience – that a horse towers above me, that the lead rope is still in my hand, which is burning because the rope was pulled through my clenched fingers, and that the offending JoJo has ducked behind a pitchfork. This knowledge is certainly primary, being in no way based upon any other person's knowledge. But, given my other beliefs at that moment, in particular my belief that all my experiences are caused by an evil demon for the express purpose of deluding me, it would seem that something is epistemically wrong with these perceptual beliefs. For one thing, they do not cohere with my settled view regarding perceptual beliefs. There is, therefore, a problem with the corpus of my beliefs as a whole, since it does not form a coherent system. Moreover, there is a problem with these perceptual beliefs in particular. For, we are supposing, these beliefs are, so to speak, the intruders. They result from my momentary loss of attention, from my epistemic weakness. They conflict with more strongly held settled convictions, and as a result, if I were to reflect upon the matter, I would regard these perceptual beliefs as mistaken, and chastise myself for having slipped into holding them. Thus, although my perceptual beliefs, about the cat and horse, would arguably constitute primary knowledge, they would stand apart from the sort of coherent system we want our beliefs to form. Finally, in virtue of conflicting with more strongly held, settled convictions, in a certain sense, these beliefs would not be rational.[16]

Similar cases seem to be possible in the moral realm. Imagine that I am a professional philosopher who specializes in meta-ethics. (This may take more or less imagination depending upon what you have thought of this book so far!) I have come to hold a skeptical position regarding morality. I did not begin my career as a skeptic, and I was at one time not entirely happy about being one, but I have been convinced, as a result of considering the relevant theories and arguments over a number of years. One evening, I am in a bar with a colleague who has been pressing objections to moral skepticism for the last hour or so. But I have heard all of this before, and I have been able to answer his objections without having to think through any aspect of my position anew. The experience has only served to refresh my memory, and further confirm me in my view that we can have no moral knowledge, because there are no moral truths, that morality is an empty sham. Suddenly my attention is drawn away from our philosophical conversation, as a man and woman at the end of the bar raise their voices. The woman starts to leave, but the man grabs her by the arm and violently spins her around to face him. She begins screaming at him. He raises his fist and punches her in the face. The woman falls backward, hitting her head against the brass foot rail along the bottom of the bar, and sits dumbly upon the floor. Some blood runs from her lip, and an ugly bruise begins to rise on her cheek, as the man storms out of the bar. I cannot believe that I have witnessed such a senseless act of violence. I am appalled. I *believe* that the man has committed a serious wrong. As in the case involving perceptual knowledge, it is arguable that I would have knowledge in the situation just described. I would know that the man had done wrong, but this bit of moral knowledge would stand at odds with all my considered beliefs about the nature of morality. My moral beliefs would lack a coherent, systematic structure, and my belief about the man's act would, again in a certain sense, fail to be rational.

The sort of moral knowledge just described is not derivative. It may even be fundamental, for I might believe not merely that the man did something wrong, but that this action was wrong because the man harmed a person far weaker than he, who posed no threat, and this could well be what makes the action wrong. But surely, knowledge, like that I have of the wrongness of the man's violent act, is not the goal of a philosophical inquiry into morality. We want to come to a systematic view, or at least to a view that is as systematic as it is possible for a moral view to be,[17] and we want to be explicitly aware of this systematic structure. We want to come to hold this view in a way that makes it rational for us to adopt it. We do not want the belief to stand in conflict with more strongly held convictions that would lead us, upon a moment's reflection, to dismiss the new belief.

There is another reason for our wishing to attain such rational, systematic knowledge. Recall the way I began in the first chapter, i.e., with the fact that all of us, or anyway nearly all of us, start out thinking about morality with a stock of moral beliefs in hand, or perhaps better, in mind. Whatever the explanation of our having them, the fact is, we do hold moral beliefs when we undertake a philosophical inquiry into morality. For most of us, these beliefs are not in terribly good shape. Our moral beliefs are patchy, not covering certain areas where we feel important moral questions arise. They are disconnected: indeed, they are likely to conflict in various ways. Yet, coming back to our practical aims, these beliefs are important – they are *supposed* to guide us, and, for most of us, they *in fact* guide our behavior, at least some of the time.[18] We begin our inquiry, therefore, in a doxastic predicament. We have these moral beliefs, and we can see what sort of a mess they present us with. It seems we must do something. But what, exactly, are we to do about this insistent rabble of moral convictions that we find residing in our minds? This is one of the questions to which our method of inquiry is supposed to provide an answer. Hence, we are brought once again to the conclusion that one of the things we are out to accomplish is to mold our moral beliefs into some sort of orderly, coherent system.[19]

So, the goal of our inquiry is rational, primary, fundamental, and systematic moral knowledge. Equally significant is the fact that we are, in a sense, pushed into the inquiry. Despite the practice of speaking as if we can choose what to believe, which philosophers, particularly epistemologists, have fallen into, we clearly cannot just decide to believe this or to disbelieve that. We do not have any direct volitional control over our beliefs. Thus, we cannot, somehow, turn off our moral beliefs when we recognize their deplorable condition. Neither can we do nothing. Once we recognize our moral beliefs are not coherent, that, in fact, some of these beliefs are inconsistent with one another, our natural inclination is to try to do something about it. We must try to sort things out. As we attempt to do this, our lack of volitional control over our believings will constrain our procedure. A procedure, or method, that simply directed us to believe, or to stop believing, some proposition would not, in general, be a method we could follow. A method that is viable, *for us*, must direct us to do things that are within our power, e.g., examine the logical and evidential relations among certain propositions, or consider an alternative theory, or seek to acquire additional experience. Finally, if we are to be able to follow a method's directives, they must operate on features that are accessible to us. Thus, for example, the instruction to believe the truth about morality cannot provide an adequate method of moral inquiry, given that we do not have direct access to the whole truth about morality. But a method could direct us, for example, to consider an alternative theory, or to seek additional information about the facts of a particular case.

The goal of moral inquiry, we have identified, is complex. The method must aim at systematic, primary moral knowledge. This goal involves at least four key components: true belief, warranted belief, rational belief, and beliefs with a coherent, systematic structure. We have already seen that there is no guarantee that the radical method of reflective equilibrium will bring us to the truth. Not only is there no guarantee, but we cannot even say that it is likely that this method of inquiry will bring us to believe the truth. There is, then, no guarantee that, just by following the method, we will reach our entire goal. But it does not follow that the method could not increase our chances of attaining our goal by helping us to attain parts of our goal. Surely, the method of reflective equilibrium is likely to lead us to a coherent, systematic set of beliefs, and bring us to an explicit awareness of this systematic structure. What of the other two epistemic components of the goal? Perhaps, the method can guarantee, or make probable, rational or warranted belief, in which case, I suppose, we should say that following the method does increase our chances of attaining our goal. Moreover, we must bear in mind the practical significance of our inquiry, and the fact that the inquiry is forced upon us. For both of these factors will incline us, so to speak, to lower our standards for an acceptable method. We must, therefore, consider what we can expect following the radical method of reflective equilibrium to do for us in the way of attaining rational and warranted moral beliefs. As a first step, I shall try to provide a more precise understanding of these concepts.

2.3 RATIONALITY AND WARRANT

I have used the terms "rational" and "warranted" in describing what I take to be the complex epistemic goal we seek in moral inquiry. But there is no agreement, even among philosophers, in the use of the terms. I cannot, therefore, expect that, when I use these terms, all readers will call to mind the same things. I need to indicate, or perhaps stipulate, what concepts I have in mind when I use these terms, and also to say something about the broad contours of these concepts. I do not believe that my use of the terms 'rational' and 'warranted' is particularly unusual, and I think the concepts I have in mind are familiar enough, so I will sometimes rely upon what we commonly say, or think, in trying to explain myself.

Even the little I said in the last section indicates a few things about my use of "rationality" and "warrant." First, and most generally, I use these terms to refer to evaluative concepts, and, more specifically, concepts of *epistemic* appraisal. Regarding the concepts individually, I have stipulated that warrant is the epistemic feature which plays the preeminent role in distinguishing mere true belief from knowledge. Specifically, that it is necessary for knowledge, and that warranted true belief is nearly sufficient, i.e., ignoring Gettier problems, it is sufficient, for knowledge.[20] I supposed that rationality is distinct from warrant, and is not required for knowing.

In trying to indicate the contours of these concepts further, I might begin with the reflection that, as evaluative concepts, both warrant and rationality involve the notion of a standard. To say that a belief is rational, or warranted, is to say that it meets certain standards. But just what evaluative standards are involved here? A common answer is that, just as moral standards are identified from a distinctive "moral point of view," epistemic standards are identified from the "*epistemic point of view*." As the passages I quoted in Section 2.1 amply illustrate, the received view among epistemologists identifies the epistemic point of view as the view of one whose aim is to believe truths and to avoid believing falsehoods. I have already said that I am not in sympathy with this position, but in this section, I shall make use of it for expository purposes. In the next section, I will detail my reasons for differing from the received view, and complicate my account accordingly.

Saying that the evaluative concepts of rationality and warrant involve standards that are identified with reference to the goal of believing truths and not believing falsehoods does not take us very far towards an understanding of these concepts. As a next step, let us note that evaluative standards can be of two broad types. Sometimes, when we compare a person's performance with a standard, whether it be a standard for believing, or some other activity, the standard defines what is, in the relevant sense, *required of* or *permitted to* the person. Such standards invite talk of rights, duties, and obligations. Failure to live up to such standards is, characteristically, culpable:[21] We blame persons for doing what is not permitted, or failing to do what is required. I shall call such standards *deontological*. Other evaluative standards define *good* or *excellent* states that a person might attain, rather than requirements and permissions. Examples are provided by standards for native intelligence, physical beauty, athletic talent, or good physical health. It would be good, or perhaps best, again from the relevant point of view, for the person to live up to such standards, but when the person falls short, he is not characteristically open to censure on this account.[22] I shall say that standards of this type are *simply evaluative*.

Someone of a rigoristic nature might shy at this distinction, thinking that we should always expect the best of people, and that we can always blame them for falling short of excellence. There might be something to this attitude, in a case where the distinction between what is merely good or bad, and what is worthy of praise or blame is grounded in some notion of what we can *reasonably* expect of persons. For example, in our common-sense thinking about morality, we distinguish between obligatory and supererogatory actions. There is no question here of a person's not being able to perform a supererogatory action, or of its being outside the person's voluntary control. Nor would we want to say that the person should not be blamed for failing to perform a super-erogatory action, because he is unable to determine the relevant standards, or assess his conformity to them. For we can presumably tell not only our duty, but also what is above and beyond the call of duty.

Acts are considered supererogatory because, while they are fine, good, or even best, they place demands upon the individual that we consider *unreasonably* high, e.g., requiring a person to risk his life, against long odds, to save the life of a stranger. There is, however, room for disagreement about what demands are unreasonable. One might even think that for certain ends, e.g., moral ones, nothing is too much to expect. Such a rigoristic skepticism, about the notion of the super-erogatory, might not be implausible. In other cases, where we do not hold persons responsible for failing to meet standards defining excellences, however, it is either because the person has no voluntary control over whether he meets these standards, or because he either cannot determine what the standards are, or monitor his conformance to the standards, not merely because we feel the standards require rather too much. In these cases, the rigoristic view does not seem plausible. Even if in some important sense, for example, altruistic or prudential, it would be best for a person to perform a certain action, we can hardly condemn the person for not performing it, if he either could not perform it, or had no way of telling that the action would be best.

We can say, then, that some evaluative standards are simply evaluative, where although, in some sense, it would be good or best for a person's state or activity to satisfy the standards, we do not blame nonconformance, while other evaluative standards are deontological, and we do hold persons responsible for falling short of these standards. What sorts of standards are involved in the concepts I refer to as "warrant" and "rationality"? We should begin our answer to this question by noting that we have only limited voluntary control over what we believe. A person has direct control over something, when he can perform the relevant action, assume the relevant state, or what have you, by a simple act of will, as, e.g., when I pet Merle, the grey cat, or think of Max, the chestnut horse. Beliefs are not within our direct voluntary control at all. Human beings cannot simply decide now to believe this, or to stop believing that. However, not all voluntary control is direct. A person has indirect control over a state, action, or what have you, when it is not within his direct control, but can be influenced in the right way by things that are in his direct control. We have more or less indirect control over a number of the examples of good or excellent states cited above, e.g., physical beauty, athletic talent, or good physical health. We do seem to have some indirect control over our beliefs. We can, for example, influence what we believe by seeking additional evidence, critically evaluating the grounds of our beliefs, considering, with an open mind, alternatives to theories, explanations, or accounts we accept, and by seeking to cultivate some habits of belief formation, and to extinguish others. But this indirect control is limited, so we have some initial reason to suspect that the standards involved in rationality and warrant are simply evaluative, and not deontological. For violations of deontological standards are characteristically blamed, and it is inappropriate to blame someone for failing to do something that was not within his control.

In the case of warrant, we can back up the suspicion that the relevant standards are simply evaluative by reflecting upon the connection between warrant and knowledge. For, we can imagine a person being as epistemically scrupulous as it is possible to be, thinking carefully about the evidence he has for some claim, considering whether additional evidence is required, and gathering data accordingly, and critically working through the arguments from his evidence to the claim in question. Yet, even if the person has done all that he can along these lines, and is confident that his evidence for the claim is strong, he might be completely mistaken about this. Perhaps, although it seems intuitively obvious to him, and has stood up to all the criticism he can muster, one of the steps in his argument embodies a probabilistic fallacy. Thus, as a matter of fact, the person's conclusion is not likely to be true, given his evidence for it. In cases such as this, the objective insufficiency of the person's evidence counts against his belief being an instance of knowledge, and thus against its being warranted. Yet we cannot blame the person for holding the belief, for he has been as dutiful as he could possibly have been in forming it. The person may fall short of an important epistemic standard, and his doxastic state may not be one of epistemic excellence, but he cannot be blamed for this. Notice that the question of whether believing is within the person's voluntary control is not at issue here. Rather, what makes blame inappropriate is that the relevant standards are objective, in such a way that it is possible for either the standards to be inaccessible to the believer, or for whether he has satisfied them to be inaccessible. Hence, even after the believer's best efforts to determine the relevant standards, and to satisfy them, he may fall short. In the example above, either the believer does not recognize the probabilistic fallacy he has committed, as a fallacy, or he does not realize that the form of argument he is using is an instance of the fallacy.

We can now consider rationality. One factor that makes it more difficult to say something helpful about how I am using "rationality" is that, even when we rule out concepts of practical or prudential rationality, and confine ourselves to the epistemic realm, we are left with a number of different concepts of rationality.[23] Let me give just a few examples. We commonly describe the beliefs of insane people as irrational. We describe beliefs that are contrary to what is commonly known as irrational (as in the case of people who believe that the earth is flat). Conclusions drawn on the basis of fallacious reasoning are said to be irrational. In legal proceedings, beliefs are sometimes held up to a standard of rationality defined by what a sane and reasonable man would believe. Distinct from some, and perhaps all, of these is the sort of rationality philosophers strive after. It is easy enough to say that this is the concept I mean to use "rational" to indicate. But can I say anything helpful about this concept? Well, the first thing to say is that there is something puzzling about the concept. For in spite of the fact that we have only limited, and no direct, voluntary control over our beliefs, when a philosopher labels a belief *irrational*, he seems intent on conveying a sense of condemnation – he holds the person responsible for his belief, and blames him for it. Indeed, it sometimes seems that philosophers think that the worst thing they could possibly say about a person is that one of his beliefs is irrational.[24] Although I do not think that saying it is irrational is the worst or only bad thing that can be said about a belief, I do wish my use of the term "irrational" to agree with what I take to be common philosophical usage in somehow conveying a sense of blame. For I want my argument that reflective equilibrium is the only rational method of inquiry to have some mustard on it! However, as we have seen in the case of warrant, holding people responsible for their beliefs is a tricky business. So, I need to explain how rationality, in the sense I am using it, can have some deontological force, despite its various similarities to warrant, and most importantly, that it applies to beliefs, which are outside our direct voluntary control. If I cannot explain this, I will be open to the charge that I am using a concept of rationality that is simply inconsistent.

Perhaps, there is a way to avoid this charge. As we have already seen, the fact that we cannot just decide to believe, or not to believe, does not entail that our beliefs are entirely outside our control. For we can *indirectly* influence what we believe in various ways. We can certainly evaluate these sorts of indirect influences upon our beliefs. Since these influences are within our direct voluntary control, it is, at least so far, possible that the relevant evaluation is deontological. The only thing that might bar deontological evaluation is if either the relevant standards, or their satisfaction, is inaccessible to the believer. But if the standards are appropriately subjective, or internal, we can avoid these last two obstacles to deontological evaluation. Hence, it might be that rational belief is, at bottom, a matter of meeting a simple evaluative standard, rather than a deontological standard, but a standard that a person would almost necessarily meet, if he fully satisfied his obligations regarding the indirect influences he brings to bear upon his beliefs. If this suggestion is correct, even when we confine ourselves to the philosopher's epistemic sense of rationality, we find two different notions of rational belief that, in practice, tend to apply to the same beliefs. For example, if a person holds two beliefs that are incompatible, we would likely regard at least one of these beliefs as irrational.[25] Since it is not just up to the person what he believes, we cannot blame him for holding these beliefs. His beliefs are irrational, in the sense that it is not a good thing, from the epistemic point of view, for him to hold them. But the person is not entirely off the hook. There is something that is directly under his control, i.e., considering the connection between these beliefs, and it is probable that, if the person had considered the connection between these beliefs, he would have seen the inconsistency, and his beliefs would have adjusted themselves accordingly. And finally, in many cases, the person should consider the connection between his beliefs, and he realizes that he should. Thus, it will not only be the case that the person's beliefs are not as good as they might be; there will also be something the person should have done that very probably would have saved him from having these less than optimal beliefs. Thus, we might say, his beliefs are irrational, in the sense that they fall short of an excellence, because he behaved irrationally, in the sense that entails blame, in forming them.

If warrant and rationality (in one sense) involve meeting standards that define a good or excellence, just what are these goods or excellences? I have said that this will be determined from the epistemic point of view, and that the *received* view is that this is the point of view of one interested in believing truths, and not believing falsehoods. One might think that nothing could better satisfy our epistemic interest than believing a truth, but warranted false beliefs have generally been thought to be possible.[26] Thus, the received view takes having warranted beliefs, very roughly, to be a matter of believing in a way that is *objectively likely* to produce true beliefs.[27] Rationality, on the other hand, will, again very roughly, have to be a matter of believing in a way that *seems to the believer* to be likely to produce true beliefs. If the standards are not thus subjectivized, there will be no guarantee that the inquirer can monitor his conformance to the standards, and rationality will lose even the indirect deontological force I tried to explain above. But we must say something about the conditions under which it seems to the person that he is believing in a way that is likely to produce true beliefs. For, we surely do not want to count as rational whatever a person believes, provided only that he thinks the belief is likely to be true. Thinking this may not even be distinct from believing. And if it is distinct, there obviously can be cases where a person believes something, and believes the belief to be epistemically above board, when a little reflection would reveal to him that the belief is incompatible with other things he believes, or that the belief was formed in a way that violates the epistemic standards that he accepts, and to which he attempts to conform his believings. We will, therefore, want to say that rationality, still very roughly, is a matter of believing in a way that the person would consider likely to produce true beliefs, were he to reflect upon the belief and its connections with the other things he believes.[28]

These characterizations allow us to see why irrational beliefs tend to be blamed in a way unwarranted beliefs are not. For, even if we try, there is no guarantee that we will be able to believe in a way that will in fact probably yield truth, but generally, we can, with a little effort, live up to our own standards, i.e., believe in a way that, after reflection, we would think is likely to yield the truth. We are also in a position to call attention to two important differences between rationality and warrant. First, the account of warrant is externalist, while that of rationality is internalist. Epistemologists have variously characterized the distinction between internalism and externalism. What I mean to call to our attention is that we do not, in general, have immediate, or direct, access to the objective likelihood of truth, which is the core notion of warrant, while we do, or can, have such access to what we take to be likely to be true, which provides the core of rationality.[29] Secondly, warrant is an objective notion, while rationality is subjective. To have warranted beliefs, one must satisfy an objective standard, which one may not even be aware of, or if one is aware of it, may not accept. Having rational beliefs is a matter of living up to one's own standards, regardless of the objective validity of these standards.

I hope that I have said enough to indicate which concepts I intend "warrant" and "rationality" to refer to, as well as enough about the general contours of these concepts for me to be able to move on to describe the strategy I will employ in defending the radical method of reflective equilibrium. (I will describe this strategy in Section 2.5 of this chapter.) I recognize that I have not said very much of substance about these concepts. In the next section, I will have more to say about warrant, in connection with a discussion of the received view of the connection between warrant and truth. And of course, throughout the discussion of the various epistemic statuses we can expect a method of moral inquiry to furnish our beliefs, I will be filling in little bits of detail regarding these concepts of epistemic assessment. However, I have no intention of providing anything like a substantive account of them. For any effort to provide such an account would not only take me too far afield, but would undoubtedly lead to a parochial defense of the method of moral inquiry. Any substantive account of warrant, or rationality, I might provide, or appeal to, would surely be controversial, and any argument for a moral methodology, based on such an account, would inherit this controversy.[30] I prefer, therefore, to develop the main argument of the book, while assuming as little about warrant and rationality as I can, thereby remaining as neutral among the various live alternative accounts of these concepts as is possible. Having affirmed my intention to remain neutral, let me summarize what I have assumed.

Warrant

This is the primary epistemic ingredient in knowledge. It plays the most significant role in elevating mere true belief to knowledge. While warrant is evaluative, it is not evaluative in a way that implies responsibility, praise, or blame. Rather, having warranted beliefs is a matter of meeting standards that identify what would be epistemically good, excellent, or best. The relevant standards are objective and external. The *received* view, regarding the sense in which believing in conformance with these standards is good, is that it is good with respect to the epistemic aim of believing truths and not believing falsehoods. If one accepts this view, to have warranted beliefs is to believe in such a way that it is objectively likely that one's beliefs are true.

Rationality

Having rational beliefs in the sense I intend is a matter of one's beliefs conforming to one's own standards, that is, of believing what one would take to be true upon reflection. Rationality is, therefore, subjective and correctly explicated along internalist lines. Standards for rational belief define a good, or excellence, rather than rights or duties, but nonetheless labeling a belief irrational seems to convey a sense of condemnation, or blame, that is generally inappropriate for such evaluative concepts. I wish to retain this implication, and have suggested that we might account for it as follows. There are various things we can do to affect our beliefs, e.g., gather evidence, consider alternatives, or critically evaluate arguments. Since these activities are within our control, we can reasonably be said to have rights and obligations respecting them. Moreover, since rationality is a matter of believing in accord with our own standards, irrational beliefs will frequently be the result of a failure to meet these obligations, e.g., by failing to consider the relations among our beliefs. Thus, we have come to associate irrational belief with violation of epistemic obligations, even though rationality is not correctly thought of in terms of rights or duties.[31]

2.4 WARRANT AND TRUTH

Although in the last section I made use of the received view, which closely ties warrant to truth-conduciveness, I have repeatedly said that I do not agree with this view. In this section, I will try to detail my reasons for doubting the received view, and to suggest something about the alternative I prefer. In the opening section of this chapter, when I first called our attention to the dominant view regarding the connection between truth and warrant, I quoted Laurence BonJour. The passage from which I drew that quote provides an excellent statement of the position I wish to challenge. Here is a more complete quotation of the passage:

> What then is the differentia which distinguishes epistemic justification, the species of justification appropriate to knowledge, from these other species of justification? The answer is to be found, I submit, by reflecting on the implicit rationale of the concept of knowledge itself. What after all is the point of such a concept, and what role is epistemic justification supposed to play in it? Why should we, as cognitive beings, *care* whether our beliefs are epistemically justified? Why is such justification something to be sought and valued?
>
> Once the question is posed in this way, the following answer seems obviously correct, at least in first approximation. What makes us cognitive beings at all is our capacity for belief, and the goal of our distinctively cognitive endeavors is *truth*: We want our beliefs to correctly and accurately depict the world . . . . The basic role of justification is that of a *means* to truth, a more directly attainable mediating link between our subjective starting point and our objective goal . . . . If epistemic justification were not conducive to truth in this way, if finding epistemically justified beliefs did not substantially increase the likelihood of finding true ones, then epistemic justification would be irrelevant to our main cognitive goal and of dubious worth. It is only if we have some reason for thinking that epistemic justification constitutes a path to truth that we as

cognitive beings have any motive for preferring epistemically justified beliefs to epistemically unjustified ones. Epistemic justification is therefore in the final analysis only an instrumental value, not an intrinsic one.[32]

I wish to argue against both the general approach to understanding warrant, in terms of some sort of truth-conduciveness, that is manifested by this quotation, and the received view that naturally leads to such an account of warrant – the view that our epistemic end, good, goal, or aim is simply believing truths and not believing falsehoods. I shall begin with the suggestion that we can provide a plausible rationale for the concept of knowledge only by supposing our epistemic aim to be truth. I shall argue that the rationale for knowledge suggested by BonJour is not as coherent as he seems to suppose, and develop an alternative rationale that does not presuppose the received view. I will then present examples that are intended to break warrant away from truth-conduciveness, and to show that our cognitive, or epistemic, activities are directed at more than merely believing truths rather than falsehoods.

Far from it being the case that the rationale of the concept of knowledge supports the truth-conduciveness of warrant, it seems to me that BonJour's view, which takes believing truths and not believing falsehoods, simpliciter, to be our epistemic or cognitive goal, provides us with a very poor, indeed, a nearly incoherent concept of knowledge. If what we really want, the epistemic summum bonum, is true belief, why should we feel that there is an important distinction between true belief and knowledge? The answer apparently must rely upon the concept of warrant, since warrant is supposed to account for the difference between true belief and knowledge. Taking warrant to be a matter of truth-conduciveness, BonJour, and others, apparently have the following answer in mind. "There is all the difference in the world between a mere true belief and a warranted true belief, for the warranted true belief is not just true, it was formed in a way or on a ground,[33] that makes it likely to be true." But if we abide by the assumption that the epistemic summum bonum is true belief, is this really an adequate answer? Allow me to begin by speaking metaphorically. If our team is down in the bottom of the ninth and our goal is to win, just to win, and nothing but to win, what difference does it make if the guy who hits the winning home run is batting .180 or .380? The answer is that it makes absolutely no difference, if our sole goal is winning. Likewise, if my sole and complete goal is believing what is true and not what is false, then right at that moment, when I have the true belief, I have just what I am after, and all that I am after. As far as that belief is concerned, I have made as much of a positive contribution to attaining my goal as I possibly could. From the epistemic point of view, it should make no difference to me whatsoever whether my believing the truth is a matter of dumb luck or the most careful planning.

It might be the case that, over the long haul, if my beliefs are warranted, I will get more epistemic gold than otherwise. Perhaps this fact provides warranted beliefs with some sort of positive status by association or by ancestry: The belief is a member of a class in which something of value is commonly found, or was produced by a mechanism that commonly produces things that have this value, so we value it. But this is just silly. What would we think of someone who told us that his gelding has a significant value, solely in virtue of being sired by Native Dancer, even though it is one of his few get that has poor conformation and is slow?[34] In addition, it is not even necessarily the case that I will get more true beliefs over the long haul by believing only what is warranted. Some people are lucky at love, others lucky at the track. It is also possible for a person to be epistemically lucky. It is possible for an individual consistently to form beliefs in ways that, over the long haul, would most often lead to false beliefs rather than true, and yet beat the odds time after time. If our goal, as epistemic beings, really is believing the truth, the man with such epistemic luck has it all. Warrant is nothing to him. He has no need of knowledge. Having these things would not improve his epistemic lot one whit.

It seems to me that the view I have been sketching is entirely wrong-headed. The sort of lucky man I have described would not be epistemically fulfilled. He would not have satisfied his goal as a cognitive being. He would not have attained the epistemic summum bonum. And the reason is true belief and the absence of false belief are not all that we are after. What we are after, epistemically and as cognitive beings, is not mere true belief, but knowledge.[35] True belief is a part of what we are after, sure enough. And false belief is inimical to our goal. But truth and the absence of falsehood are not all that we are after. For knowledge is not a matter of succeeding at something, i.e., believing the truth, and succeeding at it in a way that can be counted on to produce success. Rather, knowledge is a matter of simultaneously achieving two goals. It essentially involves two distinct goods coming together. One of the goods is truth; the other is warrant. There is no necessary connection between these goods, but as epistemic or cognitive beings we do want them both. The happy coincidence of these goods is what we call knowledge. Or perhaps I should say that we want to attain one, i.e., truth, by way of attaining the other, i.e., warrant.

This avoids suggesting that truth and warrant come together to form knowledge in the simple conjunctive way being warm and having a belly full of cream might come together in a contented cat. For I believe the interaction between truth and warrant that constitutes knowledge may be more complex than mere conjunction, so that knowledge might best be thought of as a sort of organic unity, the good of which exceeds the sum of the goods of warranted belief and true belief. But in any case, knowledge is not a matter of pursuing a good in a way that is likely to succeed, and in fact succeeding, like seducing someone as a result of following a plan calculated to overawe the object of one's ardor.[36] Knowledge is a matter of attaining two goods at once, like the consummation of a relationship that grew upon behavior that honestly expresses one's character.

It is not as though epistemologists have ignored the concern I have been trying to voice. William Alston has provided a particularly forceful statement of the concern:

> If goodness from an epistemic point of view is what we are interested in, why shouldn't we identify justification with truth, at least extensionally? What could be better from that point of view than truth? If the name of the game is the maximization of truth and the minimization of falsity in our beliefs, then plain unvarnished truth is hard to beat. However, this consideration has not moved epistemologists to identify justification with truth . . . . The logical independence of truth and justification is a staple of the epistemological literature. But why should this be?[37]

The problem is that, having given voice to the concern, Alston allows it to be smoothed over all too easily. He tells us that we cannot identify warrant with truth, because warrant has an "internalist" character.

> When we ask whether S is justified in believing that *p*, we are, as we have repeatedly been insisting, asking a question from the standpoint of an aim at truth; but we are not asking whether things are in fact as S believes. We are getting at something more "internal" to S's "perspective on the world."[38]

Alston goes on to explain how this general idea applies to the concept of warrant that he is out to elucidate, which he labels 'J_e.'[39]

> With respect to J_e the analogous point is that although this is goodness vis-à-vis the aim at truth, it consists not in the beliefs fitting the way the facts actually are, but something more like the belief's being true "so far as the subject can tell from what is available to the subject." In asking whether S is J_e in believing that *p*

we are asking whether the truth of *p* is strongly indicated by what S has to go on; whether, given what S had to go on, it is at least quite likely that *p* is true. We want to know whether S had *adequate* grounds for believing that *p*, where *adequate* grounds are those sufficiently indicative to the truth of *p*.[40]

In a way, I would not want to disagree with what Alston has to say here. I do believe that questions about the warrant of belief are asked, so to speak, "from the subject's own point of view." But what I would want to challenge is that Alston has succeeded in answering his own question, that is, in explaining why, assuming that our epistemic aim is believing the truth, and that warrant is "goodness vis-à-vis the aim at truth," we should not just identify warrant with truth. If what we are really up to, when we speak of warrant, is evaluating effectiveness with respect to believing the truth, why do we back off from truth itself, and concern ourselves with how close to the truth we could expect the subject to come *given what he has to go on?* There is, of course, an answer to this question, if we take warrant to be a *deontological* concept, that is, an evaluative concept that involves rights, obligations, and permissions, and allows for praise and especially blame. For surely, it makes no sense to blame a person for not doing better if the person had no way of gauging his own performance. But Alston has been among the leaders in the fight against the deontological conception of justification, and I made it clear above, in Section 2.3, that I believe Alston has taken the right side.

The challenge I wish to present to Alston, and the others who adhere to the received view, then, is to justify being an internalist about warrant, while really holding both that believing truths and avoiding errors is our complete epistemic good, and that warrant is not a concept of deontological evaluation. I issue this challenge, not because I doubt that warrant has an essential internalist element, or because I think that warrant is deontological. Rather, I agree with internalism regarding warrant and Alston's criticisms of possible deontological accounts of warrant. I issue the challenge, therefore, in the hope that efforts to answer it will encourage rejection of the position that takes truth to be our epistemic good, and then, in some way, ties warrant to truth-conduciveness. More generally, I challenge proponents of the received view to provide a rationale for the concepts of knowledge and warrant that makes it clear why warranted true beliefs are so much more valuable than true beliefs, if our epistemic summum bonum is nothing more than believing the truth and not believing falsehoods. The rationale for knowledge I have suggested, which is based upon the idea that our epistemic goal is an organic unity comprised of two elements, at least provides an answer to this challenge.

Having suggested an alternative to the received view regarding our epistemic goal, and an alternative rationale for the concept of knowledge, and having done what I can to reveal the incoherence of the rationale for knowledge that springs from the received view of our epistemic good, I shall now try to mount a more direct assault upon the connection between truth and warrant. The assault will be based upon two examples. I turn immediately to the first.

Imagine a demon constructing cognitive beings, or if you prefer, imagine this demon tinkering with us. But do not imagine a Cartesian demon who is out to deceive. The demon I am asking you to imagine wants beings who will believe the truth! But this demon finds the straightforward way in which beings like us come to have perceptual beliefs rather boring. He is irked that philosophers can plausibly propose simple epistemic principles that relate our being appeared to in a certain way with our being warranted in believing that the world is as it appears. So the demon sets about disrupting the connection between how the world is and how it appears to the beings. But remember, the demon is not out to deceive, so he does not want his disruptions to render the beings' beliefs inaccurate. The demon wants it to be the case that these beings believe the world to be pretty much the way it actually is. He just wants his beings' perceptual experience to match neither their beliefs nor reality. Thus, he constructs his beings in such a way that, no matter what they are doing or looking at, their visual experience is like the experience we would have if we were watching old Laurel and Hardy movies. Just as with us, the beings can accurately describe their visual experience, and an essential part of the experience of being so appeared to is the strong temptation or inclination to believe the world is as it appears. But the demon's creatures do not believe the world to be anything like their experience. They believe the world to be pretty much the way it actually is. To alter the case slightly, we might imagine these beings to be our perceptual twins, in the sense that each of them has a complete lifetime of perceptual experience that exactly matches the train of perceptual experience enjoyed by one of us. But each of the demon's beings would have beliefs about its world that are very different from the beliefs of its perceptual twin. Nonetheless, the beings' beliefs about their world would be correct about as frequently as our perceptual beliefs are. Now, I assert that the demon's creatures would have no knowledge of their world, because their relevant beliefs would not be warranted.[41] Yet, to repeat, if the demon did his work well, there would be as close a connection between the beliefs of these creatures and their world as there is between our perceptual beliefs and our world.[42]

If you are comfortable with thinking of our cognitive apparatus as something like a computer, and you are content with thinking of consciousness as involving something like representation that is capable of being monitored by some particularly significant "module" of our cognitive system, and finally, you are comfortable with thinking of believing as having a sentence stored somewhere by some module, being written in the belief box, as is sometimes said, you can picture the examples I have just described in the following way. In the normal case, somewhere along the way, the output from the eye, after various sorts of processing, is projected onto a screen that is monitored by another module of the system. The monitoring here gives us consciousness. The monitoring module writes sentences of two sorts into the belief cache, sentences about what is actually up on the screen, and sentences about the world outside. What I am asking you to imagine is something like this: Unplug the line going from the eye to the screen, and plug a VCR with an "endless" Laurel and Hardy tape into the screen. But don't leave the line out of the eye dangling. Presumably, it conveys in some form all the information necessary for the formation of beliefs about the world. So plug it into some other module, perhaps one made just for the purpose, and have this module write sentences about the outside world into the belief cache, without, so to speak, "the conscious module looking over its shoulder." As before, the "conscious" module can still write sentences about what is up on the screen into the belief cache, but it does not write sentences about the external environment there. The other example, where the beings are thought of as our perceptual twins, can be similarly conceived, only rather than connecting the screen the "conscious" module watches to a VCR playing old movies, the output from one of our eyes is copied and used as input for the screen.

I take these examples to show two things. First, they show that truth-conduciveness is not sufficient for warrant. More importantly, I think they show that true belief is not our epistemic summum bonum. For I believe that the beings created by this non-deceiving demon would be in nearly as unfavorable a cognitive or epistemic condition as beings within the power of a standard Cartesian demon. If we deviate from the practice of epistemologists for a moment, and think of the totality of the cognitive or mental lives of these beings, rather than simply what they believe, we will see their lives to be incoherent. For if their perceptual experiences are like ours, these experiences will draw the beings towards believing the world to be as it is experienced. But at the same time, upon minimal reflection, it will not seem to the beings that the world is as they experience it. Rather, it will seem obvious to these beings that the world is otherwise, and they will always believe that the world is other than as they experience it to be. A cognitive life, at odds with itself in this way, is clearly not the most choice-worthy of mental lives. It cannot be one that has reached the highest epistemic good.

Returning to the first thing I said the example of the non-deceiving demon shows, i.e., that truth-conduciveness is not sufficient for warrant, one might respond to this by claiming that it remains possible that truth-conduciveness is necessary for warrant. And in fact, apart from the most naïve forms of reliabilism, truth-conduciveness, by itself, is not identified with warrant. It is only taken to be an essential part of warrant. However, in my estimation, it is easy to show that truth-conduciveness is not necessary for warrant either. We need only reflect upon the nature of our own experience. When a person has exactly the sort of visual experience I now have, and he has no beliefs or experiences that lead him to doubt his present perception, the person is warranted in believing that there is a keyboard before him. And this is not altered at all by supposing that the person is subject to some sort of massive deception by a Cartesian demon or clever neuro-psychologist. Likewise, again supposing that no other beliefs or experiences get in the way, the experience of remembering the barn out back – the door, the isle down the middle with stalls on either side, hay stacked in front of some of the stalls, and pitchforks and wheelbarrow leaning against the front of the last stall on the right – is such that in the face of this experience it is appropriate to believe that the barn is as I remember it. If I so believe, my beliefs are warranted. And the connection between my beliefs and the facts has nothing to do with it. No demigod, or clever demon, could alter the fact that these beliefs are warranted, although presumably such a one could insure that my memory beliefs were rarely true.

If I am right, and truth-conduciveness is neither necessary nor sufficient for warrant, how should we think of this central epistemic concept? I would say that having a warranted belief is a matter of believing appropriately. I realize that this will not be very helpful, until I spell out *how* it is appropriate. But this I cannot do. I have tried to make clear what appropriateness is not; it is not simply a matter of believing what is likely to be true. But on the positive side, I can only work by example. All I can do is ask the reader to reflect upon one of his sensory experiences. I, for example, take a look out of my back window. The sun is shining. Up close are smaller muddy paddocks. In the nearest, a bay colt and a chestnut filly are contentedly munching hay. On the other side of the paddocks are larger, grassy pastures. In the nearer, a large bay horse is grazing, and in the back of the farther pasture, a large chestnut is stretching his neck over the fence to pluck leaves from a sassafras tree. Standing there, having this experience, in the absence of any experience or belief that gives me any reason to doubt my senses, I am as convinced as I could be of anything that it is appropriate for me to believe the horses to be there as I see them. And given the totality of my experience, no contradictory belief would be appropriate. If it is asked, "Appropriate for what?," I can say no more than appropriate for believing in the face of experience, or appropriate for attaining knowledge. This is unsatisfying, but true, or so I submit.

It would be remiss of me not to address a certain obvious objection before concluding. Given my identification of warrant as the positive epistemic status that is primarily responsible for distinguishing knowledge from mere true belief, and my claim that warrant is a matter of believing what is appropriate in the face of experience, it will occur to many that my position is subject to a familiar sort of counter-example. Consider a more standard sort of demon example, where the person's perceptual experiences seem to be normal, fit together in a coherent way, and so on, and where the person quite naturally forms the same sorts of beliefs as a result of these experiences as we would, but where the person's perceptual experiences are wholly fabricated by the demon, so that the beliefs the person forms are false. Now, the false beliefs formed by such a person do not cause me much discomfort. Being false, there is no question of these beliefs constituting knowledge. And the claim that these false beliefs are nonetheless warranted is a familiar enough pill that swallowing it is not too much of a chore. And of course, I have plenty of company in taking this medicine. The problem with my view rather arises, oddly enough, when the demon allows the person to form an isolated true belief. So, for example, suppose that on one occasion the person is having an experience as of standing leaning against a fence post, and forms the belief that he is leaning against a post. In addition, suppose that the person, who is in fact shaped like a longish tube and is usually kept lying in a sort of large mail-slot in the demon's workshop, has, at the very moment he believes himself to be standing, been removed from his "mail-slot" and leaned against a post in the workshop, so the demon's assistant can dust. Now, I have already committed myself to saying that such a person's beliefs are warranted, so it seems I have no choice but to say that the person knows that he is standing. This is obviously not a consequence I can swallow.

While I would have to admit that I am not sure exactly what to say about the problem illustrated by this example, it is far from clear that there is no way for me to avoid it. Indeed, there are three possible escape routes I would wish to investigate in detail, before conceding that I have been trapped. First, we do not, strictly speaking, have a counter-example to my view before us. For what is clear, in the example, is that the person does not *know* that he is standing. Had I claimed that warrant, all by itself, turns true belief into knowledge, I might be in serious trouble. But because of Gettier-type examples, I made no such claim. I hold that a complete account of knowledge requires an account of warrant, which has been my focus in this section, as well as an analysis of Gettier-style examples, and an account of how they are ruled out in cases of knowledge. Perhaps, the element of the account of knowledge that deals with Gettier examples will also deal with the purported counter-example to my account of warrant.

Secondly, I am not exactly sure where to go with it, but there is something that bothers me about the example. It seems to focus on, and seeks to evaluate, too narrow a chunk of the subject's experience, or cognitive state. It is difficult to state exactly what I mean by this, so let me try to convey the point with an example. Notice that, in the example described above, the person's perceptual experience, at the moment he forms the belief that he is standing, warrants (supposing that I am right about warrant) many more beliefs, and presumably, he forms at least some of these beliefs, and he is disposed to form very many more of them. Moreover, I have doubts about whether it is accurate, or even possible, to think of a person's perceptual experience at an instant.[43] It seems to me that individual perceptual experiences, in so far as there are such things at all, are actually extended through a certain period of time. Taking this into account, even more beliefs seem to be warranted by a given perceptual experience, and not just beliefs about properties that it is possible for things to have at an instant, such as a color or shape, but also beliefs about such matters as how things are moving in the environment. Now, instead of supposing some one isolated belief that is formed on the basis of a perceptual experience to be true, while all the others are false, imagine, instead, a case where all these beliefs are true (and we might also add that this goes on for a short period of time). Altering the example above in this way, we are now thinking of the person having not an experience of leaning against a fence post, but to him, a very sudden and bizarre experience, and coming to believe, on the basis of this experience, that he is in fact a tube-shaped thing, leaning against a post in a large, cluttered, and very odd workshop. Before him is a large shelf that seems to have something like mail-boxes built into it, mail-boxes that contain other tube-shaped things like himself. And perhaps most oddly, a queer sort of creature is carefully dusting out the one empty slot in the shelf. Now, perhaps, I am speaking only for myself, but it is far less obvious to me that the person fails to know in the example as I have altered it. I am more inclined to think of the person as somehow catching a sudden, terrifying glimpse of reality, of suddenly really perceiving his actual state for a moment, before slipping back into his accustomed state of ignorance.

Thirdly, I have doubts about whether the original example, as described, is really possible. In particular, I wonder whether it is possible for the person to believe, or even conceive, the proposition that he is the tube-shaped thing I have described. This is because I think that many of our concepts, and in particular our concepts of the objects we ordinarily see, hear, and so on, of ourselves, and of our positions in space, are much more intimately tied to our perceptual experience than the proposed counter-example, and other examples like it, presuppose. I believe that we conceive of these things as characteristically appearing to us in certain ways. Thus, to consider a different, but similar and familiar enough, sort of example, when we think of the brain in a vat believing that there is a tree before it, and there is a tree before it, it is not clear to me that this is a case where the brain has a true belief. For the brain's concept of the tree is, in large part, of a thing that characteristically appears to it in various ways, and the real tree before it is no such thing. Similarly, the person in the original example, in part, conceives of himself as having a body that appears to have a certain shape, color, feel, etc., and that he experiences in certain characteristic ways. In addition, I would say that his concept of his own standing against something includes the various kinesthetic sensations that he characteristically has when standing and leaning against something. As a result, when he believes that he is leaning against a fence post, and he, the tube-like thing, really has been leaned against a post for a moment, it is not entirely clear that he has formed a true belief.

I realize that none of the three suggestions I have just made about ways of avoiding the purported counter-example has been worked out sufficiently to be able to tell whether it really will allow me to avoid the counter-example. In fact, I might as well confess that I am concerned that I have not worked the second and third out enough even to convey an idea of what I am driving at. And there are obviously serious questions about the plausibility of my last two suggestions as well. However, my aim here was only to suggest that the purported counter-example does not clinch the case against me, and perhaps it is not too far-fetched to hope that my suggestions are sufficiently well worked out and plausible to support this meagre claim.

As I see it, my example of the non-deceiving demon, and careful reflection on particular sensory experiences, and the power of such experiences to warrant belief, reveal an important failing of much epistemology. By focusing primarily non belief, and assessing beliefs exclusively with reference to truth, many epistemologists have missed the epistemic significance of experience. No one, of course, has failed to see that experience has an important role to play. But the role has been seen as purely instrumental, as a means to belief, and, it is hoped, true belief. Adopting this conception of the epistemic role of experience leads one to ignore the phenomenological character of our experience, and in particular, to ignore that this phenomenological character can, in itself, either correspond to reality and belief, or not. Thus, if given his experience and circumstances, a person's belief is likely to be true, and it is in fact true, one will likely think that there can be nothing epistemically amiss. But when one recognizes the possibility of correspondences among experience, belief, and reality, it is easy to see that such a person's cognitive state may fall short of epistemic excellence. For it might be that there is the same sort of incoherence between the person's experience and his belief as epistemologists fear to find between belief and reality. And, I maintain, where there is such an experiential incoherence, we fall short of warrant and knowledge, no matter what the connection between our beliefs and truth.[44]

I hold that attaining knowledge is a matter of attaining two independent epistemic goods in the same act of believing. These things are good in themselves, but the good of knowledge exceeds the good of these parts. Knowledge, then, is best thought of as an organic unity. The one good, true belief has been at the heart of epistemology for quite some time. Indeed, it has received so much attention that epistemologists have sought to subsume under it the second good, viz., warrant. But this is an effort that is doomed to fail. For it takes only a little thought to see that true belief is not our epistemic summum bonum. We seek more than truth, and this is why knowledge has always been thought to be more than mere true belief. Knowledge also incorporates the second thing we seek as cognitive beings: to believe in the way that is appropriate to our total experience. Warrant, that which distinguishes mere true belief from knowledge, is this second epistemic good. It is good in itself, not merely as a means to truth.

Now, I really do believe what I have been saying in this section, both about the lack of a significant connection between warrant and truth-conduciveness, and about the nature of warrant. But at the same time, I cannot help but recognize that what I have been saying will be controversial. Indeed, by calling it controversial, I may be revealing rather too high an opinion of my own arguments. For, saying that my views are controversial might be taken to imply that I think a controversy will spring up around them, and I suspect that I have gone so far out on a limb here, that not only will no one wish to join me, but no one will want to get close enough to try to shove me off! In any case, I certainly would not want to compromise what I consider the important argument, i.e., the defense of an approach to moral inquiry, by saddling it with such a "controversial" epistemological position. As I said in the previous section, I want to develop my defense of the radical method of reflective equilibrium, while remaining as neutral as possible with respect to substantive theories of such key epistemic concepts as rationality and warrant.

Fortunately, I think there is a way to take into account the worries about the received view of warrant that I have just tried to spell out, without committing the entire argument to the particular substantive view of warrant that I happen to accept. Allow that my arguments, regarding warrant and truth-conduciveness, have established this much: At least in the case of some beliefs, e.g., perceptual beliefs, there is something to the idea that it is a good thing to believe in a way that straightforwardly corresponds with one's experience, where this good is independent of any connection between being appeared to in that way and things really being as they seem to be. We need not assume that the relevant epistemic good is warrant. It is in the spirit of the approach we have taken so far, an approach that recognizes a multiplicity of epistemic values, and epistemically evaluative concepts, to grant that a certain unique value attaches to beliefs that conform to experience in an appropriate way, where the relevant sort of appropriateness has to do with the connection between the felt character of the experience itself and the content of the belief, rather than any relation that might hold between the experience and reality. It will be convenient to have a term for this positive epistemic status, so let us dub it *experiential warrant*, and resolve to be careful to resist any temptation to think that it is a particular type of warrant, the positive epistemic status required for knowing.[45]

It is easy enough to factor experiential warrant into what we have said about the goal of moral inquiry. To do so, let us reconsider one of the examples I used in Section 2.2. As part of my argument that we seek more than primary moral knowledge, I imagined that I had come to doubt all my senses as a result of skeptical arguments. On the basis of careful consideration of all the relevant arguments, I believed that there was no world as we ordinarily conceive it, and thus, that any beliefs I might form about the world, on the basis of sense experience, were bound to be mistaken. In this case, my beliefs might surely have a systematic, coherent structure, and given that I had exercised sufficient care, I see no reason for denying that these beliefs might be rational. Nonetheless, I claimed that in a case where a startling event caused me spontaneously to form a belief about my environment in accord with my visual experience, this belief would count as knowledge. At the time, I relied solely upon what I hoped would be the intuitive plausibility of this claim. But notice that this result is supported by various familiar accounts of warrant. If we adopt the received view of the connection between warrant and truth-conduciveness, e.g., in the form of a crude reliability account, we would argue that the belief is knowledge on the ground that my perverse doubts about perception in fact do nothing to alter the reliability of my visual system. On Plantinga's version of externalism, which represents a more sophisticated interpretation of the received view, we would say the belief is warranted because it is produced by a component of my cognitive architecture, functioning properly, in an appropriate environment, where the function of that component is to produce true beliefs. And of course, on the account of warrant I favor, I would argue that the belief is warranted because it is experientially warranted.[46] But we want to suppose that I am wrong. What would I say about the example in that case? Well, I would argue that even if experiential warrant is not warrant, it nonetheless represents a positive epistemic value that we would want our beliefs to have. I would claim, therefore, that just as knowledge is not enough to satisfy all our epistemic goals, even systematic, coherent knowledge is not enough to satisfy these goals. Where there is a possibility of attaining it, we want to have experiential warrant for our beliefs as well.

I can use another variation on the example of the non-deceiving demon to bolster my claim that experiential warrant is of epistemic value, even if it is independent of warrant. Suppose that a whimsical demon sets out to tamper with our visual system without depriving us of the opportunity of coming to know about the world around us *on the basis of* our visual experiences. The demon confines his machinations to vision, allowing our other sense experiences to go on as before, both with respect to their phenomenological character, and with respect to their connection to the external world. Even with respect to visual experience, the demon does not blind us, or restrict in any way the range of visual experience we can enjoy. He allows us to go on having visual experiences that are qualitatively just like the visual experiences we ordinarily enjoy. What the demon does is disrupt the connection between the phenomenological character of our visual experiences and the nature of the external world. As a result, if we were simply to form the beliefs we are naturally inclined to form in the face of our visual experiences, for example, that a red thing is before us when we were appeared to redly, we would not very often form a true belief. However, while the demon disrupts the connection between the phenomenological character of visual experience and the nature of the external world, he does not want his disruptions to render us incapable of using these very visual experiences as a guide to the nature of the world. He thus insures that there is a reliable connection between the phenomenological character of our experience and the world, but a connection that is complex and highly non-standard. What we are imagining, therefore, is that the demon has subjected us to some sort of systematic transformation of visual experience, akin to a spectral inversion, but amounting to more of a scrambling than an inverting, and involving shapes, position, depth, etc. in addition to color.

Now, because there is a systematic connection between the nature of the visual experiences we would have as victims of this demon and the world, and because we could use our other senses to check many of the same features of the world as vision is ordinarily sensitive to, e.g., the shapes and positions of objects, and perhaps with a little help from the demon nudging us in the right direction, it should be possible for us to figure out the function that describes the transformation that the demon has wrought on our visual experiences. Once we had thus cracked the code, it would be possible for us to form warranted beliefs about the world on the basis of our visual experiences. It would not come naturally to us. Because of the strong phenomenological liveliness, or force, of visual experience, our natural inclination would be to believe, in the face of a particular visual experience, the same thing normal perceivers would believe, in the face of that experience. But over time, we could learn to use our visual experiences as a reliable guide to the nature of the external world, indeed, a guide that is every bit as reliable as ordinary vision. Now, while I am willing to allow that, even as victims of this demon, we could come to have warranted beliefs about the world on the basis of our visual experiences, and thus that we could attain knowledge in this way, I do not think that our epistemic situation would be ideal. In fact, even though, as victims of this demon, we would be as reliable as we actually are with respect to beliefs based upon visual experience, and the range of the beliefs we would form on the basis of visual experience would not be diminished, I would not want to say that our epistemic situation would be no worse than it actually is. For it is better that our visual beliefs have experiential warrant, so that we can believe what our experiences, in virtue of their phenomenological character, naturally prompt us to believe, and we do not have to bear the burden of always correcting for some sort of bizarre connection between the phenomenological character of visual experience and the nature of the world around us.[47]

Moving over to moral judgments, I will want to say that something of the same thing applies. When we actually see, or hear about, or vividly imagine morally significant actions, we often form moral judgments about the action that share many of the features of perceptual beliefs. The judgments are immediate, spontaneous, and can be extremely forceful.[48] Something similar can be said about some of the moral principles we accept. We are strongly inclined to accept them simply on the basis of considering, or understanding, them; we do not feel we need to have any sort of argument, or evidence, for these principles, and we are inclined to say such things as that we can simply *see* that they are true. Now, I do not want to involve myself in any kind of intuitionism that would say that such beliefs necessarily constitute knowledge, that we can't be wrong about them, or anything else of the sort. I would not even want to say that we cannot change our minds about these beliefs. All I want to claim is that we can speak of experiential warrant here, as in the case of perceptual beliefs, and that, in the moral realm, there is a certain epistemic value that attaches to believing what is experientially warranted. Other things being equal, it is a good thing to be able to believe those moral propositions that have experiential warrant. Recall the example of forming a spontaneous judgment about the man who struck the woman that I gave in Section 2.2. We can easily take that example to illustrate the point I am now making. For, even if there is some hesitancy about saying that the spontaneous judgment I imagined myself forming, in that case, is an instance of knowledge, given that the judgment does not cohere with the settled conviction that moral skepticism is true that I imagined myself to have, I think it must be admitted that my epistemic situation, in that example, would be less than ideal. It would be better, if either I were no longer to feel the particular, strong, immediate inclination to form moral judgments, in virtue of which these judgments are experientially warranted, or I were to abandon my commitment to moral skepticism. And I would want to say that, in the example as described, it would be best, if I either conformed my meta-ethical views to the moral judgments that are experientially warranted for me, or ceased to feel the strong inclination to form such moral judgments and began to feel the same strong inclinations to form beliefs compatible with my moral skepticism. In either case, my moral views would have the positive epistemic value of experiential warrant, in addition to whatever other positive epistemic values they might have attained.[49]

2.5 A STRATEGY FOR DEFENDING A METHOD OF MORAL INQUIRY

It is time to return to the main course of the argument. In particular, I need to describe the overall strategy I will employ to defend the acceptability of the radical method of reflective equilibrium. The argument of Chapter 1 forced me to grant that this method of inquiry is most probably not reliable. We cannot say that the method is likely to lead inquirers to beliefs that are true. But even if our goal were true beliefs, pure and simple, the method's unreliability would not necessarily force us to conclude that the method is unacceptable, as other writers apparently suppose. As I suggested above, the end of moral inquiry is very important, and we are, in a way, forced to embark upon the inquiry. Under such conditions, we might regard a method as adequate, even though it is not very likely to succeed. For, perhaps, the method is more likely to succeed than any alternative, and, although it offers but slim hope for success, this hope may be sufficient for us to feel that it would be better to go on and use the method, rather than give up on the inquiry entirely. I shall not, however, attempt to mount such a defense of the radical method of reflective equilibrium. For doing so would require some sort of assessment of the method's probability of success, as well as similar assessments for other methods.

My strategy for defending the radical method is grounded in the complexity of the epistemic goal at which moral inquiry aims. To simplify, if we have a tripartite goal, of any sort, we may well regard a method for pursuing the goal as adequate, even if it does no better than chance at attaining one part of the goal. For the method may be very good at helping us attain one or both of the other parts of the goal. Although the case of moral inquiry is more complex, this general idea still applies. In pursuing moral inquiry, our epistemic goals are complex. We seek moral knowledge, which entails that we seek moral beliefs that are true and warranted. We also seek *rational* moral knowledge, which adds a third epistemic value to the list. As I have argued, the radical method is probably not reliable, but this does not mean that we cannot come to have true beliefs by following the method. For all I have said, then, it remains possible that, by following the method, we will attain even this element of the goal of moral inquiry. What, then, of the other two elements of our goal? Considering the rationality of belief, we will find that, because rationality is subjective, there are many systems of moral beliefs that a person could rationally accept. And there might be any number of unexpected, and improbable, methods that could bring a person around to accepting one of these systems of belief, e.g., being "brainwashed." But I shall argue that radical reflective equilibrium leads inquirers to accept a rational system of beliefs by a series of rational steps, indeed, that it is the *only* method that does so. This is the first element of my two-pronged strategy for defending the method.

If reflective equilibrium is the only rational method, then the question of the method's adequacy reduces to the question of whether the method does enough. There is, after all, no other option. By adopting any other method, we give up on one component of the end we seek when we undertake a philosophical inquiry into morality. One way in which the method might not do enough for us would be if we could not attain the third element of our goal, i.e., warranted belief, by employing it. Perhaps, even if we could not attain moral knowledge, since we could not attain warranted moral beliefs, we would be willing to settle for rational, and possibly true, moral beliefs. But settling for so little would constitute a disappointing retrenchment. I will, therefore, attempt to establish that it is *possible* to come to hold warranted moral beliefs by following the method of radical reflective equilibrium. Even if I can establish this possibility, we still might conclude that the method does not do enough. But the cost of this conclusion would be very high indeed, for if I can make out the case for reflective equilibrium's being the only rational method of inquiry, it would follow that there is no adequate method of moral inquiry, that we should not undertake a philosophical inquiry into morality at all. The second prong of my strategy, therefore, is to show that it is possible for a person employing the radical method of reflective equilibrium to come to have warranted moral beliefs.

The portion of the argument dealing with warrant is bound to be controversial, since, as we have seen, the notion of warrant is controversial itself. The received view holds that warrant is to be understood in terms of some sort of truth-conduciveness, while I have argued that warrant consists, not in any sort of truth-conduciveness, but in believing in a way that is appropriate, given the phenomenological character of one's experience. Regardless of whether or not I am right about this, it seems safe to conclude that our epistemic goals are even more complex than I have supposed up to this point. For if warrant is to be understood in terms requiring truth-conduciveness, then believing in a way that is appropriate to experience, i.e., in a way I would call experientially warranted, represents yet another epistemic value that we would prefer our moral beliefs to attain. (And of course, if I am right, and warrant is not to be understood in terms of truth-conduciveness, I suppose I can be big enough to allow that there is something to the received view, specifically, that the received view does succeed in identifying *something* of positive epistemic value, viz., truth-conduciveness.) So when we move away from rationality to consider warrant, we will actually need to consider two epistemic values, truth-conduciveness and experiential warrant, both of which, under the worst scenario, might turn out to be distinct from warrant. I plan to proceed by first describing how certain perceptual judgments are warranted, and then arguing that it is plausible to think that the warrant of certain moral judgments might be analogous. The analogy will also serve to illustrate how the moral judgments we are led to make, as a result of following the radical method of reflective equilibrium, might be experientially warranted, and truth-conducive, in an interesting sense. I hope that the argument of this section will accomplish two other goals as well: First, that it will illuminate the role reflective equilibrium plays in our moral beliefs coming to be warranted and experientially warranted; and secondly, that it will make it seem more than barely possible that the method will lead to beliefs that are warranted, experientially warranted, and even truth-conducive.

At this point, many readers will surely think that I have lost track of my own argument. For only a few paragraphs above, at the beginning of this section, I admitted that the argument of the first chapter established that the radical method of reflective equilibrium is probably not reliable. And now I have just said that I plan to argue that it is "more than barely possible" that the method will lead to beliefs that are truth-conducive. Moreover, the more important part of the argument to follow must make out the claim that it is possible to come to hold warranted beliefs by following the radical method of reflective equilibrium, and I have freely admitted that the received view holds warrant to be some manner of truth-conduciveness. Doesn't the argument of my own first chapter stand in the way of the argument I am now promising to give?

If we are sufficiently careful about what that argument showed, and what I am now promising to argue, it should become clear that I am not bound to break the promise I am now making. In the first chapter, I argued that the radical method of reflective equilibrium is probably unreliable. The argument turned upon the fact that reflective equilibrium seems unlikely to yield a consensus. Strictly speaking, what I meant by "unreliable" was that the proportion of true moral beliefs, among the beliefs of all inquirers who employed the method, would not be large. We can say, then, that the method, by itself and regardless of who is employing it, is not reliable. It will not lead everyone to true beliefs. But all this is compatible with *some* of the individuals who have employed the method ending up reliable moral judges. This would be one sort of "interesting truth-conduciveness" that might be had by beliefs that are formed as a result of following the method of reflective equilibrium. I see no reason to suppose that these beliefs might not be truth-conducive in other interesting ways, as well. Therefore, on many versions of the received view, the argument of the first chapter is compatible with the claim that some of those who employ the radical method might thereby come to hold warranted moral beliefs.

To see this point, we might consider the nearly blind cartoon character Mr Magoo, who forms the most bizarre beliefs about the world around him, and manages to navigate safely through his environment only as a result of a prolonged series of lucky coincidences between his wildly mistaken beliefs and the actual nature of his surroundings. Now, instead of one Magoo, imagine a whole world full of Magoos trying to formulate a systematic picture of their environment. If the Magoos used anything like the methods we use to develop our view of the world, we can pretty well guess what the results would be. It is highly unlikely that, by following this method, the Magoos would reliably be led to the truth. Nonetheless, we could not say that it is not possible to come to have warranted beliefs by following the methods they use, for there might be a small number of people in the Magoo world with the sort of visual acuity we consider normal, and these people would be reliable when using the method. The beliefs they came to hold as a result of following the method would be warranted. The same thing might be going on in the moral case. While being unreliable for the population as a whole, the method of reflective equilibrium might be a very reliable method for some individuals. Thus, even assuming the received view of warrant, and granting the overall unreliability of reflective equilibrium, it might be possible for some individuals employing the method to be led to warranted moral beliefs.

2.6 CONCLUSION

It is certain many will think that, when all is said and done, even I, a defender of the radical method, can come up with very little to recommend it. "Why," it will surely be asked, "should we settle for what reflective equilibrium can offer – rational beliefs and maybe, just possibly, true and warranted beliefs as well? Can this really be enough?" In all fairness, I think that a large part of the answer to this question must be provided by the remainder of this book. Rather than just asking ourselves, in the abstract, whether it is enough, we must consider, carefully, just what the method can do in the way of rationally bringing us to have warranted beliefs. When I have spelled out in detail what the method can do, then we will be in a position to decide whether it is enough. My belief, of course, is that we will conclude that it is; indeed, that the method can do a great deal.

I think that I can also say a little now, even on the very abstract level at which I am speaking, about why a rational method that holds open the possibility of moral knowledge is adequate. I have already mentioned two points a number of times. First, we are, in a sense, forced into moral inquiry. As a matter of fact, nearly all of us acquire all sorts of moral beliefs long before we think of undertaking a philosophical inquiry into morality, indeed, long before we know what either philosophy or morality is. In all but the most unusual cases, these moral beliefs comprise a motley crew. If we compare them with one another, it is not at all apparent how they fit together; indeed, in most cases, what becomes apparent, after a little thought, is that they do not fit together. Thinking about the relations among our moral beliefs and other types of belief does not obviously improve the situation. We are likely to find, for example, that our moral beliefs do not live up to the epistemic standards which we insist that other beliefs meet. Or, perhaps, we discover that persons we consider highly trustworthy do not share our moral beliefs. Yet once we have these beliefs, we cannot avoid them. We cannot just turn them off. And if we ever become aware of the shape they are in, we must do something about them. We can try to start sorting our beliefs out, which is, in reality, to take up a philosophical inquiry, or we might try to go on as we have, although I do not think this is so much as a possibility. When an activity is forced upon us in this way, we cannot afford to be overly demanding when we consider how we are to proceed.

Secondly, it should go without saying that the complex goal of moral inquiry is terribly important. Our moral beliefs have practical import: They guide our actions. They cannot fulfill this function well, if they are incoherent. And, in so far as they bear upon the question of how best to live, we do not want just any old coherent set of beliefs to guide us – we want to be guided by the right set. Attaining rational, systematic moral knowledge is, therefore, a goal of the first order. If the best we can do with respect to attaining this goal is not very much, so be it. The goal is sufficiently important to outweigh the long odds of success we might face.

The final point in behalf of my strategy has to do with how much work we can expect a method of inquiry to do. There is a tendency to think that a method must take care of every significant feature of inquiry, that a method should be a mechanical thing that will take any person, no matter what his beliefs, the epistemic status of those beliefs, or the person's perceptual and intellectual capacities and the degree to which these capacities have been developed, to systematic knowledge, and that features of the method, not the person, will play the preeminent role in accounting for the epistemological status of the theory that the person ends up accepting. It is this thought that grounds the no contact and no credibility objections. And, it is this thought that leads one to think that, if a method cannot guarantee truth, it must at least be able to guarantee warrant for our beliefs. But we must give up the idea that the warrant of an inquirer's beliefs must always be accounted for primarily in terms of features of the method employed in forming those beliefs. Once we do, our expectations regarding what an adequate method of inquiry can accomplish are free to become more realistic. Consider, for example, the method each of us employs in forming a common-sense conception of the world around us. Surely, if this method were to be employed by Mr Magoo, his picture of the world would be very odd. I'm inclined to say that his picture would be rational in spite of its oddity, since presumably Magoo would be living up to his own standards, and, given the strange ways things always work out for him, his subsequent experiences would never conflict with his evolving picture of the world. But few of us would be inclined to think that Magoo's beliefs are warranted. It is quite clear that they are not truth-conducive. And if we suppose that he is forming beliefs about the world on the basis of fuzzy, indistinct, perceptual experiences, beliefs that vastly outstrip the content of these experiences, then we cannot even say that his beliefs have experiential warrant.[50] The important thing to see, however, is that these failures to achieve positive epistemic values in his believings count against *Magoo*, not *the method* he employs. We can only expect a method of inquiry to do so much. In Magoo's case, the method would have done its job, in spite of Magoo's failings.

If we shift the emphasis from the method of inquiry to the individual inquirer, and hold that various features of the inquirer play the most significant role in accounting for the epistemic status of the beliefs he comes to accept, we will tend to think that an adequate method should *aid* a person in his quest for knowledge, or perhaps simply not be a hindrance to the person's efforts. And, rather than requiring that an adequate method provide guarantees, we will simply require, at a minimum, that it be possible for some persons to come to have warranted beliefs as a result of following the method, viz., those who make the right contribution to the process. We would, then, wish to go on to show that the method does *more* for those who employ it than alternative methods that also meet this minimum requirement. In the moral case, however, since radical reflective equilibrium is the only rational method, and since being rational is an essential requirement, to establish the bare adequacy of the method, we need only an argument for the possibility of warranted beliefs.

To sum up, our epistemological goals in pursuing a philosophical inquiry into morality are complex. Any consideration of the adequacy of methods that might be employed in such an inquiry must be sensitive to the complexity of these goals. Insensitivity to just this complexity has plagued contemporary efforts to assess the adequacy of reflective equilibrium. My strategy for establishing the adequacy of a radical version of this method of moral inquiry is as follows. I require of an adequate method that it do all it can for those who follow it – it must put them in as good a position as possible with respect to attaining the goal of moral inquiry, which is rational moral knowledge. I do not think that any method of moral inquiry can guarantee true, or even warranted, moral beliefs, and I have argued for the former claim. But this opinion does not entail either that no moral methodology is adequate, or that my requirement on adequate methods can be ignored. For it may be that some methods bring us, or allow us to come, so to speak, closer to rational knowledge. In particular, it would seem that we should rule out entirely any method that leaves one in no position rationally to know at all, that is, any method such that it is not possible for a person who follows it to come to have either rational or warranted beliefs. When we consider what radical reflective equilibrium can do for us with respect to rationality, it will emerge that it is the only rational method. I devote Part II to making out this claim. In Part III, I will turn to warrant, and the related notions of experiential warrant and truth-conduciveness. It will become clear that the method I defend can play a significant role in bringing it about that our moral beliefs are experientially warranted. Even if this has nothing to do with these beliefs being warranted, and the received view tying warrant to truth-conduciveness is correct, I will be able to argue that it is possible for an inquirer to come to have warranted beliefs. This, I claim, will be enough to show that the method is adequate.

Part II
Rationality

3 The case for the rationality of radical reflective equilibrium

3.1 INTRODUCTION

I have promised to argue that the radical method of reflective equilibrium is the only rational method of moral inquiry. But the careful reader will have realized that this is not a promise I intend to keep. In the last chapter, I spoke *as if* I were out to defend the radical method only for the sake of convenience. In reality, I plan to defend a different, but related, method, which I call the method of balance and refinement. Having said this, so that I cannot be charged with being an out and out cheat, I will find it convenient to go on for a while longer without laying all my cards on the table. I will, accordingly, continue throughout this chapter to speak as if I will be defending the radical method of reflective equilibrium. My aim in this chapter is to offer a preliminary argument for thinking that radical reflective equilibrium is the *only* rational method of moral inquiry. One might think that I am therefore committed to holding that all the various critics of reflective equilibrium, and proponents of alternative methods, proceed irrationally, but in fact I am more inclined to believe that these critics do not actually succeed in employing alternatives to reflective equilibrium. So, more specifically, what I wish to show is that apparent alternatives to reflective equilibrium are either, at bottom, particular implementations of that very method, or they are irrational.

The argument I will offer against alternatives to reflective equilibrium turns on a particular factor that is relevant to assessing the rationality of belief, namely, whether all relevant beliefs held by the inquirer have been taken into account. My claim is that the alternative methods that have been proposed systematically exclude certain types of belief, and hence, are liable to lead inquirers to make revisions of belief that are irrational, in the subjective sense I identified in the last chapter. Since the method of reflective equilibrium excludes none of the inquirer's beliefs, at least in this respect, it is apparently a rational method. However, as we ordinarily think of rationality, the rationality of a given belief, or revision of belief, is not determined solely by the belief's connections with the inquirer's other beliefs. In some cases, we consider a belief to be irrational, even though all the evidence the inquirer accepts supports it, for example, when the inquirer has not bothered to gather sufficient evidence. I will show that the same holds for my subjective conception of rationality. When we consider this element of the rationality of belief, in terms of my subjective conception, it will once again turn out that the radical method of reflective equilibrium constitutes a rational method of inquiry. We will have, then, by the end of this chapter, discovered that the sorts of alternatives to reflective equilibrium that have been proposed are either irrational or not really alternatives. We will also have, what I consider, a fairly strong positive argument for thinking that the radical method is a rational method of inquiry. But this positive argument is only preliminary.

In the next chapter, we will consider another factor that is relevant to the rationality of belief. It will turn out that, where this factor is concerned, even the radical method of reflective equilibrium falls short. I will respond by making an addition to the radical method of reflective equilibrium. The amended method, the method of balance and refinement, is the approach to moral inquiry that I advocate. Although the addition I introduce might not seem particularly substantial, I believe that, in practice, the method of balance and refinement would look quite different from reflective equilibrium, even when reflective equilibrium is understood in the radical way I have proposed. However, the method of balance and refinement will share those features of reflective equilibrium that are involved in the argument I shall offer, in the present chapter, for thinking that it is the only rational approach to moral inquiry. So it will emerge, by the end of Chapter 4, that the method of balance and refinement is the only rational method for moral inquiry.

In the previous chapter, I adopted a subjective, internalist conception of rationality, according to which believing rationally is a matter of believing what, from the believer's own perspective, seems likely to be true, or better, would seem likely to be true upon reflection. I also characterized this sense of rational belief as believing in a way that satisfies one's own epistemic standards. This conception of rationality can be used to evaluate beliefs held at a given time, or to evaluate alterations of belief over time. The latter use plays the most significant role in my overall argument, but it is worth explaining, in some detail, why the former use of the concept plays a comparatively unimportant role in determining the acceptability of methods of moral inquiry. I therefore devote the next section to this use of the concept, and come back to evaluations of the rationality of revisions of belief in Section 3.3. Then, in Section 3.4, I will argue that alternatives to radical reflective equilibrium allow irrational revisions of belief.

3.2 THE RATIONALITY OF SYSTEMS OF BELIEF

One way of applying the subjective conception of rationality I've adopted is to apply it to beliefs held at a certain time. One asks, for example, whether some belief held by a person at a particular time is rational, or whether a whole system of beliefs that a person might hold at a particular time is rational. What is important here is that we are considering a belief, or set of beliefs, as held at a moment of time, not requiring that the beliefs *actually* be held. For we can be asking essentially the same question when we ask whether a system of beliefs no one actually holds is rational, or whether it would be rational for a person, in a given set of circumstances, to accept a certain belief that the person does not in fact hold. Since we are concerned to evaluate the outputs of methods of moral inquiry, we will be focusing on the rationality of systems of belief, rather than individual beliefs. We want to know whether reflective equilibrium can be counted on to lead inquirers to a system of beliefs, and in particular, a system of moral beliefs, that it would be rational to hold, and whether any other methods of moral inquiry can be counted on to yield such a rational system of beliefs as output.

It will, however, be easier to work up to systems of belief from a consideration of the rationality of individual beliefs. Now, when we ask whether an individual belief is rational, we are asking whether the person who holds the belief would consider her belief likely to be true, were she to reflect upon the belief. A large part of this reflection would involve considering the connections between the belief in question, or target belief, and the other things the person believes. One thing the believer will want to determine is whether any of her other beliefs conflict with the target belief.[1] If she finds any conflicting beliefs that seem to her to be more likely to be true than the target belief, we would say that the target belief is irrational. But it will not necessarily follow, from the existence of a conflict, that the target belief is irrational; for it might be that the believer is more strongly committed to the target belief than to the belief that conflicts with it, and would remain firm in this commitment upon reflection. In this case, the target belief would be rational, and the conflicting belief irrational. It might also turn out that neither belief is rational; for upon discovering the conflict, the believer might come to doubt both.

It is important to realize the various forms that conflicts between beliefs can take. One sort of conflict that will be especially significant will involve epistemic principles and non-epistemic beliefs. Such a conflict might arise, if a person's belief, and beliefs about the conditions in which the belief was formed, put the belief at odds with an epistemic principle accepted by the person. Thus, for example, a person might believe that her young colt has excellent gaits and conformation, but also believe that she bred the colt out of a favorite old mare; she is therefore especially attached to it, and believes that judgments formed under such circumstances are likely to be biased. Most people have not, of course, worked out a system of epistemic principles, so one might think that conflicts of the sort just described cannot be terribly common. However, since rationality is determined by what a person would think *upon reflection*, conflicts involving epistemic principles will become more common. For reflecting about a given belief will involve considering the circumstances under which the belief was formed, whether those circumstances are propitious for forming true beliefs, whether they at least do not make it so likely that false beliefs will be formed that one would be better off forming no belief at all, what precautions against forming false beliefs might be taken in such circumstances, etc., which in effect is to say that reflection will involve deciding upon something like epistemic principles, although perhaps not a systematic theory of normative epistemology. This is the reason I tried to convey the intuitive sense of the concept of rationality we are employing, by saying that it involves both believing what one would think likely to be true upon reflection, and believing in accord with one's own epistemic standards.

Having recognized the more ordinary role epistemic principles will play in reflection, we are in a position to note that such principles might also serve to make *both* members of a conflicting pair of beliefs rational. Consider, for example, the following sort of case. A particular person believes that it is extremely important that she form judgments regarding three moral issues. It is not apparent, even after a fair amount of reflection, that the issues are related. So the person considers the three issues separately. She gathers evidence, constructs arguments and counter-arguments, and finally resolves each issue to her own satisfaction. During the course of her deliberations, the considerations relevant to each issue apparently remain separate, at least to this extent: The inquirer at no point concluded that the three issues shared some deep or important similarity, the sort of similarity that would have indicated that her resolutions of the three issues ought to be coordinated, and in the end, the reasons grounding the person's final beliefs about each issue are different. Now, even given all this, it is still possible that, if the person were to undertake the sort of reflection that determines the rationality of belief, she might become convinced that her resolutions of the three moral issues are, in fact, inconsistent, at least given certain background beliefs that she takes to be beyond doubt. I can see no reason for thinking that she could not be right about this. Having come to believe that her resolutions of the three issues were not consistent, she would set about trying to eliminate the inconsistency. But suppose that she could not. Careful reflection upon her resolutions, driven by the knowledge that all three could not possibly be true, reveals nothing to choose among them: The considerations that individually led the person to adopt each of the resolutions continue to seem compelling, and the background beliefs that are necessary to generate the inconsistency among the resolutions continue to seem beyond question. If we recall that we are working with a conception of rationality as living up to one's own epistemic standards, we can see that we need not conclude that a person in this epistemic predicament would be forced, on pain of irrationality, to drop either all three resolutions or one resolution, which would apparently have to be selected in some epistemically arbitrary fashion. For the person might accept epistemic standards according to which, in cases of precisely this kind, the best balance between her interests in believing truly and avoiding error is attained by holding onto her beliefs in all three resolutions, even when she knows they are inconsistent. She might even reassure herself with the thought that each resolution has a 0.667 chance of being correct.[2] If a person accepts such a standard, certain inconsistencies among beliefs, i.e., ones for which the person has this specific sort of explanation (or excuse), would not indicate an incoherence between belief and epistemic standard, and hence, would ground no charge of irrationality.[3]

Although uncovering and resolving conflicts would play a significant role in the sort of reflection involved in determining the rationality of belief, it is not all that would be involved in such reflection. When considering the logical and evidential connections between a target belief and her other beliefs, an inquirer would be equally concerned to uncover beliefs that support the target belief. But, it is important to remember that, since what it is rational to believe is determined from the believer's own perspective, how much support a target belief might need from other beliefs, if any at all, and even what sorts of relations among beliefs constitute support, are dependent upon what would seem appropriate to the believer upon reflection. So once again, we are led back to the believer's epistemic principles, for considering whether a certain target belief needs to be supported by evidence, whether something provides evidence for something else, how strong the evidence is, and the like, can aptly be thought of as working out the epistemic principles one accepts, or at the very least, particular instances from which principles could be generalized.

I should mention one final element that reflection would presumably involve, an element that, once again, will involve epistemic principles. This is the consideration of alternatives to one's own beliefs. Perhaps the clearest case of what I have in mind occurs where one accepts a belief because it offers an explanation for certain other things one believes. We would, usually, be dubious of the first explanation of puzzling facts that popped into a person's head. We would think that the person should at least consider what sorts of alternative explanations might be offered for those facts. Suppose, e.g., that I come into the kitchen, and find a glass that had been on the counter lying broken on the floor. It would not be rational for me to believe that my wife clumsily knocked the glass over, and lazily left it there on the floor, without considering the possibility that one of our four cats, all of whom frequent the counter, was the culprit. Similarly, if a person holds a view regarding some matter about which there is considerable controversy, and a number of well-developed alternative views, we would generally think that the person needs to consider these alternatives, and form some idea of how her view stands with respect to them, not just examine how her belief relates to other beliefs of her own.

It might be objected that I have here deviated from what the subjective conception of rationality dictates, since I have appealed to what *we* think appropriate, rather than what *the believer* would think appropriate. But this objection is premature. For I realize that, having introduced the point in this way, I must go on to sing a familiar refrain, namely, that it will be up to the believer to decide what alternatives to consider, how much consideration to give them, and what to make of these alternatives, vis-à-vis her own belief. In effect, then, we might view the requirement to consider alternatives as a requirement to work out epistemic principles that bear upon the consideration of alternatives, and then believe in accord with these principles. There is another point to make in response to this objection. It is that the account of rationality we have adopted is not subjective "all the way down." For while much is determined from the believer's own point of view, not everything is. In particular, what is involved in reflection is not entirely up to the inquirer. Thus, reflection must involve examining the logical and evidential relations among beliefs, attempting to locate conflicts, and to resolve them. Moreover, while it is left to the inquirer to determine what the significant evidential relations are, logical relations are not determined from the believer's point of view.[4] Hence, what constitutes a conflict is partly an objective matter, but is also partly up to the inquirer. The most significant subjective element in rationality is, of course, that resolution of conflicts is entirely up to the inquirer. Similarly, the requirement that reflection involve considering alternatives to the believer's views is consistent with the rest of the account, so long as we leave it up to the believer's reflection to determine exactly what alternatives must be considered, and what the outcome of considering these alternatives will be.

Although this is nowhere near a complete account of what would be involved in an individual belief being rational, I think it is sufficient for us to form an accurate impression of what would be involved in a fairly comprehensive system of beliefs being rational. On the basis of this impression, it is plausible to suppose that, at the level of comprehensive systems of belief, the subjective conception of rationality we have adopted will lead to a kind of coherentism. For, in such a comprehensive system, epistemic principles, judgments about hypothetical cases, and so on will have been made explicit, so that we will no longer need further input from the inquirer to determine where conflicts lie, or how they will be resolved. Thus, whether or not a person's system of beliefs is rational will be determined by the relations among these beliefs, and the person's degrees of commitment to these various beliefs.[5] Turning to systems of propositions that may not actually be believed by anyone, we will say that the system is rational, if it contains no conflicts among propositions, where it is significant that the system will have to contain fairly well-worked-out epistemic principles, and that none of the beliefs contained in the system conflicts with these principles. It is clear that many distinct, and even conflicting, systems of propositions or beliefs will count as rational, and that one thing that allows for this is that these systems might contain diverse epistemic standards.

Assuming I'm right about what is involved in a system of beliefs being rational, it is very easy to see how to answer questions about the output of the method of reflective equilibrium. In as much as the radical method of reflective equilibrium, and for that matter, reflective equilibrium, as standardly conceived, is a method for producing a comprehensive and coherent system of beliefs, the claim that the method of reflective equilibrium will lead inquirers to hold a rational system of beliefs should need no defense. It ought to suffice to note, in particular, how one feature of that method will operate. Recall the distinction between wide and narrow reflective equilibrium. The latter method seeks to achieve coherence between considered moral judgments and a moral theory, while the former complicates the picture by bringing "background" beliefs into play, in particular, background philosophical beliefs. This will, in the end, have to include epistemic principles. So, in effect, employing the method of wide reflective equilibrium will involve settling upon a system of epistemic standards, and seeing to it that our considered moral judgments and the moral principles, or theories, we accept satisfy these standards, at least in so far as it is within our power to do so. Hence, the type of coherent system of belief required by the concept of rationality we have adopted is nearly exactly the sort of system of beliefs that the method of wide reflective equilibrium would lead inquirers to hold. It is safe to say, therefore, that the method of wide reflective equilibrium can be counted on to lead inquirers to a system of beliefs that it would be rational for them to accept.

Unfortunately, leading to rational systems of beliefs is not so much of an accomplishment as it might seem. For any number of clearly unacceptable methods of philosophical inquiry could conceivably lead to the formation of a rational system of beliefs, as well. Believing all and only the pronouncements of an oracle could produce such a system of beliefs, provided that the oracle is consistent and issues sufficiently many and diverse pronouncements. Or again, it would seem that extreme indoctrination techniques, or "brainwashing," might be capable of leading to a system of beliefs that is rational in the sense we have been talking about. Of course, neither of these "methods" could be counted on to produce such beliefs, but it does not take much imagination to conceive of clearly unacceptable methods of inquiry that could guarantee us a rational system of beliefs. There is, for example, the *inverse* method of reflective equilibrium, which is exactly like the method of wide reflective equilibrium with one exception: When inconsistent pairs of moral beliefs are uncovered, the inquirer is to revise the belief that, after due reflection, seems *more* likely to be true. This is perhaps a difficult task, since as we have noted, what we believe is not within our direct voluntary control, and it seems that, at least typically, the natural consequence of reflecting upon a pair of inconsistent beliefs is the gradual extinction of the belief that seems less likely to be correct. But nonetheless, perhaps supplemented with various psychological techniques, the inverse method seems to be possible. So we cannot say that the radical method of reflective equilibrium is unique, even in guaranteeing that it will lead inquirers to a rational system of beliefs.

Some might think that this result indicates no failing of the radical method of reflective equilibrium, but rather the deficiency of the conception of rationality I have adopted. More specifically, it will surely be thought that such crazy "methods" can produce, and even guarantee, rational systems of belief precisely because the conception of rationality I am working with is subjective, and so extremely weak. Now, I agree that we have encountered no problem for the radical method of reflective equilibrium here, but not because I think the concept of rationality with which I am operating is somehow deficient. I think that it is a good thing to have beliefs that are rational in the weak and subjective sense I have identified. It is also a good thing that the radical method of reflective equilibrium can guarantee inquirers rational beliefs. It is even a good thing that the crazy methods can yield rational beliefs. What is wrong with that? Just because a method of philosophical inquiry is clearly unacceptable, it does not follow that there is *nothing* good about it. It does not follow that the method cannot produce beliefs with *some* sort of positive epistemic status. It does not even follow that the method cannot *guarantee* the production of such beliefs. As I argued in the last chapter, because of the diversity of our epistemic goals, the acceptability of methods of inquiry is a complex matter. For the same reason, the unacceptability of methods will be complex, typically involving a failure to achieve the right sort of balance of epistemic goods, not a failure to achieve anything at all that is of some epistemic value.

"Fair enough," someone might say, "but it is still true that the conception of rationality you have adopted is just too weak. Provided only that a person's beliefs are coherent, it seems pretty clear that she could adopt all sorts of bizarre epistemic principles that would, in turn, sanction all sorts of bizarre beliefs. And we are left holding the bag, forced to admit that these beliefs are *rational*!" To my way of thinking, nearly all of the force of this objection is dissipated once one really gets it firmly in mind that rationality is not the only epistemic good we seek. Saying that a belief is rational is not saying everything epistemically significant about it. It says just one thing – that the belief has attained a certain, admittedly very weak, positive epistemic status. It is perfectly possible that the belief has all sorts of terrible epistemic faults as well. It might, for example, be false, lack warrant, be formed on the basis of unreliable methods of inquiry or information processing, or even be the sort of thing that only a crazy person would accept. With such an arsenal available to pound away at the epistemic status of a belief, the desire philosophers have for one final bomb to hurl, viz., the charge of irrationality, is surely hawkish in the extreme!

Having admitted that the conception of rationality I'm working with is indeed very weak, and even issued what might be construed as an apology for going on with its use, I want to stress that to say that a belief is rational, in this sense, is *not* to say nothing at all. In fact, it is to say quite a bit. For while it is *possible* for all sorts of bizarre beliefs to attain the sort of rationality in question, we should not presume that beliefs that are in fact rational, in the relevant sense, are to be found all over the place. It is, for example, extremely unlikely that any of the crazy beliefs we encounter in ordinary life meet this standard. Indeed, I am quite confident that none of us has attained this sort of rationality for all, or possibly even most, of our own beliefs. For it is quite clear that many of our beliefs, both moral and non-moral, are incoherent in one way or another, that many of our beliefs do not satisfy even the partial epistemic standards we ordinarily employ, let alone those we might find adequate upon reflection, and that we have not pursued to its completion the sort of reflection that would be necessary for us to uncover our own deep epistemic standards, and bring our beliefs into conformity with these standards. So, while we can easily see that it would be possible for a person rationally to hold beliefs that we would consider epistemically unsavory in various ways, we must not let this obscure what a daunting task it would be for most of us explicitly to mold our beliefs into a system that is rational, in the "very weak subjective" sense we have been talking about.[6]

There is another way in which the conception of rationality I'm employing is stronger than it might at first appear. Recall that I began this discussion by saying that one way of applying this conception of rationality is to the beliefs, or system of beliefs, a person holds at a particular time. But we also assess the rationality of revisions of belief, that is, we can evaluate changes of belief over time as rational or irrational. As I noted in the last chapter, an adequate method for philosophical inquiry into morality must not only bring us to a system of beliefs that it would be rational for us to hold, but must also do so by a series of steps that are rational for us to take. Even when interpreted using our weak subjective conception of rationality, this requirement is significant. It is this requirement that the clearly unacceptable methods suggested above violate.[7] More importantly, this is the requirement that rules out all methods other than reflective equilibrium as irrational. I shall devote the next couple of sections to defending this claim, beginning in the next section by examining how the weak conception of rationality can be applied to the revision of belief over time.

3.3 RATIONALITY AND THE REVISION OF BELIEF

We have seen that the subjective conception of rationality, according to which rational belief is understood as believing what would seem right from the believer's own perspective, leads us to view the rationality of a system of beliefs as primarily involving the interrelations among the beliefs that comprise the system, so that roughly, a system of beliefs is rational if it has a certain sort of coherence. As a result, requiring acceptable methods of inquiry to yield rational systems of belief does very little. For any number of methods can lead persons to hold coherent beliefs, including methods that are clearly unacceptable, e.g., "brainwashing," or the "inverse" method of reflective equilibrium. I've claimed that the requirement regarding rationality becomes much more forceful when it is focused upon the steps a method directs persons to take as they attempt to formulate a theory. The two methods just suggested go astray, and indeed are irrational, because they do not lead the inquirer to a rational system of beliefs by steps that it would be rational for her to take. But it isn't only such "screwy" methods of inquiry that fail to be rational in this sense. Any method of inquiry other than the method of reflective equilibrium will fail – or so I claim.

To make good on this claim, I need to draw out principles that can be applied to revisions of belief, from the conception of rationality as believing in a way that accords with one's own standards. I must admit that, in the last section, I did not offer a terribly careful argument for the conclusion that the subjective conception of rationality will yield a coherentism of sorts. But I think I can be excused for two reasons: First, I had the luxury of relying upon the efforts others have made to develop this conception in detail,[8] and secondly, I do not rely upon the notion of rationality, as applied to beliefs held at a particular time, to do much work in my argument. The situation with respect to the revision of belief differs in both respects: No one has worked out in detail the relevant conception of rationality, and I intend the application of this conception to do a tremendous amount of work for me. Specifically, this conception must ground the elimination, on grounds of irrationality, of all methods of philosophical inquiry into morality other than reflective equilibrium. So particular care is called for at this point in the argument. I shall do my best to supply it, but I am not terribly confident that I can improve markedly upon the sort of argument I offered in the last section.

It might seem that the subjective conception of rationality I have adopted would apply straightaway to the revision of belief. For, one way in which we have characterized that conception is by saying that rationality is a matter of believing in conformity with one's own epistemic standards, which would seem to lead, very naturally, to the idea that a revision of belief would be rational, just in case it conforms to the believer's epistemic standards. But there are a number of problems with this idea. For one thing, most persons will not have explicitly developed their epistemic standards. So we cannot just canvass a person's current beliefs, to locate the relevant standards, and then compare a particular revision of belief with the relevant epistemic belief. Moreover, even when the person does explicitly accept some epistemic principles, conforming to these principles will not necessarily amount to rational belief. For it might be that the person accepts the principles in question, without having given them much thought, and that, if the person were to reflect even a little on the matter, she would come to disbelieve the principle. In such a case, we would not want to say that the believed epistemic principle reflects the person's real epistemic standards.

Essentially the same point can be made without focusing on epistemic principles. Suppose that an inquirer comes to believe that two of her beliefs, A and B, are in conflict, and responds by ceasing to hold A, which seems to her to be less likely to be true than B. Should we say that this revision is rational, since it seemed to the inquirer that the revised belief was less likely to be true than the belief retained? Not necessarily, for it might be the case that even a little reflection would alter the inquirer's estimation of A and B. For example, a third proposition, C, which the believer holds to be much more certain than either A or B, might be evidentially related to these beliefs in such a way that it strongly confirms A and disconfirms B. This evidential connection might be one that the believer would take note of, upon the slightest reflection. Supposing that no other beliefs are similarly relevant, the revision of belief in question would not be rational.

It might seem that this problem can easily be solved by holding that a revision of belief, in the face of conflict, is rational, just in case the revised belief is the one that the believer would consider less likely to be true *upon reflection*. This proposal has the effect of bringing the account of rational revision of belief into accord with the account of rational belief at a time offered in the last section – in case a conflict between two beliefs is encountered, the belief to be revised is the one that it would not be rational for the person to hold. What could be more natural? Well, in a certain sense, I'm afraid that nothing, or at least nothing I will be able to come up with on this point, will be more *natural*, but unfortunately, the natural account of rational revision of belief is flawed nonetheless. It might be easiest to see why, if we consider a case involving a conflict between a belief and the epistemic principles the believer accepts. Suppose that a person is quite firmly convinced of an epistemic standard according to which it is best, given her circumstances, that she does not hold a certain belief, a belief she in fact holds, but with less conviction than she feels for the epistemic standard. She therefore revises her belief to accord with the epistemic principle. But suppose, finally, that were she to reflect fully, until she had settled upon a system of epistemic principles, she would no longer accept the standard in question, but rather a collection of principles that would sanction her original belief. In this sort of case, I do not think we should necessarily hold the revision of belief to be irrational, even though the revised belief is the rational belief, in the sense that it is the belief that would be contained in the system of beliefs it would be rational for the person to hold.

By filling in the example with specific details, I think I can make my case more compelling. Suppose that the person is a committed Bayesian, holding that beliefs ought to be altered in the face of additional evidence according to conditionalization.[9] But, in a certain case, the acquisition of new evidence has led her to alter her thinking radically, so that she no longer sees the evidence as having the same bearing upon her original belief that she would initially have thought. The believer has had a little schooling in probability theory, however. She is quite firmly convinced of the cogency of the Bayesian approach. And she is aware that people are often inclined to violate the dictates of the probability calculus. So after reflecting on the matter quite carefully, she decides that is what is happening in her case. The result of this reflection is that she gives up her radical thinking and comes to believe in accord with conditionalization. It might seem as if her revision is rational, but the story is not over. Unbeknownst to our conscientious inquirer, were she to undertake a critical, philosophical study of Bayesian epistemology, she would eventually find it unacceptable on the grounds that it is sometimes correct to "throw away the priors." And, when she had reached this conclusion, she would see that to be exactly what she had done with the belief in question. So, according to the ultimate results of reflection, the person's revision was not rational. She should have stuck with her original belief. What are we to say here?

I would want to say that the person's revision of belief is rational, in spite of the fact that reflection would ultimately result in the person's adopting epistemic principles that would not sanction the revision. For even if the believer were to reflect quite carefully, both upon her epistemic principles and the specific belief in question, it would seem to her that the relevant principle, and the belief it sanctions, are both almost certainly true. She would come to doubt the epistemic principle only if she were to press very far along a course of reflections that we might imagine running parallel to an extended debate being carried on by professional philosophers in a series of technical articles. I do not think that we should view revisions of belief as irrational because they do not accord with standards that would be revealed only by such reflection. For even though the core notion of rationality I am working with is simply evaluative, and not deontological, I did not want to lose entirely the sense of condemnation that philosophers clearly associate with the charge of irrationality.[10] And we certainly would not want to blame the believer in our example. How can we, in good conscience, hold an inquirer to a standard that is practically inaccessible to her in the way described, even if the standard is, very deep down, *her own*?

Where should we go now? We cannot say that whether an alteration of belief is rational is determined by the beliefs, including the epistemic principles, a person happens to hold at the moment, possibly without any thought. What it is rational to retain, and what it is rational to revise, is determined by what would seem likely to be true to the person after giving the matter *some* thought. In cases where epistemic standards figure prominently, we want to hold the person to the principles that she would accept after putting *some* time and effort into examining these principles. But just how much thought? How much time and effort? We have seen that we cannot hold persons to what would seem most likely to be true after some ideal series of reflections had run its course to a stable conclusion. But where are we to stop short of that? In my opinion, these are important questions. And I do hope, and believe, that there is a natural, intuitively plausible way of identifying how much, and what sort of, reflection is needed. But quite frankly, I do not have anything useful to say about the matter. I will simply have to rely upon our intuitive sense of how much reflection is required for a revision of belief to be rational. My hope is that this intuitive sense will be informed, and to some extent corrected, by two things: our awareness of the problem we have been discussing, and more importantly, the idea that when we call a belief irrational, we convey a sense of condemnation or blame. I think that keeping the latter firmly in mind will lead us to expect something of inquirers, while helping to guard against demanding that they take extraordinary measures in revising their beliefs.

Having made one stab at a rationalization for "bailing out" on this important issue, I want to offer yet another excuse for not being more specific about the amount of reflection that is relevant to assessing the rationality of revisions of belief. The most important critical claim I wish to establish is that any alternative to the radical method of reflective equilibrium can lead inquirers to revise their beliefs in irrational ways. My argument for this claim would certainly be weakened, if it involved a substantial assumption about how much reflection is needed for rational belief revision. For it would follow from such an assumption that, if that specific amount of reflection were required, the method would sanction irrational revisions, but if some different amount of reflection were involved, these same revisions would turn out to be rational. I shall offer my argument without making any such assumption. Allow me to lay out the argument against one of the "screwy" alternatives to reflective equilibrium introduced in the last section, i.e., the inverse method of reflective equilibrium. This will serve both to introduce the form of argument I shall mount in the next section against more serious challengers and to show that I indeed avoid taking a substantive stand on how much reflection is needed for rational revisions of belief.

The inverse method of reflective equilibrium proceeds in much the same way as standard versions of reflective equilibrium. It directs the inquirer to attempt to develop a system of moral principles that will account for her considered moral judgments in a simple, intuitively plausible way, while also cohering with any relevant background philosophical or empirical beliefs she might hold. Just as in standard versions of the method, as the inquirer strives to mold her moral and non-moral beliefs into a coherent system of the requisite sort, she will be on the lookout for any possible conflicts among her beliefs. When a conflict is discovered, the two methods again agree in directing the inquirer to consider the connections among the conflicting beliefs and her other beliefs, both moral and non-moral. But when this reflection has been completed, the two methods diverge. For whereas ordinary versions of reflective equilibrium direct the inquirer to revise the belief that seems less likely to be true, all things considered, when moral beliefs are at issue, the inverse method directs the inquirer to revise the moral belief that, all things considered, seems to her to be more likely to be true, while retaining the belief that she considers likely to be mistaken. Is the revision of belief recommended by the inverse method of reflective equilibrium rational? It most certainly is not! To arrive at this answer, we need make only an extremely weak assumption about rationality: that when an inquirer uncovers a conflict between beliefs, and has considered the matter fully, examining the logical and evidential connections among the conflicting beliefs, and all her other beliefs, she should not alter the belief that seems *more* likely to be correct. She should rather address the conflict by revising the belief that she considers more likely to be mistaken.

Notice that by posing the question with respect to the rationality of a revision made *after* the believer has completely reflected upon the conflicting propositions, I have avoided the problem regarding how much reflection is required for rational revision of belief. This means, of course, that the argument is less general than it might be. What a self-serving way of putting the point! The fact is, the argument applies only to a situation that has been idealized, a situation that no actual inquirer is ever likely to find herself in, since it would be nearly impossible ever to complete the relevant sort of reflection. Nonetheless, I think it remains a deficiency of the inverse method that it would lead inquirers to make an irrational revision of belief in these idealized circumstances. And, perhaps, I can get away with saying that it is a particularly telling deficiency that, even in such an ideal situation, where we are imagining a person to have reflected fully upon some conflict between beliefs, the inverse method still mandates a revision that is irrational.

Even if making bad recommendations in idealized situations is not something we should hold against a method of inquiry, consideration of how the method operates in such circumstances is of some significance, for the argument developed there can be extended to actual circumstances. It should be apparent how I will try to make the extension. Surely *some* amount of reflection, short of complete reflection, is relevant to the assessment of revisions of belief. Perhaps this amount is fixed absolutely. More probably, it varies from case to case, depending upon certain factors, e.g., the importance of the beliefs in question, the perceived likelihood that further reflection will improve the chances of arriving at a correct answer, the complexity of the issues involved, and maybe even such factors as the other interests the inquirer has, and the amount of time and resources that are available to her. But in any case, let us suppose that for a given believer who has uncovered a conflict between two of her beliefs, there is a certain amount of reflection that she must devote to the matter, before any revision of belief will be rational. If we suppose that the inquirer engages in this required amount of reflection regarding the conflict between her beliefs and then follows the directive of a version of the inverse method that has been accordingly modified for practical application, it seems perfectly clear that we should say the same thing about the revision of belief that the inverse method recommends in this case as we said about the revision of belief that it recommends in the ideal case. The revision would be irrational!

I would also like to say that when we consider the recommendation that the radical method of wide reflective equilibrium makes, in either the ideal or actual circumstances, it is equally apparent that this revision of belief is rational. Indeed, I wonder whether there is any real alternative to the revision this method directs. For it seems to me that to reflect upon a conflict between beliefs, and as a result to come to view one of the beliefs as more likely to be true and the other as comparatively less likely to be true, will, in all but the most extraordinary circumstances, quite naturally result in retaining the belief that comes to seem more likely to be true, and losing the belief that comes to seem less likely to be true.[11] My contention that the revisions of belief enjoined by the radical method of reflective equilibrium are rational might be questioned on the grounds that we have been focusing upon only one factor relevant to the rationality of the revision of belief, i.e., considering the connections among the conflicting beliefs and the other beliefs the person holds. But it seems that the rationality of a revision of belief can sometimes be determined by factors other than beliefs the inquirer actually holds. For example, in many circumstances, we would consider it irrational for a person to form a belief without gathering additional evidence. We also seem to think that considering alternatives to our beliefs is relevant to their rationality. This is perhaps most clear when we come to believe something because it offers an explanation for certain other things we believe. Must we not take these factors into account before we pronounce the revisions of belief dictated by reflective equilibrium rational?

The first thing to say is that an inquirer will often be led to address the kinds of issues I have just raised when she considers the connections among her beliefs. Recall that, in seeking wide reflective equilibrium, an inquirer must examine the connections among moral beliefs and background philosophical beliefs. The latter will, presumably, include epistemological beliefs, and for most persons, some of these beliefs will concern issues such as how much evidence it is necessary to gather before coming to a conclusion, and what sort of hearing one must give alternatives to one's favored explanations or theories.[12] As a result, it may turn out that when a person begins to reflect upon a pair of conflicting beliefs, she will discover that one or both run afoul of her epistemic principles. In such a case, eliminating the conflict might well involve gathering additional evidence and considering alternative explanatory beliefs or systems. In addition, such epistemological beliefs provide an opportunity for new conflicts to arise. For a belief that conflicts with no beliefs of its own kind, e.g., moral beliefs, might very well fail to satisfy the person's epistemic standards. To be more precise, there may be a conflict among the belief, the person's beliefs about the circumstances of the belief, and her epistemic principles. In such a case, I expect the path of least resistance to a resolution of the conflict would lead through the alteration of the circumstances of belief, specifically, by seeking additional evidence or considering relevant alternatives.

So it is not as though the mere consideration of connections among one's own beliefs were powerless with respect to propositions outside one's corpus of beliefs. But one may question whether it has sufficient power. What, for example, about cases where the inquirer simply lacks the sorts of epistemic beliefs that might force her outside what she believes already? The problem is handled readily if we idealize the method of reflective equilibrium. Then, attaining reflective equilibrium involves considering *all* the alternatives to the system of moral beliefs that one would hold in narrow equilibrium, as well as all the arguments for and against these alternatives. So, consideration of alternatives is explicitly required, and consideration of the relevant arguments can, I think, be counted on to force the acquisition of all the additional evidence that might be needed. But, having said this, we now face familiar difficulties involved in moving from the ideal case to actual cases. Since no one could consider all the alternatives to the moral theory the initial stages of inquiry led her to adopt, let alone all the arguments bearing upon these alternatives, we surely cannot require this for rational revision of belief. But neither can we rest content at the opposite extreme, allowing the believer to operate solely with the evidence she has already acquired, and to draw conclusions without considering any alternatives to her view. How many, and what sorts of, alternatives must inquirers consider, then, and how much additional evidence must they acquire?

Given that we are working with a subjective conception of rationality, our initial inclination might be to say that this question must be answered in terms of the believer's own epistemic standards. However, if we try to give this answer, we will run into familiar difficulties, for we must say which standards determine the answer. Is it the standards that the inquirer actually holds? It would seem not, since the inquirer may not explicitly accept any such standards, or accept them only because she has not given the matter any thought. Should we say that the relevant standards are those the person would accept upon completing an ideal course of reflections? As we have already seen, with an affirmative answer to this question we hold persons to epistemic standards that may well be practically inaccessible to them. So once again, we are left supposing that there must be some middle way, but with no chart of this course. We might also wonder whether the subjective conception of rationality must allow the consideration of alternatives, and the acquisition of evidence, to be determined by an inquirer's epistemic standards. We might, for example, be worried about an inquirer who, even upon reflection, holds that she need never gather additional evidence bearing upon what she believes, or consider alternatives to these beliefs. It seems that the subjective conception of rationality might allow us to dictate that evidence be gathered in certain cases, and that certain alternatives must be considered, so long as it is left up to the inquirer what she will make of the evidence and the alternatives.

What conclusion should we draw, then, about the rationality of the revisions of belief that the radical method of reflective equilibrium directs vis-à-vis the consideration of relevant alternatives and the acquisition of evidence? I am inclined to respond to this question in the same way I responded to the similar question regarding the appropriate amount of reflection on the connections among the things the inquirer already believes. We suppose that there is some level of reflection, now including consideration of *relevant* alternatives and acquisition of *appropriate* additional evidence, that is required for the rational revision of belief in actual cases. What is relevant and appropriate may be determined absolutely, or it may be determined by the inquirer's own limited reflection on epistemic principles. We may not be able to say in a precise, systematic way just what is involved here at present, but we have a pretty good intuitive sense of what is required in particular cases. Thus, for example, Rawls' suggestion that attaining wide reflective equilibrium regarding a moral theory would require consideration of those moral systems and arguments that have figured prominently in the philosophical tradition seems to be a plausible proposal as to which alternative theories must be considered.[13] In any case, I think it is safe to assume that the development of a systematic account of the consideration of alternatives, and the acquisition of evidence necessary for the rational revision of belief, will pose no obstacle to my contention that the method of reflective equilibrium directs inquirers to revise their beliefs in rational ways. Rather, it will simply allow us to improve upon Rawls' suggestion, and say more precisely just what the method of reflective equilibrium requires in actual practice.

Having offered what is, perhaps, only a rather tentative argument for thinking that the method of reflective equilibrium can be counted on to lead inquirers to approach the acquisition of evidence and the consideration of alternative theories and points of view in a rational way, I might note that, although the "screwy" method of inverse reflective equilibrium need not be offensive in this regard, other possible methods of inquiry very well might so offend. In particular, it would seem that certain methods, which we might describe as "dogmatic" or "close-minded," will be liable to direct inquirers to make irrational revisions of belief. I might also mention that we will return to this and related issues below, for the objection I intend to press against the radical method of reflective equilibrium in the next chapter concerns what might be thought of as the consideration of alternatives and the acquisition of evidence.

It will be helpful to summarize the conclusions we have reached in this section before moving on. I began by discussing what is involved in the rational revision of belief in a way that highlighted, rather than hid, the incompleteness of my account of this aspect of rationality. I then tried to show that the inverse method of reflective equilibrium would lead inquirers to revise their beliefs in irrational ways, even in ideal circumstances, where they had reflected fully upon the connections among their beliefs. The argument relied upon what I consider a minimal assumption regarding the rational revision of belief, i.e., that, when an inquirer uncovers a conflict among her beliefs, and has considered the matter fully, examining the logical and evidential connections among the conflicting beliefs and all her other beliefs, she should not alter the belief that seems more likely to be correct, but should address the conflict by revising the belief that she considers more likely to be mistaken. Although this epistemic principle, and the arguments in which it figures, apply only to an ideal case, it is not hard to see how the argument can be extended to actual inquiry. For whatever amount of reflection on the connections among one's beliefs, short of complete reflection, might be required for the rational revision of belief, the inverse method of reflective equilibrium will direct revision of the moral belief that seems more likely to be correct after the requisite amount of reflection, and this cannot be the rational thing to do.

On the other hand, it seems that the method of reflective equilibrium directs a rational revision of belief, in so far as it favors what reflection leads the inquirer to consider most likely to be true. But it would have been premature to make such a claim for reflective equilibrium, at this point in the argument. For what revisions of belief are rational is not determined solely by the connections among the things a person believes. We commonly think that failure to consider relevant alternatives, or to gather sufficient evidence, can render a belief irrational. The question of how precisely to incorporate these factors into the account of the rational revision of belief is vexed. We cannot require inquirers to believe what they would upon consideration of all the evidence and all the alternatives. We cannot even require that they satisfy the epistemic principles that they would hold were they to reflect fully upon the matter. But it seems that a certain amount of attention must be given to alternatives before a revision of belief can be rational, and likewise that a certain amount of evidence must have been gathered. Fortunately, there seems to be no obstacle to revising the idealized account of the method of reflective equilibrium in accord with a responsible account of this aspect of rational belief revision, in order to attain a conception of reflective equilibrium that is applicable in practice, and that can be counted on to direct only rational revisions of belief.

It would be comparatively easy to minimize the importance of these conclusions. For the positive argument, that the radical method of reflective equilibrium will direct inquirers to make rational revisions of belief, is rather heavily mortgaged, and the argument against the inverse method is, admittedly, not directed against a very serious target, although it is about as unencumbered as a philosophical argument can be. I hope that the arguments presented in the next section will provide sufficient motivation to resist selling short what we have accomplished in this section. For I shall extend the argument against the inverse method to the serious alternatives to reflective equilibrium. In the resulting market, devoid as it will be of competitors, the fact that the method of reflective equilibrium does not obviously lead inquirers to make irrational revisions of belief may combine with the, admittedly, weak, positive argument for thinking that all the revisions of belief it dictates are rational, to make the method seem like a very attractive buy.

3.4 THE IRRATIONALITY OF ALTERNATIVES TO REFLECTIVE EQUILIBRIUM

It might seem that, at this point, the argument would have to become involved in the details of the various criticisms of reflective equilibrium, and alternative proposals regarding the correct method of moral inquiry. Fortunately, I can avoid this sort of discussion. I shall, instead, present my argument in general terms, in the hope that it will be sufficiently simple to make the application of this form of argument to various particular critics of reflective equilibrium, and their proposed alternative methods, transparent. So let's consider, in a general way, the views of those moral theorists who have criticized reflective equilibrium. Almost all such critics focus on the fact that reflective equilibrium allows our considered moral judgments to play a significant role in the construction of a moral theory. As a rule, such critics will go on to suggest some other starting point for theory construction, usually some meta-ethical theory, e.g., regarding the meaning of moral terms. I claim that there are only two ways to understand this position: Either it constitutes no real alternative to reflective equilibrium, or it offers directions for the revision of belief that would lead some inquirers to revise their beliefs in irrational ways.

If the critics are offering a genuine alternative to the method of reflective equilibrium, this alternative method must be granting epistemic principles, specifically those that ground the criticism of our considered moral judgments or other background theories, e.g., views regarding the meaning of moral language, a privileged status. For, in effect, the critics begin by highlighting a conflict between certain epistemic principles and our considered moral judgments, and then direct that the conflict be resolved in favor of the epistemic principles. Those who advocate the construction of a moral theory on some other basis, e.g., claims about moral language, do essentially the same thing. For they generally make a great point of the fact that their views regarding the meaning of moral terms will lead to moral directives that are at odds with at least part of what we commonly think, which is to say, their views conflict with the considered moral judgments of a sizable number of individuals. And, of course, the critics direct that what we commonly think give way to their position on moral language. Notice, then, exactly what these critics of reflective equilibrium are advocating. They direct inquirers – all inquirers – to revise their moral beliefs so that they accord with certain epistemic principles and background theories, *regardless* of what other propositions the individual inquirer might believe, and *regardless* of which beliefs the inquirer would consider more likely to be true, after thinking the matter through. I do not see how this can be rational. Indeed, it seems that the method apparently advocated by the critics of reflective equilibrium is irrational, and irrational in exactly the way that the screwy inverse method of reflective equilibrium is irrational.

Suppose an inquirer holds certain considered moral judgments (e.g., judgments about morally significant situations she has actually had to confront, and deal with, on numerous occasions) to be much more likely to be true than certain epistemic principles, theories regarding the meaning of moral language, or other background beliefs she found to be initially compelling, specifically, those put forward by some critic of reflective equilibrium. Suppose, in addition, that the inquirer's estimation of her moral judgments remains firm after thoroughly considering her own view, alternatives to this view, and relevant arguments that might decide the issue, where this consideration will, obviously, have to involve particularly careful consideration of the positions and arguments advanced by the critics of reflective equilibrium. I do not see how it could possibly be rational for such a person to try to go on believing what she thinks is more probably wrong, i.e., the views advanced by the critic, and stop believing what she takes to be true, i.e., her considered judgments. But this is what the opponents of reflective equilibrium would have to be recommending if theirs is truly an alternative method of moral inquiry. And, of course, the situation is actually much worse than I have portrayed. For I have supposed the individual inquirer shares the background theories, e.g., epistemic and linguistic principles, that ground the critic's arguments, at least in that she found them attractive initially. But there is no guarantee that this will be the case. Indeed, the inquirer may not hold these non-moral beliefs at all, accepting instead principles that not only pose no serious threat to her considered moral views, but actually cohere with them. Such a person would have no reason at all to make the alterations in belief that would be required by the alternatives to reflective equilibrium. It seems, then, that the method advocated by the critics of reflective equilibrium could possibly direct inquirers to make irrational revisions of belief. I strongly suspect that this is more than a mere possibility.

I am worried that I might have been unfair to the critics of reflective equilibrium. There is another way of interpreting their proposals, so that they do not direct irrational revisions of belief. According to this interpretation, the critics suppose that we are strongly committed to epistemic principles, according to which our considered moral judgments are dubious, and that we are also very confident of their favored meta-ethical views, e.g., regarding the meaning of moral language, which both suffice for the construction of a moral theory and contradict some of our considered moral judgments. Moreover, they suppose that we are much more strongly committed to these principles and views than we are to any considered moral judgments that we might have been inclined to make, or that, upon reflection, we will consider our moral judgments to be less likely to be true than these epistemic principles and meta-ethical views. Under these suppositions, the critics of reflective equilibrium clearly do not direct the sort of irrational revision of belief that is directed by the inverse method of reflective equilibrium. What is not clear, on this interpretation, is that the critic of reflective equilibrium is actually employing an alternative to that method. In as much as the inquirer does not seem to make use of her considered moral judgments in constructing a moral theory, but rather proceeds to derive this theory from meta-ethical theories, it appears that some other method of inquiry is being employed. But this appearance arises because the inquirer is systematically more committed to epistemic, linguistic, and other background principles or theories that conflict with her considered moral judgments than she is to these judgments, and remains so committed, through due consideration of relevant alternatives. As a result of these commitments, the inquirer is forced to reject her considered moral judgments, in order to bring her moral beliefs into coherence with her background philosophical beliefs. However, the important point is that the inquirer is seeking to mold her moral and philosophical beliefs into a coherent system, where the course of the required revisions is determined by the relations among the propositions she believes, and how likely she thinks these various propositions are to be true. So it turns out, on the present interpretation, that the critics of reflective equilibrium are actually employing the method of reflective equilibrium.

As far as the overall defense of the method of reflective equilibrium I wish to present is concerned, this portion of the argument could end right here. My aim was to show that there is no rational alternative to the method of reflective equilibrium. And the fact of the matter is that methods that have been put forward as alternatives to reflective equilibrium all face the dilemma I have outlined. For, in essence, the method of reflective equilibrium directs inquirers (i) to consider, or reflect, on various things, e.g., the connections among their own beliefs, alternatives to their own system of belief, and arguments that might decide among these alternatives, and (ii) to believe what comes to seem likely to be correct through the course of these reflections. Therefore, in order to offer a genuine alternative to the method of reflective equilibrium, a critic would have to issue some sort of directive to all inquirers, requiring them either to leave something out of account during their reflections, or systematically to favor some particular propositions or types of propositions, regardless of what they believe or would come to believe as a result of their reflections. Clearly, either directive will lead some inquirers to revise their beliefs in irrational ways. Fortunately, the critics of reflective equilibrium do not issue such blanket directives, or so I think. But, of course, the cost is that the methods they propose only *appear* to be genuine alternatives to reflective equilibrium. They are, in fact, no more than particular workings through of that method, albeit by inquirers who are much more confident of certain epistemic principles, or meta-ethical theories, than they are of their own considered moral judgments.

As I have said, respecting the overall structure of my argument, this portion could end right here. However, I foresee a line of response that, I think, the critics of reflective equilibrium would want to offer. The trouble is, this line of response carries us away from the main course of the argument. Indeed, it is, strictly speaking, beside the point. For it begins with the suggestion that the critics were attacking a narrower understanding of reflective equilibrium than the one I have adopted, and it proceeds to consider not whether it would be rational for any inquirer to employ this method, but whether it would be rational for us contemporary moral theorists to employ it. Although considering this line of response will take us rather far afield, I think it is quite important, so I shall devote the remainder of this section to following it through.

Against my charge that the critics of reflective equilibrium have in fact employed this method, these critics will likely protest that I have construed reflective equilibrium so broadly that they no longer mind being accused of employing it. What they wanted to object to was allowing our considered moral judgments to play the leading role in the construction of a moral theory. If, in offering their objections, they can somehow be construed as, nonetheless, employing the method of reflective equilibrium, so be it. As long as they have ruled out the use of considered moral judgments, they will be content. I have granted that these critics may be rational in paying no attention to *their* considered moral judgments and seeking, instead, some other ground upon which to build a moral theory. Have I thereby conceded that we should not use *our* considered judgments in constructing a moral theory? Not at all. It is important to bear in mind that, as I have construed it, the method of reflective equilibrium is a method for the *individual* to use. It is a method that is sensitive to the individual's beliefs, degrees of belief, and even propensities to believe. Indeed, if it were not sensitive in this way, it would not be a rational method. For the conception of rationality we have been working with is subjective, and is, accordingly, sensitive to various features of the individual. Because of the individualistic character of reflective equilibrium, it is liable to lead different individuals to very different substantive moral views. And because the notion of rationality is subjective, different inquirers can rationally accept very different moral theories. Thus, from the fact that some inquirers employing the method might be led to doubt their considered moral judgments and to construct a moral theory on some other basis, and might even be rational in so proceeding, it does not follow that all inquirers should proceed in like fashion. The method of reflective equilibrium will allow those inquirers who are sufficiently confident of their considered moral judgments to make use of these judgments in constructing a moral theory, and even to modify their epistemic principles, and theories about the meaning of moral language, so that they conform with their considered moral judgments, and it will be perfectly rational for such inquirers to do so.

At this point in the argument, certain critics of reflective equilibrium might respond by claiming that, although what they advocate might be irrational for some inquirers in *my* sense of "irrational," what they advocate *is rational* for all inquirers in a more important sense of "rational." Specifically, they might claim that, when we speak of beliefs being rational, we mean to indicate that these beliefs are not contrary to the deliverances of reason. Paradigm examples of such deliverances of reason might include simple logical principles and mathematical truths, certain metaphysical principles, e.g., the indiscernibility of identicals, and even certain moral principles, as for example, the claim that moral goodness is supervenient, in the sense that no two individuals could share all their non-moral properties and differ with respect to moral properties. The critics would then claim that the epistemological and meta-ethical principles on which their approach is grounded are among the deliverances of reason. It would follow that their approach to moral theorizing is rational not in my sense, but in the important sense they are concerned about, while any alternative approach, e.g., the method of reflective equilibrium, is liable to lead inquirers into irrationality, again in the sense that really matters.

While there is some reason to think that this is what some opponents of reflective equilibrium have in mind, particularly proponents of rationalist approaches to ethics, this line of reasoning is clearly not without its problems. Most obviously, it is based upon the notion of "deliverances of reason." This notion is not entirely clear; indeed, it is controversial whether it is possible to spell out a viable notion of deliverances of reason. And even if we could develop a clear notion of deliverances of reason, that was adequate to the most central paradigms, it would surely be controversial whether any of the propositions which ground alternatives to reflective equilibrium could be included among the deliverances of reason. In addition, pending an explication of the notion of deliverances of reason, we cannot say that a method based on such propositions would constitute an alternative to the method of reflective equilibrium. Consider what happens, for example, if we identify deliverances of reason as those propositions which we can see to be true simply upon grasping or understanding them. Presumably the inquirer would encounter these propositions as she engaged in the sort of reflection required to bring her beliefs into a state of reflective equilibrium, particularly since such reflection involves the consideration of alternative moral conceptions and relevant philosophical arguments. Upon grasping these propositions, the inquirer would see that they are true, and presumably believe them to a high degree. It would, then, be entirely consistent with the method of reflective equilibrium for these propositions to play a guiding role in the inquirer's moral theorizing of precisely the sort the critics of reflective equilibrium desire. This result suggests that, for so-called deliverances of reason to ground a serious alternative to the method of reflective equilibrium, it must not be the case that all inquirers can be expected to come upon, and then accept, these propositions during the course of their moral theorizing. And if the propositions that actually have been proposed as grounds for moral theory construction by critics of reflective equilibrium are any indication, we can be quite sure that they will not be accepted by all who grasp them. At this point, I would be inclined to push the argument I offered above, but without using the term "rational," to avoid begging any questions. I would simply ask, how can a method for philosophical inquiry be accepted if it directs inquirers to jettison beliefs of which they are quite confident after due consideration in favor of propositions that, again after due consideration, they consider unlikely to be true? I cannot imagine such a method being acceptable.

The critics of reflective equilibrium are likely to respond that they were never fans of deliverances of reason and their ilk. They will complain that, in particular, they never intended to offer some sort of *a priori* argument showing that everyone had to accept their starting points, or that no one could rationally employ their own considered moral judgments in the construction of a moral theory. Rather, they took themselves to be speaking to the members of a certain intellectual community, a community that shares certain beliefs, propensities to believe, a certain overall intellectual outlook, and so on. Their aim was, surely, to convince the members of this community, and their assumption was that these members would, or should, in a sense of "should" that is appropriately relativized to the community's overall outlook, find the epistemic principles, and meta- ethical theories, that ground their critique, much more compelling than any considered moral judgments they might be inclined to make. If the critics of reflective equilibrium are assuming that the relevant persons would, as a matter of fact, agree with them in doubting their considered moral judgments, we can say with considerable confidence that they are mistaken. It seems quite clear that many, and maybe even most, moral theorists take some of their considered moral judgments to be much more likely to be true than either the epistemic principles that have been presumed in criticizing these judgments or the meta-ethical theories that have been offered as new grounds for the construction of a moral theory.

So we are thrown back onto the claim that, whatever moral theorists might, as a matter of fact, place their confidence in, they *should not* trust their considered moral judgments. The idea here is presumably that there are certain things we all know or believe, e.g., that persons in different cultures and at different times have made different moral judgments, and a certain outlook we all share (I expect that an important part of this outlook involves taking science to be the producer of rational belief, and knowledge, *par excellence*), and given that we hold these beliefs, and share this outlook, those of us who place any confidence in our considered moral judgments will have incoherent beliefs. Now the critics of reflective equilibrium would surely have a powerful position if, in fact, the epistemic principles and meta-ethical theories that they employ were somehow grounded in the beliefs and outlook shared by all, or nearly all, contemporary moral theorists. However, I doubt that they are so grounded.

Let's begin with the epistemological criticism of considered moral judgments. I have not said, specifically, what epistemic principles the critics of reflective equilibrium employ, but this is not a bad thing. Different critics will employ, or presuppose, different principles, and I would like to be able to offer a response to this line of criticism that is as general as possible. Rather than asking what epistemic principles might be used to criticize our considered moral judgments, let us ask instead about the nature of epistemic principles, and how such principles are constructed. The first thing to note is that epistemic principles are evaluative, just as certain moral principles are. As a result, such principles cannot be established by empirical methods. They must be uncovered by philosophical inquiry. If we can take the practice of epistemologists as a guide to the nature of this inquiry, we will find that considered judgments about actual and hypothetical cases, as well as intuitive judgments about various principles, play a crucial role in such inquiries. It would seem, therefore, that considered *epistemic* judgments play a role in establishing epistemic principles, a role that is similar to the role advocates of the method of reflective equilibrium take our considered moral judgments to play in the construction of moral theories. If this is so, why should we find epistemic principles to be universally favorable to considered moral judgments? I don't think we are generally better judges of epistemic matters than we are of moral matters. A common view among analytic philosophers is that both moral and epistemic judgments are linguistic – they are judgments regarding what we would say. Anyone sharing this view would apparently have to say that, at least at first glance, moral and epistemic judgments should be on exactly the same footing. Perhaps, then, epistemic judgments are not to be favored in principle over moral judgments, but are to be favored because they form a much more orderly, unified system of judgments – a system of judgments that can be codified in epistemic principles and then turned against our considered moral judgments, which suffer in comparison, because they do not form a similarly coherent system that has yielded to codification by a set of elegant, compelling principles. If it were clear that our moral judgments were much more disorderly than our epistemic judgments, this might well provide a strong reason to think that they should systematically lose out to epistemic judgments in cases of conflict. On the view that holds both epistemic and moral judgments to be linguistic, such disorder might be taken to reveal that moral terms have no straightforward meaning, or that we do not understand the meanings of moral terms, e.g., we might have misconstrued these terms, in something like the way the emotivists have suggested, by taking them to attribute properties to things when, in fact, they serve to express our reactions to these things. The trouble is that it is not the case that our moral judgments are in much worse shape than our epistemic judgments. In neither realm have simple, elegant principles that uncontroversially account for our judgments emerged. In both realms, we find strongly held judgments that are apparently explicable only if contradictory principles are adopted. In both realms, we are inclined to make different judgments about cases, where it is not at all clear that the cases differ in a way that can support a difference in judgment. And so on. Once again the two realms appear to be on all fours.

It seems to me, therefore, that nothing in the current situation provides a strong reason for thinking we must favor epistemic judgments or principles over moral judgments and principles. Moreover, I would be willing to go out on a limb a little by claiming that, in the long run, we may well end up with reason for siding with moral, rather than epistemic, judgments when they conflict. In the last paragraph, I dwelt on the mutual disorder of the epistemic and moral realms, but this should not be taken to indicate any sort of pessimism on my part. I hope, and perhaps even expect, that the disorder will eventually be resolved, or at least that different individuals might each resolve the disorder to her own satisfaction. But being in optimistic spirits, let's suppose that a whole community of philosophers shares a sufficiently similar overall outlook that all its members are able to accept, more or less, the same resolution of the conflicts among their moral and epistemological beliefs. Now, if the members of this community employ the equilibrium method, their moral and epistemic beliefs will be mutually adjusted, so there will be no conflicts between these realms. In order to pose our question, then, we need to suppose that the members of the community have been working at ethics and epistemology, more or less independently, without taking careful stock of how their results in the two areas fit together. So, we are imagining a community of inquirers who begin with rather disorderly moral and epistemic beliefs, which are pretty much the sort of moral and epistemic beliefs we actually have. The members of this community proceed to reflect upon the conflicts within the moral realm, and the conflicts within the epistemic realm, and to revise and refine their views in each of these realms. Eventually, the beliefs that form each realm begin to take the shape of a coherent set of judgments and principles. At this point, feeling good about the progress they have made, the inquirers begin to reflect upon how the moral system that is emerging from their reflections squares with the epistemic principles that are similarly emerging. Unfortunately, when the inquirers begin to reflect upon the connections between these two realms, they discover that their moral beliefs do not meet the epistemic standards that they have come to hold. If the inquirers were following something like the equilibrium method, they would revise their beliefs according to what judgments, or principles, they considered more likely to be correct upon due reflection. But, let us suppose that the members of this community are about equally strongly committed to their moral and epistemic principles, so that they are forced to pose just the kind of question with which we are concerned. They must seek to uncover some reason for preferring either their moral or their epistemic beliefs. Now, this question is, of course, a little odd, since it will presumably be answered by an epistemic principle. One might be worried, for example, about whether a verdict in favor of our moral principles would be subject to self-referential difficulties. But I don't think the answer need be involved in any such funny business, so let's just move ahead.

How, then, might these inquirers decide whether to adjust their moral or their epistemic principles? It seems to me that the following considerations might prove to be weighty. Consider what is involved in the epistemic realm and what is involved in the moral realm. On the epistemic side, we have a vast array of beliefs that we have formed, or might form, in various circumstances about various things. We have procedures we follow, or might follow, in forming, testing, and revising beliefs. And we have what appears to be a sophisticated set of concepts that we use to evaluate and criticize these beliefs, procedures of belief formation, and the like. On the moral side, it might *initially* appear that we find a similar cast of characters: actions performed in various circumstances, and a sophisticated set of concepts used to evaluate and criticize these actions, traits of character, and a set of concepts for the evaluation and criticism of these, states of affairs, and concepts for evaluating the moral value of these, and so on. But I am a little suspicious of this appearance. A description of why will serve as a nice preparation for the main point I wish to make. Although the kinds of judgments made within the moral and epistemic realms are obviously sophisticated, various, and complexly related to one another, I doubt whether the epistemic realm can really match the moral, in terms of overall complexity and sophistication. What, for example, would be the epistemic analog of the kind of moral evaluation of whole lives that some interpreters see as playing a central role in the moral thinking of such diverse characters as Aristotle and Nietzsche? And, though we can talk of praise and blame in the epistemic realm, surely it does not seem that the judgments we make regarding these are anywhere near as highly articulated as the judgments we make regarding moral praise and blame. What, for example, might provide epistemic analogs for supererogatory and suberogatory action? And again, although we can speak of epistemic, or better, intellectual virtue and vice, surely we find, once again, that our concepts and judgments regarding moral virtue and vice are vastly more complex, and subtle, than anything we find on the epistemic side. As a final example, I might mention epistemic, as opposed to moral, value. While we can, and do, talk about what might be of epistemic value, and even ultimate epistemic value, such judgments pale in comparison with the similar judgments that are made in the moral realm. It is apparent, therefore, that the system of concepts involved in the moral realm, and consequently the judgments and principles that this realm includes, are considerably more numerous, complexly interrelated, highly articulated, and so on, than are the concepts of the epistemic realm.

There is an even more significant difference between the two realms. For as much as is involved here in the conceptual and judgmental systems, it seems to me that this is all pretty thin, highly intellectualized stuff. What will be operative in determining the shape of moral and epistemic theories, given what I've said so far, are beliefs that such and such belief, or type of belief, has thus and so epistemic property, and beliefs that such and such action, or trait of character, or state of affairs, has thus and so moral property. But, surely, there is more to the moral realm than this. There is clearly a whole range of peculiar emotional reactions that are associated with morality, e.g., feelings of guilt, outrage, shame, repentance, admiration, and so on. Now, I would want to insist that these emotional reactions make up a central, and significant, element of the moral realm. These feelings must be integrated into any coherent moral system, every bit as much as concepts and judgments must be integrated within such a system. When we turn to the epistemic realm, I think we find a near complete lack of any similar emotional reactions. And so, we have uncovered yet another way in which the moral realm is, to describe the situation in more or less neutral terms, rather more complicated and varied, and to adopt a less neutral term, much *richer* than the epistemic realm.[14]

What might follow from these differences? Well, it seems to me that *if* it should turn out that both realms are, or can be turned into, well-integrated, coherent systems, the construction of the moral system would be much the more impressive accomplishment. For it seems to me, initially, unlikely that such a diverse set of beliefs, judgments, principles, and even emotional reactions should turn out to form a coherent whole. In science, or perhaps I should say the discussions of philosophers of science, it is commonly taken to be an asset when a theory can provide an integrated account of a wide range of apparently disconnected phenomena. I am inclined to think that an integrated account of all the apparently diverse judgments, and emotional reactions, encompassed within the moral realm would inherit an analogous asset. And since the moral realm is much richer than the epistemic realm, we would have a reason to favor the moral judgments that might comprise a part of a system that fully integrated this realm over epistemic principles that might cast these judgments in a negative light, even if these epistemic judgments were part of a system that adequately integrated the epistemic realm.

Even if these last speculations of mine are incorrect, and we would have no principled reason for preferring a reasonably well-worked-out moral system to a similarly developed epistemic system that might conflict with it, my main point against the critics of reflective equilibrium still holds. There does not seem to be any generally compelling reason for preferring epistemic principles to considered moral judgments that might conflict with them. Thus, I would want to allow that it is open to individual inquirers to decide the matter as they see fit. Without the epistemic criticism of considered moral judgments, the critic's proposal to build up a moral theory from meta-ethical principles surely loses some of its force. But there might still be reason to be tempted by this proposal. R. M. Hare, for example, seems to be motivated in part by a desire to build a consensus regarding morality. He fears that people differ too much in the considered moral judgments they are inclined to make for them to reach agreement regarding moral principles if they base these principles on their considered judgments. He thinks that there will be more agreement regarding meta-ethical principles, indeed, nearly universal agreement, so that the prospects for reaching a consensus regarding morality would seem to be good if we build upon meta-ethical principles. The question we must answer, however, is not whether there is some reason for preferring the approach that favors meta-ethical principles over considered moral judgments, or whether it might be rational for some inquirers to adopt this approach. Indeed, I am more than willing to admit that there are such reasons (I have just described one, after all) and that inquirers who find these reasons compelling proceed rationally. The question we must address is whether some element of the outlook shared by all, or nearly all, contemporary moral theorists provides a compelling reason to favor meta-ethical principles over our considered moral judgments. For the critics of reflective equilibrium maintain not only that they proceed rationally, but that the other parties to the current discussion regarding morality must proceed in the same way.

It is difficult for me to imagine that there is any such compelling reason for preferring meta-ethical principles over considered moral judgments. Just consider what these principles are like. For one thing, they are extremely general, indeed universal. If one thinks of these principles as concerning the logic, or meaning, of moral language, one might think that their universality is bought at the price of being empty or trivial, and hence, that their extreme generality poses no serious epistemological problems. But, of course, those who propose to erect a moral theory upon such principles think of them as anything but trivial. They think that these principles have all sorts of substantive moral consequences, consequences that are at odds with the moral judgments that many of us commonly make. If this is what these principles are like, I think that their generality does pose a problem. If you bit off one of these principles, you would clearly get a mouthful and then some.[15] I should think most inquirers would, therefore, exhibit a healthy reluctance about wholeheartedly accepting any such principle. Their reluctance should, I would think, be bolstered when they noted that the relevant principles tend to be very abstract. They are not the sorts of propositions with which most inquirers have a lot of experience. Even philosophers have vastly more experience with ordinary normative judgments, including judgments about general moral rules, than with such abstract principles. Moral judgments are the stuff of everyday life. We live and work with them. Our natural first inclination, when presented with an abstract meta-ethical principle, is to apply it to more familiar cases, both to figure out what it comes to, and to "test" it against some of the intuitive judgments of which we are most confident. Given our relative lack of experience with meta-ethical principles on their own, their detachment from our daily lives, our natural inclination marks the only proper approach. But note that our natural inclination is basically to favor our considered moral judgments over meta-ethical principles.

The power and abstractness of meta-ethical principles, and our lack of experience with them, are aggravated by the fact that it is unclear what sort of epistemic access we might have to these principles, as well as what their ontological status might be. Of course, the ontological status of, and our epistemic access to, ordinary moral judgments is no more clear, but then these judgments are not so abstract and powerful. And we are used to making such judgments, being the subject of such judgments, participating in the criticism of such judgments, etc., and we are used to living with the consequences of all this. They are a part of our lives, for better or worse, not something some theorist is proposing to add. So we are, I think justifiedly, inclined to be more tolerant of epistemological and ontological vagaries surrounding such familiar things. There are more uncontroversial cases of propositions we think we can trust, even though we do not clearly understand the relevant epistemology and ontology, cases such as mathematics, where the relevant principles are even abstract and universal. Some critics of reflective equilibrium might wish to develop the analogy with mathematics in defense of their use of meta-ethical principles. They might note that one finds the same sort of conflict between intuitive judgment and abstract principle in the case of mathematics as we find in the case of morality. Consider, for example, our judgments of the "sizes" of roughly spherical objects. We are inclined to think of the "size" of such things in terms of something like their diameters, and as a result, we tend to underestimate differences in the volumes of such objects. We will think one such object only somewhat bigger when it in fact has twice the volume. There is no question how to resolve the conflict here, and the fact that geometrical principles are abstract and universal, and that we do not well understand their epistemology, or ontology, does not matter a bit. Why, then, the critic of reflective equilibrium might ask, should we be so suspicious of her proposal regarding moral theory? She merely wants to accomplish for ethics what we have already accomplished in the case of mathematics.

One thing we might say about this line of response is that, although there are some, there are nowhere near as many conflicts between our intuitive judgments and the principles of mathematics as the critics of reflective equilibrium seem to think there are between meta-ethical principles and considered moral judgments. It might be that this difference in number, on its own, justifies us in being more dubious of meta-ethical principles than we are of mathematical principles. A more significant dissimilarity between mathematical and meta-ethical principles emerges if we consider the role experience plays, both with respect to intuitive judgment and mathematical principle. We cannot say that mathematics is quite so unfamiliar and removed from our daily lives as meta-ethics, at least, if we are thinking of the rudiments of arithmetic, geometry, trigonometry, and perhaps even calculus and set theory. We are introduced to these subjects at an early age and make nearly daily use of some elements of some of them, and more occasional use of much more. Indeed, we almost surely do simple mathematics much more frequently than we make moral judgments. Moreover, I think that when there are conflicts between intuitive judgments and mathematical principle, we will find that those making the intuitive judgments are lacking in relevant experience. Consider, again, the example of our judgments of the "sizes" of roughly spherical objects. I would be willing to bet that the people whose intuitive judgments are at odds with the truths of geometry tend to be those who lack practical experience. People who commonly have to move large ball bearings, or boulders, or even logs can, I think, be expected to make intuitive judgments that do not conflict with conclusions derived from geometric principles. I do not, therefore, think that the analogy with mathematics is close enough to blunt the argument I have offered, particularly if we bear in mind that I have only been concerned to establish the modest conclusion that there is nothing within the overall outlook we share that compels us to favor meta-ethical principles over our considered moral judgments. I have tried to establish this conclusion by highlighting what I take to be some elements of our common outlook that should incline us to favor our considered judgments and be dubious of meta-ethical principles.

Since I have just finished a rather long section with a rather long digression, it might be wise to get our bearings before closing this chapter. My primary aim in the last two sections has been to argue that the radical method of reflective equilibrium will lead inquirers to revise their beliefs in rational ways, while any alternative method of inquiry is liable to lead inquirers to revise their beliefs in irrational ways. This is because the essential feature of reflective equilibrium is that it directs inquirers to revise their beliefs according to what would seem most likely to be correct to them, upon reflection. Any genuine alternative to the method of reflective equilibrium must pick out some type of belief, e.g., epistemic or meta-ethical principles, for preferential treatment, and it is, therefore, liable to direct some inquirers to make irrational revisions of belief, namely, those inquirers who would, after the appropriate amount of reflection, consider their moral judgments to be more likely to be true than the beliefs that are supposed to have a privileged status. Given that I have been employing a weak, subjective conception of rationality, I had to allow that this argument does not really engage the various critics of reflective equilibrium. These critics are most probably concerned to offer a less than fully general indictment of that method, hoping only to convince those of us who share a certain contemporary outlook that we ought to be suspicious of our considered moral judgments, and favor certain epistemological or meta-ethical principles. Although it is not crucial to my argument, I have sought to defuse this idea by showing that we can find quite a lot in our shared outlook that might be taken to support our considered moral judgments over any epistemological or meta-ethical principles that might conflict with them.

4 Naïveté, corruption, and the method of balance and refinement

4.1 INTRODUCTION

Having just spent a chapter arguing that the radical method of reflective equilibrium is the only rational method of moral inquiry, I now want to present some reasons for thinking that even it cannot claim to be an entirely rational method. My aim is not to push for some sort of skeptical conclusion by first arguing that reflective equilibrium is the only possibly rational method, and then pulling out the rug by arguing that even it falls short of being rational. And I hope that I do not suffer from some sort of perverse urge to assert contradictions. What, then, is the structure of the argument I am out to present? The argument of the last chapter may be understood in the following way. Both defenders and critics of reflective equilibrium seem to proceed on the basis of a tacit agreement as to what might be relevant to the rationality of moral inquiry. This agreement recognizes the following to be relevant to the rationality of moral inquiry: (i) the inquirer's considered moral judgments, (ii) background philosophical theories, such as theories regarding the nature of persons and personal identity, (iii) background social scientific theories, such as theories regarding the role that a moral conception plays in a society, (iv) the various alternative moral theories that have been developed, and defended, within the inquirer's cultural tradition, and possibly within alien traditions with which the inquirer's tradition has had to interact, and, of course, (v) the various philosophical arguments that have been constructed for and against all these moral conceptions. In the last chapter, I did not question this tacit agreement as to what might be relevant to the rationality of moral inquiry. Proceeding on the basis of the agreement, I argued that while the method of radical reflective equilibrium does not exclude any of these features from playing a role in a person's moral inquiry, where this is appropriate, any alternative method is liable arbitrarily to exclude something that ought to influence a person's inquiry. Hence, no alternative to reflective equilibrium can guarantee that it will not lead an inquirer to make irrational revisions of belief. So ends the argument of the last chapter.

Now, if the agreed view of what might be relevant to the rationality of inquiry were correct, specifically, if nothing more or less than what this view takes to be relevant to rational moral inquiry might be relevant, it would follow that radical reflective equilibrium is the only rational method of inquiry. Unfortunately, the agreed-upon view of what might be relevant to the rationality of moral inquiry is not correct. The problem is not that it includes too much, as certain critics of our considered moral judgments might be interpreted as holding. The problem is that the agreed view leaves something important out of account. As a result, since reflective equilibrium is, perhaps unwittingly, a party to the agreement, not even it can guarantee rational inquiry. My first aim in the present chapter is to substantiate my claim that the agreed-upon view is incorrect, and hence, that not even reflective equilibrium is a rational method of moral inquiry. My second goal is to describe how radical reflective equilibrium ought to be embellished, to obtain a method that allows a proper role to everything that might be relevant to the rationality of moral inquiry.

To prepare the way, I need to say a little about the role of experience in moral inquiry, a task to which I devote the next section. In that section, I will identify, as best I can, the type of experience that I take to be relevant to the rationality of moral inquiry that has been left out by reflective equilibrium. I call this sort of experience *formative experience*. In Section 4.3, I describe, in detail, a person whose moral views are epistemically deficient as a result of his limited range of formative experience. The person suffers from what I take to be a form of naïveté. Then, in Section 4.4, I argue, in detail, that the method of reflective equilibrium, whether it is construed narrowly or widely, radically or conservatively, cannot be counted upon to remedy the epistemological deficiency of the naïve person. In Section 4.5, I consider a modest revision of the method of reflective equilibrium that might be thought capable of relieving naïveté. However, this remedy places inquirers at risk of becoming victims of another sort of epistemic deficiency involving formative experience: corruption of moral judgment. In Section 4.6, I argue that the epistemic deficiencies involved in naïveté and corruption are, in part, a matter of irrationality, and hence, that an adequate method of moral inquiry must contain some element for dealing with them. Finally, in Section 4.7, I describe how the method of reflective equilibrium should be amended, thereby arriving at the method of balance and refinement.

4.2 EXPERIENCE AND MORAL INQUIRY

Let's take a familiar passage from Aristotle as our point of departure:

> a young man is not a proper hearer of lectures on political science; for he is inexperienced in the actions that occur in life, but its discussions start from these and are about these.[1]

This remark invariably evokes a strong reaction from students today, as it must have when Aristotle made it. But we should not let the obvious humor of the comment conceal the common sense it expresses – in ethics, as in any other study, a certain breadth of experience is necessary if one's inquiry is to be fruitful.

No one would want to deny this platitude. Yet it is questionable whether reflective equilibrium, even though it is arguably the heir to Aristotle's method of moral inquiry, has so much as managed to capture Aristotle's insight, let alone improve upon his formulation. Reflective equilibrium rather seems to represent the attitude that, since the experience of any ordinary adult will do for moral inquiry, there is no need to describe in any detail the role of experience in moral inquiry. Perhaps this attitude is a remnant of the old-fashioned view that substantive ethical theory is entailed by the meanings of moral terms, and hence that no more than the ability to understand or, less mentalisticly, to use moral language is required. We seem to be told that the experience we have had is good enough for constructing a moral theory, whatever our experience happens to have been. By taking this facile view of the role experience plays in moral inquiry, proponents of reflective equilibrium have left entirely out of account a type of experience that is crucially important to the rationality of moral inquiry.

It might seem that I am being unduly harsh with reflective equilibrium here. For reflective equilibrium directs the inquirer to consider all the arguments that might be offered for and against his moral conception, which would presumably involve considering all the relevant evidence. And, according to what is, perhaps, the most straightforward construal of Aristotle's concern, it has to do primarily with the acquisition of evidence or factual information. Aristotle thinks the young are unfit for moral inquiry, because they do not have enough information about life. There are certain psychological, and sociological, facts having to do, e.g., with such things as the motivations that characteristically influence people to act in certain ways, and the likely consequences of certain types of conduct. Because of their lack of experience, the young lack this important information. However, although it is probably true that the young lack such information, and that further experience would likely supply them with it, I do not think that this can really be Aristotle's concern.[2] For why would it be that only experience can supply such information? Why cannot those who have acquired such information simply present it to the young, who lack it, along with evidence to convince them of the veracity of the relevant claims? If the problem Aristotle was concerned with were a simple lack of information, it would seem that he would have gone on to say that lectures regarding ethics, intended for the young, cannot dig right into questions of substantive ethics, but must rather take care to begin by supplying young listeners with the practical information that is necessary for them to follow the moral arguments about to be presented.

If Aristotle's worry about the young's lack of experience did not have to do primarily with the information such experience can supply, what was he concerned about? This question is very much more complicated than one might suspect. Indeed, I suppose that, in some sense, the remainder of this book constitutes my effort to describe a possible answer. In the next section, I will present an example that illustrates the kind of experience I suspect Aristotle was worried that the young lack. Of course, my immediate concern is not with Aristotle's view, but with reflective equilibrium. Accordingly, my example is intended to illustrate a kind of inexperience, and hence, an epistemic deficiency, that reflective equilibrium cannot be counted on to remedy. However, although I will not be structuring the discussion to follow around an interpretation of Aristotle, reflection on his view of who is fit for moral inquiry has had such a strong influence upon my thinking about reflective equilibrium that I thought I ought to acknowledge my debt at the outset. As I have said, I shall devote the next section to presenting an example of inexperience. But before presenting that example, it will be useful to distinguish between two different types of experience. In the remainder of the present section, I shall offer a sketch of this distinction.

I am not going to pretend that I understand very much about experience or the other factors that lead persons to form, to hold onto, and to alter their moral beliefs. Fortunately, one needs to understand very little in order to become aware of the problem I wish to pose for reflective equilibrium. Basically, all I need to get the argument going is a distinction between two kinds of experience that can lead a person to form or to alter his moral beliefs.[3] The first kind of experience should be very familiar to philosophers. It involves such things as constructing an argument from propositions one already believes, appreciating a counter-example to a moral principle one accepts, or seeing a proposition as obvious upon considering it. This kind of experience, which I shall call *reasoning experience*, provides the engine that drives reflective equilibrium, and nearly every other philosophical method as well.

There are two paradigms of reasoning experience. The first involves a person changing or acquiring a belief, as a result of considering the logical or evidential relations among the various propositions he believes. For example, a person might realize that two propositions that he believes very strongly entail the negation of some third proposition that he believes much less strongly, and, as a result, come to disbelieve the third proposition. Or again, a person might accept a general moral principle, because he discovers that the principle is inductively supported by the total set of more particular moral judgments that he makes about a certain type of action. I also include, under the first paradigm, cases that turn on the acquisition of factual information. For example, a person who evaluated some actual action in a certain way might be led to alter his evaluation by the discovery of additional facts regarding the action.

Reason has traditionally been thought to give us new beliefs, in addition to carrying us from one belief to another. The second paradigm of reasoning experience involves the acquisition of new beliefs, where the acquisition is not mediated by reflection on the logical or evidential connections between the proposition which the person comes to believe, and propositions the person already accepts. The purest examples of this sort of belief acquisition involve simple necessary truths that seem to the inquirer to be absolutely obvious and necessary upon first consideration. The reasoning experience, in such a case, would include the grasping, or understanding, of the proposition, and the feeling that this proposition obviously must be so that accompanies the person's grasping it. It would seem that moral belief acquisition sometimes fits this paradigm, for sometimes, when we first direct our attention upon a moral principle, even a very general principle, it strikes us immediately, and on its own, as something that must be true. The "ought implies can" principle arguably fits this bill. It might be argued that less formal moral propositions fit the bill as well, e.g., that it is wrong to cause suffering gratuitously.

According to one understanding of how counter-examples work, they provide a familiar case that in part falls under the second paradigm, and in part falls under the first. When confronted with a successful counter-example, a person makes an intuitive judgment about a hypothetical case, which judgment is not the result of applying already-believed general principles. Indeed, the intuitive judgment is inconsistent with at least some of the general principles the person already accepts. Appreciating the counter-example, therefore, begins with a reasoning experience that conforms to the second paradigm. It also contains elements conforming to the first paradigm. For, one needs to see the logical connection, specifically, the contradiction, between one's intuitive judgment about the example and the relevant previously accepted principles, and then to revise these principles accordingly.

Do all alterations in moral view result from reasoning experience? I think not. Consider, for example, what happens to Raskolnikov in the Epilogue of *Crime and Punishment*.[4] Even after he has broken down and confessed to the murder of the old pawnbroker and her sister, and been sent in chains, dressed in rags and with his head shaven, to do hard labor in prison, Raskolnikov continues to hold himself above others. He is contemptuous even of his only friend, the prostitute Sonia Marmeladov, who loves him, and has followed him to prison. He treats her coarsely. He does not believe that he has done anything wrong. He feels no guilt, no remorse. He views his actions as though they were no more than a simple blunder. The following passage reflects his thinking:

> "Why does my action strike them as so hideous?" he kept saying to himself. "Is it because it was a crime? What does 'crime' mean? My conscience is clear. No doubt I have committed a criminal offense, no doubt I violated the letter of the law and blood was shed. All right, execute me for the letter of the law and have done with it! Of course, in that case many of the benefactors of mankind, who seized power instead of inheriting it, should have been executed at the very start of their careers. But those men were successful and so *they were right*, and I was not successful and therefore had no right to permit myself such a step."
>
> It was that alone he considered to have been his crime: not having been successful in it and having confessed.[5]

We can see here, quite clearly, the same line of reasoning that led Raskolnikov to commit the murders in the first place. The more Raskolnikov thinks about the morality of what he has done, the more he constructs arguments and reasons about his situation, the more firmly committed to his "theory" he becomes.[6] He only manages to dig a deeper hole for himself!

But the novel does not end with Raskolnikov in this frame of mind. He has a profound change of heart, particularly towards Sonia. He finally accepts the love of this simple, virtuous woman, whom he has treated quite cruelly, and admits to his love for her. He does not tell her this; indeed, he says nothing to her at all. But his profound change of heart is evident to Sonia, and to the reader as well. Lying in his prison bunk, in the evening after he has had his change of heart, Raskolnikov reflects:

> And what did all, *all* the torments of the past amount to now? Everything, even his crime, even his sentence and punishment appeared to him now, in the first transport of feeling, a strange extraneous event that did not seem even to have happened to him. But he could not think of anything long and continuously that evening or concentrate on anything. Besides, now he would hardly have been able to solve any of his problems consciously; he could only feel. Life had taken the place of dialectics, and something quite different had to work itself out in his mind.[7]

Dostoyevsky does not explicitly tell us that Raskolnikov now judges his actions differently, or that he now accepts a completely different moral view. But this goes without saying. The change of heart Raskolnikov experiences could not occur without a corresponding change in moral judgment and outlook. What led to this change? It isn't entirely clear what caused it, and perhaps it was no one thing. Of the few things that happen to Raskolnikov in prison, before his change of heart, two seem to be worth mentioning. The first is a dream he had while in the prison hospital with a fever. The dream is of a terrible plague that caused people to go mad:

> But never had people considered themselves as wise and as strong in their pursuit of truth as these plague-ridden people. Never had they thought their decisions, their scientific conclusions, and their moral convictions so unshakable or so incontestably right. Whole villages, whole towns and peoples became infested and went mad . . . . They did not understand each other. Each of them believed that the truth only resided in him . . . . They did not know whom to put on trial or how to pass judgment; they could not agree on what was good or what was evil. They did not know whom to accuse or whom to acquit. Men killed each other in a kind of senseless fury.[8]

The second thing that might be worth mentioning also occurs while Raskolnikov is in the hospital.

> Sonia had been able to visit him only twice in hospital . . . . But she often used to come to the hospital yard and stand under the windows, towards evening, sometimes to stand in the yard for only a minute and look at the windows of the ward from a distance. One evening Raskolnikov, who had by then completely recovered, fell

asleep. On waking up, he just happened to walk up to the window, and he suddenly saw Sonia in the distance at the hospital gate. She was standing there, and seemed to be waiting for something. Something seemed to stab him to the heart at that moment: he gave a start and withdrew quickly from the window.[9]

The next time Raskolnikov saw Sonia, a few days later, he experienced his profound change of heart. It is not easy to say how the delirious dream, and seeing Sonia in the hospital yard, precipitated this change of heart, but it seems perfectly clear that no reasoning experience was involved. Indeed, in the case of his seeing Sonia, it is hard to see how one would go about constructing the necessary argument or contemplation of some proposition. And while it might be possible to construe Raskolnikov's dream as some sort of counter-example to his utilitarian/Thrasymachean moral view, there is absolutely no reason to think that Raskolnikov construed the dream in this way, although we are told that the dream troubled his memory.

It would seem, then, that not all changes in moral view are the result of some sort of reasoning experience. We really should have expected this result. Perhaps I need not have turned to such a troubled character as Raskolnikov to find an example. For people alter their beliefs, particularly their moral beliefs, in a vast range of different circumstances. All of the following, for example, have the potential to provoke an alteration in a person's moral view: actually performing an action he considers right or wrong, living with a person who has a certain virtue or vice, and closely interacting with people who value markedly different things.[10] This short and nowhere near exhaustive list only mentions what we might call "real-life" activities or experiences. It seems obvious that alterations in moral belief can result from other kinds of experience as well, for example, watching a powerful theatrical production or film, reading a novel, memorizing a moving poem, or perhaps even listening to a piece of music or viewing a painting. Just as Raskolnikov's dream might have provoked him to construct an argument, experiences of all these different types *might*, sometimes, provoke a person to consider an argument, or realize that his views are inconsistent in some way, or to have some other sort of reasoning experience, and thence to alter his moral views. But again, just as in Raskolnikov's case, I find it difficult to believe that careful analysis will uncover a reasoning experience that is the real cause of belief revision, in every instance, of all these various types of experience.[11] For want of a better term, I shall call experience that leads to alteration of belief, but does not fit the mold of reasoning experience, *formative experience*. Unfortunately, I will not be able to get much beyond characterizing formative experience as I just have, by contrast with reasoning experience, as "not being like this." But even though I am afraid I will only be able to say a little more about formative experience, I will try to add what I can.

One obstacle in the way of saying something helpful about formative experience is that the examples of types of experience which are apt to cause alterations of belief that I gave in the last paragraph are not really examples of formative experiences. They are, instead, examples of occurrences, activities, or experiences that commonly give rise to formative experiences, or in the case of some of the experiences, can sometimes be formative themselves. Even the most provocative works of art do not influence everyone in the same way, and some people are not affected by them at all. So, of a group of people engaged in a given activity apt to cause a change in moral beliefs, without causing the change by way of a reasoning experience, it is entirely possible, and even quite likely, that only some will have a formative experience. Secondly, even when an activity commonly associated with formative experiences, e.g., reading a compelling novel, causes an alteration in belief, it may be that no formative experience is involved. For the activity can cause a change in belief by way of a reasoning experience, as when a novel serves to make one aware of new facts. Thirdly, while emotions are somehow connected with formative experience, and they are crucially involved in our responses to theater, film, and the like, the connection between formative experience and emotion must be complicated and contingent. In particular, a real-life experience that is intensely emotional, or a work of art that provokes an intense emotional reaction, may not involve or provoke a formative experience, while an experience or work of art or literature that minimally engages our emotions could give rise to a formative experience. Finally, activities that can lead to a formative experience may not produce their effect upon a person's moral beliefs all at once, during a flash of what the person takes to be insight. It is more likely that repeated involvement in the activity will be required, with the pursuit of the activity subtly influencing a person's moral outlook over a prolonged period. Although Raskolnikov's change of heart was sudden and radical, a series of formative experiences occurring over a prolonged period was required to provoke it. Particularly because of these last two points, it may not be clear, even to a person who has had a formative experience, that he has had such an experience. The occurrence of a formative experience is more likely to be revealed when we set about trying to explain why a person changed his mind about some moral matter, and find that the experience that provoked the change resists assimilation to one of the paradigms for reasoning experience.[12] However, although we are most likely to become aware of a formative experience where there has been a change in moral judgment, change in belief is not necessary for a formative experience. This is because it is possible for the ground of a person's believing to change, even though the person continues to believe the same thing.[13]

In spite of these difficulties, I hope that the occurrences, activities and experiences mentioned above will be recognized as having the potential to influence a person's moral beliefs, where this influence need not consist in imparting factual information, bringing to light latent conflicts within a person's system of moral beliefs, or anything else that we would regard as a reasoning experience. I hope it is clear that sometimes, when one reads a novel, or becomes deeply absorbed with a piece of art, or carries through with a significant moral decision, the activity or experience causes one to adopt a subtly, or even radically, different moral perspective, and causes this change directly, rather than by way of some reasoning experience. After this kind of formative experience, one no longer has the same moral beliefs, but, as in the case of Raskolnikov, it is not clear why, in the way it would be if one were taken by argument from already accepted propositions to the negation of other believed propositions. Having such a formative experience is not a matter of working out the consequences of a system of more or less explicit moral beliefs that are the product of, if I can be excused the expression, one's moral sense. Rather, formative experiences feel more as if they influence one's faculty of moral judgment, intuition, or perception, so that one sees situations in a different way, and feels drawn to make different moral judgments or accept different moral principles. Let me emphasize this last point, for although it will not allow me to provide a definition or a criterion for discerning formative experiences, it does, I think, indicate the core of the concept I am after. Suppose we can think of a person's moral faculty as a sort of mechanism that operates by taking the person from input beliefs to output beliefs. Then we might conceive of two sorts of things happening to this mechanism. On the one hand, the mechanism can function in the ordinary way, performing operations upon input and churning out an output. This is, in effect, what a reasoning experience involves. On the other hand, something might happen that affects the way the mechanism operates, causing it to operate in a different fashion, and forcing us to describe it with a different function. This is what occurs when one has a formative experience.

I would like to be able to say more about reasoning and formative experience. I recognize that the notion of a formative experience, in particular, could benefit from further discussion. But I am afraid I have said all I can, and so I will have to be satisfied if I have made the two kinds of experience clear enough for it to be granted that they are distinct types of experience, and that people enjoy both.[14] If these concessions are granted, I have enough to raise the difficulty for radical reflective equilibrium that I wish to discuss. The problem arises, quite simply, because reflective equilibrium ignores formative experience entirely. What if a person who has had a very limited range of formative experience, a person we might aptly call naïve, sets out to construct a moral theory using this method? Or worse, what if the method is employed by a dogmatic person, a person who has systematically avoided formative experiences that regularly lead others to question or abandon the moral beliefs about which he is fanatically certain? Because reflective equilibrium says nothing about formative experience, it would seem that naïve and dogmatic persons could mold their beliefs into the sort of coherent whole that constitutes a state of wide reflective equilibrium without ever supplementing their inadequate moral experience as they brought their beliefs into equilibrium. Unless they somehow supplement their moral experience along the way, the moral beliefs of such persons would be epistemically deficient, even after they had brought their beliefs into reflective equilibrium. Moreover, I believe such persons may well have proceeded irrationally, in the sense that they did not do all that they could, as seen from their own point of view, to insure the truth of their views. Hence, if it is to constitute a rational method, reflective equilibrium must have some element which prevents naïve and dogmatic persons from constructing a moral theory without adding to their base of formative experience.

If my claim that persons with deficient formative experience could bring their beliefs into reflective equilibrium seems grossly implausible, consider Raskolnikov again. He was an extremely intelligent, thoughtful young man. And he apparently had well-worked-out moral views. We are told, for example, that he published an article explaining these views, which I described above as "utilitarian/Thrasymachean," and which he referred to as "Napoleonic." And throughout the novel we see him reasoning out his views, without ever being led by his reasoning to doubt them. Given all this, there does not seem to be any reason to suppose that he would not continue to hold his moral theory in reflective equilibrium. Indeed, ignoring the *emotional* contradiction Raskolnikov embodies, and focusing only upon his beliefs, we might as well suppose that he has brought his beliefs into a state of reflective equilibrium already. I would have to say more, of course, to really make out these claims concerning Raskolnikov, but I think they are initially sufficiently plausible to illustrate the kind of charge I want to make against the method of reflective equilibrium, and to show that this charge is not outlandish.[15]

Although I have made a prima facie case, we must consider more carefully whether reflective equilibrium contains a mechanism for bringing naïve and dogmatic inquirers to enjoy new formative experiences. Also, since I have done no more than assert that this method is not rational, unless it contains such a mechanism, some convincing on this point is in order, as well. In the following section, I will present an example intended to provide an intuitively clear case where a person with an impoverished range of formative experience has moral beliefs that are epistemically deficient, precisely because his formative experience has been inadequate. I shall then argue, in Section 4.4, that such a naïve person could employ the method of wide reflective equilibrium without ever having the formative experiences he needs to lose his naïveté, and hence that we cannot be sure that this method will not lead us to epistemically deficient beliefs. In the next two sections, I shall not, however, try to show that the epistemic deficiency involved in naïveté constitutes irrationality. I will take up that task in Section 4.6, after I have, in Section 4.5, introduced another sort of epistemic problem that we are liable to encounter while pursuing a moral inquiry.

4.3 NAïVETÉ

Jay is a young man who does not see war as a great evil, but as a rather good thing, an opportunity for developing and testing one's courage, and attaining personal honor and glory. Jay has had no first-hand experience with war. However, what he lacks in the way of first-hand experience Jay more than makes up for in imagination. He likes nothing more than listening to the stories the old timers tell about the Second World War, and the Korean and Vietnam Wars, down at the local American Legion Hall. In addition to these stories, Jay unfortunately feeds his extensive imaginary access to war by immersing himself in literature and films that romanticize it, e.g., *Soldier of Fortune* magazine, and John Wayne, Chuck Norris, and "Rambo" movies. During the Persian Gulf War, he was in his glory, glued to his television watching CNN. In spite of all this, we can still suppose that Jay's evaluation of war is not the result of any insensitivity on his part. He would be moved by experiences that generally move others. Actually fighting in a war would have a profound effect on him, but he would be moved by other experiences as well, e.g., viewing films like *The Deer Hunter*, *Full Metal Jacket*, or *Glory*, or a documentary like the one produced by

Ken Burns on the American Civil War, or reading such novels as *All Quiet on the Western Front* or *Johnny Get Your Gun*. Were Jay to have any of these experiences, his view of war would be affected. Not all at once, of course. For particularly in the cases of the novels and films, he would initially respond to the "wrong" parts, resonating primarily with the vivid representations of battles, the courage of the characters involved, the glory won by the victors and the nobly vanquished. But over time, if Jay were either to acquire first-hand experience of war or to immerse himself in the sort of literature and film that presents more of an anti-war message as well as, rather than exclusively, literature and film that romanticize war, he would begin to alter his moral evaluation. So Jay's view of war is not rigidly fixed, immune to any sort of input. It is grounded upon the experiences he has had, and it would be responsive to experiences he might have in the future. Unfortunately, Jay is rather naïve. The experience, reasoning and formative, that grounds his view of war is very narrow; none is first hand, and the rest is exclusively of reports, essays, novels, and films that romanticize warfare.[16]

It is obvious that Jay's moral evaluation of war does not enjoy any very impressive positive epistemic status. I suppose it is also quite clear that any moral theory Jay might devise incorporating his position on war would inherit a similarly unimpressive epistemic status. But what does any of this have to do with reflective equilibrium? Jay sounds like the sort of fellow one might find hanging around in a small-town gas station, not a moral theorist! So what difference does it make if his moral beliefs are epistemically deficient? The answer, of course, is that it does not make any difference at all, so long as Jay's beliefs about war would either be eliminated, or grounded on a wider range of experience, as a result of his employing the method of reflective equilibrium to conduct an inquiry into the morality of war. However, if Jay could use this method to construct a moral theory *around* his beliefs about war, without substantially enriching his experience, this would constitute a problem for reflective equilibrium. The question we must consider, then, is whether Jay could carry his views about war into a state of wide reflective equilibrium.

Before addressing this question, I want to make three points. First, I must confess to playing loose with the term "experience." I have spoken indiscriminately of Jay's naïveté resulting from his exposure to an insufficient range of formative experience, and from his inadequate life experience and experience with novels, films, and so on. And I have done this after I made it clear that these are not the same thing. Reading a novel might occasion a formative experience, but it is not a formative experience, and it cannot even be counted on to occasion one. Nonetheless, I am not going to tighten up my usage. I continue to believe that the root problem of naïveté is an inadequate range of *formative* experience. However, as I pointed out above, formative experiences are difficult to identify. Moreover, formative experiences are not within our control, so we cannot choose to expose ourselves to them as we can choose to read a book or go to a play. It is, therefore, much easier, as well as more useful, to approach formative experience by way of the events, activities, and sometimes even the experiences that are apt to be or cause them. I shall, therefore, continue to speak of naïveté where a person has had neither a wide range of life experience nor a wide exposure to literature, film, and such, and I shall continue to talk as if the remedy for naïveté is broadened life experience, and exposure to literature, film, art, and so on.

Secondly, the method of reflective equilibrium is not so exact that, given the minimal description of Jay's doxastic structure supplied above, his path to reflective equilibrium is determined. Various states of reflective equilibrium might be open to Jay, depending on the other beliefs we suppose him to have, and also his dispositions for forming beliefs and resolving conflicts among beliefs. Thirdly, I have, so far, said only that Jay's moral judgments about war are epistemically deficient, not that they are irrational. But the issue before us is whether reflective equilibrium is a rational method of inquiry. Therefore, to produce an objection to the method of reflective equilibrium, I must do more than find some way in which Jay might bring his beliefs into reflective equilibrium while retaining his evaluation of war. I must show that there is something irrational about his doing this. Given the weak subjective notion of rationality with which we are operating, we should, by now, be aware that there may well be circumstances in which Jay might bring his beliefs into reflective equilibrium without altering his view of war, and do so rationally. We must, therefore, be careful that we uncover states of reflective equilibrium that include these beliefs, and that can be used to show reflective equilibrium to be an irrational method of inquiry. However, having just issued a reminder that our concern is with the rationality of reflective equilibrium, I am going to slip back into talking about Jay's epistemic situation more vaguely. Then, after offering, in Section 4.4, my reasons for thinking that reflective equilibrium cannot, as it stands, be counted on to remedy Jay's epistemic deficiency, and exploring, in Section 4.5, an unsuccessful attempt to amend reflective equilibrium, I shall, in Section 4.6, take up the question of whether Jay's deficiency is one of *irrationality*, in particular.

4.4 THE IMPOTENCE OF REFLECTIVE EQUILIBRIUM

Bearing in mind the three points I made at the end of the last section, we must now imagine that Jay embarks upon an inquiry into the morality of war, employing the method of reflective equilibrium. There are, apparently, only three points at which this method might force him either to alter his views about war or to acquire additional experience: (1) when he refines his initial moral judgments to obtain his considered moral judgments, (2) when he brings these considered moral judgments into narrow reflective equilibrium, and (3) when he moves from narrow to wide reflective equilibrium. Let's consider each in turn.

(1) Rawls describes considered moral judgments as those made "in circumstances where the more common excuses and explanations for making a mistake do not obtain."[17] He gives as examples of initial judgments which will be eliminated those of which a person is not confident, those made in a state of emotional distress, and those made in circumstances where a person stands to gain or lose depending upon his decision.[18] Hence, it does not seem that the minimal sort of screening involved in attaining considered moral judgments will serve to eliminate Jay's initial judgments about war. For we can suppose that he is quite confident of these judgments, that no reward or punishment is attendant upon his making them, and that he coolly and carefully considers the cases about which these judgments are made.

It might be thought that another condition often placed upon considered judgments, although not explicitly mentioned by Rawls in *A Theory of Justice*, would do the trick here – the requirement that considered judgments be formed after reflection upon all the relevant facts.[19] For it is tempting to think that Jay's problem is that his narrow experience with war has obviously left him ignorant of relevant facts, e.g., those having to do with the terrible suffering, loss of life, and devastation of property caused by modern war. There is, however, no reason to suppose that he formed his opinions about war in ignorance of this information. Indeed, it is, in some sense, to be expected that a person like Jay would know much more about these matters than the average person. For, it is more than consistent with his character that he have a deep interest in military history, military strategy and military hardware, and, as a consequence, that he be very knowledgeable when it comes to the actual facts about recent military conflicts, and a much better judge of what would be likely to happen in any future military conflict than most of us. Speaking loosely, then, we might say that Jay's problem is not that he is ignorant of the relevant facts, but that they somehow don't strike him the right way, and, as a result, that he does not respond to them as he ought. But however we describe the case, it seems clear that we cannot expect the moral judgments regarding war that we find offensive to be excluded from the set of Jay's considered moral judgments.

We should not be surprised at this result. The kind of "filtering" involved in obtaining considered moral judgments is unlikely to help with a person who is naïve. The problem with the beliefs of such persons is not that they are formed in circumstances where errors are likely to be made. The problem has more to do with the person than the circumstances. The naïve person has not had certain formative experiences, and, as a result, neither does he make any judgment about such experiences nor, more importantly, are the judgments he does make influenced by these experiences. Thus, a procedure that weeds out judgments formed in circumstances where errors are likely to be made cannot completely correct the deficiency in a naïve person's beliefs. Such a person most needs fertilizing, not weeding, i.e., the addition of experiences that will bring new judgments and influence existing judgments.

(2) In a state of narrow reflective equilibrium, a person accepts a moral theory that explicates his considered moral judgments. This theory will not be a mere generalization of his initial set of considered judgments, however, since the effort to account for these judgments with general principles might bring problems with them to light. For example, the considered moral judgments a person begins with might require a very complex, unintuitive moral theory, while a slight alteration in these judgments would allow him to accept a much simpler and more appealing theory. In such a case, the method of reflective equilibrium allows the person to respond by altering his considered judgments. Whether the theory or considered judgments are altered will depend upon the person's degrees of confidence in the judgments involved.

In moving to a point of narrow reflective equilibrium, Jay might be forced to abandon his evaluation of war. It might, for example, turn out that a simple utilitarian theory accounts for all of his other considered moral judgments, and that, when Jay realizes that this theory is inconsistent with his view of war, he will revise this view and retain the utilitarian theory. However, Jay need not respond in this way, for he could be more strongly committed to his judgments about war than to any judgments that conflict with them. In any case, these considerations are beside the point. Bringing one's beliefs into narrow reflective equilibrium is a purely intellectual exercise, apparently involving only reasoning experiences. So, whether or not Jay retains his view of war in narrow reflective equilibrium, it is quite clear that he will not be forced to enrich his *formative* experience, while attempting to bring his considered moral judgments into a narrow equilibrium with a moral theory. Whether he retains his romantic conception of war, or abandons it for some moral principle, Jay will remain naïve. It is important to remember that the objection to reflective equilibrium that I wished to raise is not that one could hold a romantic view of war in reflective equilibrium, but that one could do so naïvely.[20]

(3) The transition from narrow to wide reflective equilibrium is commonly described in two ways. It is sometimes described in terms of considering alternative moral conceptions and philosophical arguments that might be advanced to decide among these alternatives, and it is sometimes described in terms of bringing the inquirer's background philosophical beliefs into play. These descriptions are not commonly taken to pick out two different approaches to moral inquiry, the idea being that the background philosophical beliefs referred to by the second description will constitute the premises of the philosophical arguments referred to by the first. Nonetheless, it is not clear that these descriptions do identify the same method of inquiry. For the first clearly forces the inquirer to move outside the circle of his own beliefs, at least, to consider alternative moral conceptions and philosophical arguments, while the second does not, clearly, move the inquirer outside his own beliefs. If one is thinking only of the conservative conception of reflective equilibrium, this difference is not, perhaps, terribly significant. For on this conception, revisions of belief must be required by something the inquirer already believes, and as a result, the only way the consideration of alternative conceptions could motivate a change in belief is if this consideration serves to bring some conflict in the person's system of belief to light, where the conflict will presumably involve a background belief.[21] However, if we have the radical conception of reflective equilibrium in mind, we will allow the possibility that the consideration of alternative moral conceptions and philosophical arguments might lead to a discontinuous revision of belief, i.e., a revision that is not required by one of the inquirer's background beliefs. So understood, the consideration of alternative moral conceptions has the potential to be more than merely a heuristic device, a means of calling the inquirer's attention to an incoherence in his system of beliefs that has been there all along. According to the radical conception of reflective equilibrium, the transition to wide reflective equilibrium has the potential to move the inquirer outside the circle of his own antecedent beliefs. I have already made it clear that I favor the radical conception of reflective equilibrium. But there is no reason for not considering what resources the conservative conception might possess

for dealing with Jay. I shall, therefore, begin by considering whether moving to wide equilibrium, conservatively understood, might serve to remedy Jay's naïveté, and then consider whether the radical conception can do any better.

According to the conservative conception, the transition to wide reflective equilibrium primarily involves bringing one's background beliefs into play. Philosophical arguments beginning with these background beliefs serve to illuminate the logical and evidential relations between these beliefs and one's moral beliefs. The consideration of alternative moral conceptions apparently plays a purely heuristic role, serving to insure that one has not overlooked any possible conflicts between background beliefs and moral beliefs. It is not at all clear that any of this can be counted on to force Jay to abandon his romantic conception of war in any very direct way. For one thing, I just cannot see what sort of background belief might conflict either with Jay's overall moral view or with his considered moral judgments, in particular, his considered judgments about war. But I am willing to allow that this is entirely my fault. I will confess that I have never fully appreciated how background theories regarding, e.g., the nature of persons, or the role of morality in society, might force significant revisions of explicitly moral judgments and principles. So, it is no surprise that my imagination fails me in Jay's case. I shall just suppose, then, that some background belief of his, perhaps his ideal of a well-ordered society, is in conflict with his moral evaluation of war, even though I do not really understand the nature of such a conflict. Can we be sure that reflection on this conflict will serve to force Jay to improve his epistemic situation? No. There are two significant obstacles standing in the way of supposing that consideration of his background beliefs can be counted on to force Jay to improve his epistemic situation. First, given that reflective equilibrium directs that conflicts be revised according to the inquirer's degrees of commitment to the relevant propositions, the existence of a conflict between Jay's romantic view of war and one of his background beliefs does not, by itself, require revision of the view of war. If Jay is sufficiently confident of his judgments regarding war, and there is no reason for supposing he is not, it is the background belief that will have to be revised. Secondly, and more importantly, while a revision in his view of war forced by strong commitment to some background theory might bring Jay's moral views more into line with ours, it isn't clear that his epistemic situation will have been improved. For while Jay will have thought some about his view of war, realized that this view does not cohere with his broader philosophical views, and made revisions, so that his overall system of belief is more coherent, he will not have broadened his range of formative experience. He will still be every bit as naïve as he was when he held to the romantic view of war, although he will now naïvely hold a view that *we* find more acceptable.

There is another way in which the consideration of his background beliefs might force Jay to improve the epistemic status of his moral beliefs. Rather than asking whether any of his background beliefs are somehow in direct conflict with the moral view that he accepts in narrow equilibrium, we might instead ask how Jay's acceptance of this view, and the considered judgments that led to it, comport with the epistemic standards he accepts. For an effort to live up to these standards might exert a sort of indirect influence upon Jay's final state of reflective equilibrium. There is even reason to hope that this effort might force Jay to remedy his naïveté by broadening his experience. Suppose that he accepts our usual common-sense epistemology, an epistemology that dictates such things as that one not form beliefs about matters one is not familiar with, and that one not form opinions about controversial matters without considering what has been said on all sides of the question. If he accepts these epistemic principles, there will be an opportunity for Jay's views about war to be altered when he attempts to bring his moral beliefs into coherence with his background philosophical beliefs. For example, if Jay believes that he has no accurate information about war, then his epistemological beliefs will conflict with his having formed an evaluative judgment about war. Another way in which Jay's moral and epistemological beliefs could be incoherent would be if he realizes that there are various films and novels that present war in a negative perspective that he has not taken into account. In either case, it seems that the natural way for Jay to resolve the conflict is by broadening his experience in the way required by his epistemic beliefs. In the case of acquiring more information, Jay's efforts will involve only reasoning experience, but in case his epistemic principles require exposure to films, novels, etc., the effort to achieve coherence will actually lead him to broaden his range of formative experiences. According to our supposition that Jay is not insensitive, this broadening of experience will lead him to alter his moral views. More importantly, he will not only alter his moral evaluation of war, but he will be forced to acquire the sorts of formative experience needed to relieve his naïveté.

So there is, within the method of reflective equilibrium, a mechanism for driving a naïve person to improve the epistemic status of his beliefs after all. Unfortunately, the limitations of this mechanism are more significant than its assets. If a person's epistemological beliefs are to drive the person to acquire more experience, in order to achieve reflective equilibrium, several conditions must be met: (i) the person must have the right sorts of epistemological beliefs, (ii) the person must believe that his moral beliefs do not meet the standards represented by his epistemological beliefs, and (iii) the person must be at least as strongly committed to his epistemological beliefs as he is to his moral beliefs. It is by no means clear that the naïve inquirer will either begin with the right kinds of epistemic principles, or be led to hold such principles in the course of trying to bring his beliefs into a state of equilibrium. But I am willing to grant that the naïve inquirer either holds, or will be led to hold, the right epistemic principles, so let's focus on (ii) and (iii).

In my original description of Jay, I referred to him as naïve. He had a limited experience with war, and the experience he had enjoyed tended to romanticize it. Given this description, there is no reason to suppose that Jay would believe his information about war to be inaccurate – "After all," he might say, "I've already got it straight from the horse's mouth! I've spoken with the boys down at the Legion Hall, and they actually fought in wars. Hell, some of them just got back from Kuwait!" Moreover, as I suggested above, we might suppose that Jay is a sort of military history and hardware buff, which would, once again, lead him to suppose that he had very good, rather than inaccurate, information about war. Hence, even if he did accept an epistemic principle that prohibits jumping to conclusions without sufficient and accurate information, Jay may well responsibly believe that he has satisfied this requirement. Similarly, we need not suppose Jay would believe there are experiences that would lead him to alter his beliefs about war. If he is at all aware of the "anti-war" literature and film that he has ignored, he will likely think it is so much "whining pinko tripe," and not the sort of thing that could possibly alter his convictions. So once again, even if Jay accepted the right sort of epistemic principles, there is no reason to think he would feel himself to be in violation. In general, then, it seems that, even if a naïve person accepts our usual common-sense epistemology, such a person could too easily believe that his naïve beliefs do not violate these epistemic standards, thereby avoiding any pressure to relieve his naïveté.

If we suppose, instead, that Jay takes his beliefs about war to violate common-sense epistemic standards, he begins to sound more dogmatic than naïve. For we are now supposing that he realizes that there is another side to the story, maybe even that there are experiences that would lead him to alter his evaluation of war, and that he believes that one should not form beliefs without considering all sides of an issue.

Clearly, such a person will have to make some alteration in his doxastic system if he is to bring his beliefs into wide reflective equilibrium. We would hope that the alteration would involve Jay's bringing his moral beliefs into line with his epistemic beliefs by supplementing his experience. However, there is really no reason why this must be the course Jay takes. As we noted above, the method of reflective equilibrium does not play favorites. When beliefs are in conflict, the necessary revision will be guided, not by belief type, but by the degree of commitment the person has to the beliefs involved. So, if Jay is very strongly committed to his moral beliefs, reflective equilibrium may direct him to alter his epistemological beliefs, rather than acquire the experience necessary to bring his moral beliefs into conformance. Under this scenario, Jay truly sounds dogmatic in the worst sense, clinging to his moral views without giving any consideration to alternatives to his position, and altering even his common-sense epistemology, rather than allowing a possible challenge to his moral beliefs. Yet, it seems that a person could incorporate such dogmatism into a point of wide reflective equilibrium.

Let us now turn to the radical conception of wide reflective equilibrium. According to this conception, a person must consider alternatives to the moral theory he accepts in narrow equilibrium, as well as philosophical arguments designed to decide among these alternatives, in order to move to a state of wide reflective equilibrium. It might seem that this method would immediately force Jay to supplement his formative experience, thereby relieving his naïveté. For, we have supposed that there are various experiences, for example, reading *Johnny Get Your Gun*, that would set Jay on the road to abandoning his considered judgments about the value of war, and one might think that he would need to have these experiences, in the course of considering alternatives to the moral theory he holds in narrow reflective equilibrium. But it is not at all clear that this is the case. In the first place, the injunction to consider alternatives has ordinarily been taken to apply to *philosophical* theories and arguments, e.g., Kantian or utilitarian theories, and the arguments pro and con, not to such things as films and novels.[22] As a result, the consideration of alternatives required to move from narrow to wide reflective equilibrium, at least as it is ordinarily understood, can be counted on to lead Jay to do a lot of reasoning, but it cannot be counted on to lead him to have any additional formative experiences.[23] Moreover, even if we can sensibly suppose that there is a philosophical conception of morality, along with philosophical arguments, somehow contained in novels, films, and the like, and that this conception, along with the relevant arguments, might somehow be extracted and presented to Jay in a precise, analytic form, it is not clear that his consideration of such an extracted theory would provide any more of an aid in relieving his naïveté than would his consideration of other, more ordinarily constructed, philosophical theories. For, in the first place, there is no reason to think that this conception and the arguments supporting it would seem plausible to Jay if they were presented to him in a precise, analytic form, apart from any story.[24] And, in the second place, and more importantly, I do not think that by engaging in the sort of purely intellectual exercise involved in considering philosophical theories and arguments, no matter where they may have originated, Jay is likely to become any less naïve. He would merely gain a bit more of a kind of purely technical sophistication – he would know of still more alternatives to his position, other arguments that might be offered against his position, which of the premises of these arguments he does not share, and so on. But, it simply does not seem that such reasoning is equivalent to the formative experience Jay lacks, experience that might be gained from actual involvement in war, or perhaps, even better, by reading certain novels, watching certain films, and so on. The interesting thing about such experiences is that they are not at all like the kinds of reasoning or arguing experiences that have occupied the attention of moral epistemologists. And so it seems that the formative experience Jay is lacking will not be involved in his efforts to bring his beliefs into wide equilibrium, even as radically conceived.[25]

I think that the example of Jay makes it quite clear that there is something epistemically amiss with a naïve person's moral beliefs, and also that the method of reflective equilibrium cannot be counted on to correct the problem. It does not, of course, immediately follow that reflective equilibrium is an inadequate method of moral inquiry, for as we saw in the second chapter, the epistemic goals we have for our moral investigations are diverse. Before we could conclude that reflective equilibrium's ineffectiveness at relieving naïveté constitutes an insuperable objection to the method, we would need to know exactly what is epistemically deficient about a naïve person's moral beliefs, specifically, whether the deficiency involves some sort of irrationality. I will eventually try to show that this deficiency does constitute a form of irrationality, but I am going to continue to speak vaguely about epistemically deficient beliefs for one more section of this chapter. In it, I wish to consider, and reject, an appealing proposal for an easy fix-up of reflective equilibrium. My argument against this proposal will bring to light another epistemological malady to which we are susceptible – corruption. I shall then set out to show that both naïveté and corruption involve an element of irrationality. For this reason, any adequate method of moral inquiry will have to be capable of dealing with both naïveté and corruption. In the final section of this chapter, I shall describe how reflective equilibrium can be improved so that it has this capability. But before closing the present section, and setting out upon this course of argument, I would like to make one last point about naïveté.

Jay is, of course, an extreme case. I wanted an example where it would be quite clear that the naïve person's beliefs are epistemically deficient. I would not want the extremity of the example to conceal the fact that this sort of experiential naïveté is actually quite common. For example, anyone who has taught undergraduate ethics courses with any frequency has, on occasion, encountered a very clever, but naïve student. It is usually rather enjoyable, but also rather frustrating, to discuss moral issues with such a student: He can argue round and round with you in defense of some position, eventually giving the impression that he has constructed what is, probably, as close to a coherent moral system as anyone ever constructs, but there is a sort of unreality, or ungroundedness, about the student's reasoning. The student just does not seem to respond to certain things, and he has not had certain experiences that you suspect might help to sensitize him to the things to which he is not responding. In short, it seems that what the student needs is to grow up a little, that is, to have a wider range of experience, and no amount of argument or reasoning seems likely to provide a suitable substitute.

Students are not the only people who fit this bill. Occasionally, and this is perhaps most distressing, the sort of person I've tried to describe can be found within the ranks of professional philosophers. I am sure that we have all encountered a person who is totally immersed in a certain theory, who has all sorts of arguments defending and applying the theory ready at hand, who is aware of all kinds of objections and is able to produce ingenious rebuttals, and so on. Although I am usually impressed by this sort of argumentative virtuosity, even when exercised in behalf of a theory I do not accept, sometimes I am not impressed when I see it. Instead, I get the feeling that something has gone wrong. I seem to sense that further philosophical discussion would be pointless, and not merely because I would not be clever enough to win. (This happens often enough that I no longer put much stock in it.) Rather than thinking there would be any point to raising any objection, it seems that to have any hope of altering the person's views, one would have to lead the person through a certain sort of life experience, or maybe to get them to read certain novels or watch certain films, or I don't know what – but certainly, not analyze yet another argument. I don't think it is just crazy of me to react in this way. For I believe that at least sometimes when I react in this way, it is because I have encountered just the sort of naïveté that Jay is supposed to represent. And I hope that I am not alone in having this reaction to certain people, for if others have sometimes felt the same way, perhaps they will have both a better idea of the sort of character Jay is supposed to illustrate and a sense that he does not represent a rare and bizarre type of individual who may be a curiosity, but with whom we need not concern ourselves in developing a method of moral inquiry.[26]

4.5 CORRUPTION

An easy approach to the problem of naïve inquirers would be to adopt the same attitude towards formative experience as reflective equilibrium takes towards alternative moral theories: The ideal is that *all* alternative moral theories and relevant philosophical arguments be taken into account; in practice, we must settle for less, taking into consideration at least all those that are on the intellectual scene. Accordingly, one might take it that, ideally, a person in reflective equilibrium will have had at least some exposure to all the various kinds of experience that are likely to alter his moral beliefs, and, in practice, require a person to expose himself to all such experiences that are in fact available to him.[27] Unfortunately, formative experience cannot be treated in this simple and straightforward fashion. We cannot say that whenever there is a non-reasoning experience that would lead to significant alterations in a person's moral view if the person were to have it, the person has some epistemic obligation to have the experience in the course of constructing a moral theory. After all, the experiences of being brutally brainwashed or having certain areas of the brain destroyed are likely to alter a person's moral beliefs, yet we would not require a person to have these experiences. Such experiences are as likely to have a negative influence on the epistemic status of a person's beliefs as to have any positive effect.

There might be some way of distinguishing such experiences from formative experiences. The experience of having a part of one's brain damaged is, perhaps, distinguished by the fact that the experience is not directly relevant to the alterations in belief, but a by-product of the physical damage, which is the real cause of the alterations in belief. Maybe experiences like being brainwashed, which involve psychological rather than physical trauma, can be separated from formative experiences in a similar way.[28] However, even if this distinction could be drawn, there remains a deeper problem with revising reflective equilibrium, so that it requires persons to have a sampling of each kind of available, *non-traumatic*, formative experience. Let me use another example to raise this difficulty.

Suppose that Janet is a person who has been brought up to value premarital chastity and marital fidelity very highly. Janet has not simply accepted her childhood teaching on blind faith, but has thought long and hard about the morality of sexual relations outside of marriage, and considered what the proponents of such relations have to say in their behalf. She has identified what she considers to be the weak spots in the arguments offered by the proponents of liberal sexual morals, and constructed arguments for her view, from premises that she finds deeply compelling, even after long critical reflection. In short, suppose that Janet has attained a point of wide reflective equilibrium in which she holds sexual relations outside of marriage to be immoral. It seems to me that Janet might well correctly judge that there are experiences that would lead her to alter this point of view, for example, reading erotica and romantic novels with an open mind, watching (well-made) pornographic films, and having sexual relations with numerous (sensitive and experienced) partners.[29] But the natural thing for Janet would be to avoid these experiences, on the grounds that they would corrupt both her character and, more importantly in the present context, her moral judgment.[30]

I maintain that Janet's moral beliefs are in reasonably good epistemic order.[31] She is not naïve in the way that Jay is, and it is quite clear that she need not have the experiences she considers corrupting for her moral theorizing to avoid the epistemic pitfall into which Jay has tumbled. Moreover, it seems that there would be something epistemically wrong about Janet's undertaking to enjoy the formative experiences in question, given her deeply held conviction that these experiences would ruin her moral sensibility.

In case Janet seems to be an artificially contrived sort of person, allow me to present another, more realistic, example. Consider the views of an Amishman. The Amish feel morally obliged to live a simple agrarian life, apart from the modern world, working in harmony with nature. We need not suppose that the Amishman has merely gone along with the training he received as a child and the pressures to conform exerted by his tightly knit family and religious community. We shall, instead, suppose that this man has thought a great deal about the rather odd way in which he lives, as compared with the modern American society that surrounds him. He does not reject the use of various elements of modern technology on the basis of blind obedience to tradition, or some kind of simple-minded notion that the Bible forbids the use of this technology. Rather, we can suppose him to have a well-worked-out conception of the kind of life it is fitting for a person to live, and in particular, the kind of relations a man should have with his family and neighbors, and the kind of relation a man should have to nature and his work. It is this conception of the good life that grounds the Amishman's rejection of most modern conveniences, and with them, the life-style we would consider normal. In short, although he would not describe it in these terms, we are imagining that the Amishman has attained a point of reflective equilibrium in which he holds a simple nineteenth-century agrarian life-style to be morally required of him. Now, the Amishman is certainly aware that there are many experiences that he has not had: experiences that we might take to represent some of the good things about the life-style he has rejected. I have in mind such experiences as watching television, listening to radio, going to movies, using modern labor-saving devices in one's daily life, and even such things as pursuing higher education. The Amishman is unlikely to have so high an opinion of his integrity that he would not recognize that, were he to enjoy enough of these experiences, he would no longer be committed to the moral view he presently accepts. But, rather than thinking he should expose himself to both the experiences constitutive of his way of life and also those constitutive of the alternative life we live, in order to be in a position to make a rational choice between them, the Amishman will feel no need to sample our life-style.[32] He will think that the experiences he lacks would corrupt his judgment, rather than inform it, and hence, he will avoid these experiences.

I think it is quite clear that the moral views of the Amishman, like Janet's, are in reasonably good epistemic order. Lest it seem that I am willing to be much too generous with "the dogmatic beliefs of a member of an extreme religious cult and the sexual hang-ups of a prig," it is worth noting that, in the relevant respects, Janet and the Amishman are not significantly different from any of us. For our purposes, the only remarkable thing about them is that they have a settled opinion that certain experiences would be corrupting, and this is not really at all remarkable. For surely, we all recognize there are formative experiences that would probably lead us radically to alter our system of values, yet for the most part, we do not feel it would be a good idea to go out and have these experiences. We hold that they would corrupt our moral judgment, so we avoid them. This, I think, is the proper attitude to have. Only a person with an absurdly high opinion of his intellectual fortitude could think there are no formative experiences that would corrupt his judgment, and that he should therefore be open to all experiences, even those viewed by "weaker" individuals as "potentially" corrupting.

A reader exercising any care at all will have noticed that the above examples are not really examples of corruption, but of people who believe certain experiences would be corrupting to them. Is this belief really at all well founded? Is there any reason to believe that corruption is so much as a possibility? In keeping with the form of argument I have adopted in this chapter, I shall try to answer this question by describing another example. Imagine a more or less ordinary young man, whom we will call Billy Goat. Billy tends towards liberal, egalitarian views about appropriate relations between men and women. Wishing to ground his judgments on a firmer foundation, Billy decides to read a classic treatment of the topic, J. S. Mill's *On the Subjection of Women*, and he finds himself to be in substantial agreement with the position and arguments offered by Mill. But, let us suppose, Billy has not had much in the way of experience with women; he has a feeling that he is rather naïve, and in a poor position to be making judgments about what sorts of relationships between men and women are appropriate. And, while Mill has had much to say to our young man, Mill was concerned primarily with how the government should treat women, and not with what modes of personal interaction between men and women are best. At this point Billy makes a serious blunder. He correctly decides that more philosophical argument will not significantly improve the epistemological status of his moral judgments, but makes a very poor choice about how to broaden his imaginative experience – he picks up a romantic novel on his way out of the supermarket. As a result of reading this novel, which Billy really enjoys, he starts to form the opinion that what a woman really wants is to be "swept away" by a "real man," that women need to be dominated by men, both emotionally and sexually, and that rough treatment, bordering on rape, is often appropriate and even desirable. His former agreement with the egalitarian views of Mill go by the board. Of course, if Billy were to stop with this one novel, he would be just as naïve as when he began, so he undertakes to broaden his exposure in many directions, reading lots of novels, essays, and poems and watching plays and films. But, unfortunately, that first trashy romance has done its work. Images of the seductions in the novel stick in his mind, accompanied by an appealing glow. Throughout his reading, the only things which "ring true" to Billy, and resonate with his sensibilities, are those that confirm the distorted perspective he originally picked up in the romantic novel. We can plausibly imagine that we find the same thing going on in Billy's real life – the sexual encounters and relation-ships that he finds most rewarding are those that most closely approximate the paradigm laid down in the novel. The end result of the whole affair is that Billy's moral judgments regarding appropriate relations between men and women are thoroughly fouled up.[33]

I hope that this example does not seem far-fetched. For while it is vastly oversimplified, I think that what I am trying to describe goes on all the time. People pick up paradigms for relations between the sexes from the worst sorts of novels and films, and then tragically go out into the world to try to recreate these paradigms in their own lives. More to the point, the corrupting influences of such literature and art on a person's judgments about how men and women should be together can be incredibly tenacious, defying all efforts to dislodge them by convey-ing additional empirical information to the person, or confronting the person with philosophical arguments. We should not be too smug about this example, thinking that this kind of corruption is exceptional. For surely we all recognize that there are experiences that would probably lead us radically to alter our system of values. Perhaps, merely reading a novel would not have this effect, but immersing oneself in a mode of life very different from one's own, including the literature, music, and art connected with that life-style, certainly could have the effect, and probably much less than complete immersion would do the trick.[34]

The example of Billy shows that concerns about the possibility of corruption are not unfounded. When this example is conjoined with those of Janet and the Amishman, it becomes clear that we cannot correct the problem naïveté poses the method of wide reflective equilibrium by simply requiring that a person have any available experience that is likely to alter his considered moral judgments. Is there some way of modifying the method of reflective equilibrium so that it will force naïve persons to gain additional experience, while not forcing persons to have formative experiences that they have deeply held reasons for regarding as corrupting? I believe that there is, but before describing it, we need to assure ourselves that the method of reflective equilibrium really does need to be amended. For, I have yet to argue that the epistemic deficiency that a naïve person's moral judgments are subject to is, at least in part, a matter of irrationality. I shall, therefore, devote the next section to showing that the deficiency does indeed constitute irrationality, and then I shall return to the question of how to amend reflective equilibrium in Section 4.7.

4.6 ARE NAïVETÉ AND CORRUPTION IRRATIONAL?

Rather than diving right into the question of whether naïve and corrupt inquirers will be led to form irrational beliefs, or revise their beliefs in irrational ways, I am going to begin by considering the rationality of evidence gathering, and whether evidence a person does not possess can affect the rationality of his belief. I suspect that we will be able to extend our understanding of evidence to the cases of naïveté and corruption. Nearly everyone would maintain that, ideally, a person should be acquainted with all the relevant evidence before making a judgment. Of course, it is never possible for a person to meet this ideal, so we must be able to say that judgments can be rational even though they are formed on the basis of less than all the evidence. But how much evidence does a person need to have in order to believe rationally? One approach is to assume that it is rational for a person to believe a given proposition on certain evidence only if it is also rational for the person to believe that the total evidence would continue to support the proposition.[35] On this approach, cases where we would intuitively think that a person has jumped to a conclusion on the basis of too little evidence will be explained as follows. Even though the person's scanty evidence supports his conclusion, that support is not sufficient for the conclusion to be rational, because the evidence does not also support the belief that the total evidence would continue to support the conclusion. Therefore, the person would have to acquire additional evidence. It is important to see, however, that this approach does not saddle a person with an obligation to acquire additional evidence endlessly, since, in many cases, even a small amount of evidence will adequately support the proposition that the total evidence would also confirm the person's conclusion.[36] And even if a person is aware of additional evidence that disconfirms his conclusion, the person may not fall under any obligation to acquire that evidence. For the person might have reason to believe that evidence to be misleading.[37]

The kind of formative experience the naïve person lacks is not exactly evidence. And, as we have seen, we cannot take as an ideal that a person expose himself to all formative experiences. But it does seem that formative experience is subject to a similar ideal. For I suppose that there is a very large class of formative experiences that it would, in some sense, be best for a person to enjoy before making moral judgments. We can call the formative experiences in this class *enriching*. Just as with the ideal of acquiring all the evidence, as a practical matter, it is not possible for anyone to live up to the ideal of exposure to all enriching formative experiences. A person can rationally make moral judgments having had less than all enriching formative experiences. We would, therefore, like to be able to say just how much formative experience the person needs to have for his judgments to be rational. We might approach this problem, which is, after all, the problem of naïveté posed in a more general form, in the way I suggested we deal with evidence. Thus, we shall say that it is not rational for a person to make moral judgments unless he can rationally believe that his judgment will remain firm in the face of all enriching formative experiences. A naïve person will begin without any beliefs at all about either the adequacy of his experience for the judgments he is making or what experiences might be enriching. But presumably, once he considers the question, given his limited range of formative experience, the naïve person will be in no position to think that his judgments would remain firm in the face of additional experience. The naïve person will presumably have to think about how much experience he needs to be competent to make moral judgments and which of the experiences he has not had might be enriching, and then go on and acquire appropriate additional experience.[38]

This approach to the problem of naïveté squares nicely with the conception of rationality as a matter of doing what one can to insure that one's beliefs are true. Certainly, when a naïve person is aware of a formative experience that might lead to an alteration in his judgment, but avoids the experience for no good reason, we cannot say that the person has done all he can to insure the accuracy of his judgment. So we regard his judgment as irrational. And even when the person is not aware of the experience, but the experience is readily available to him, in the sense that he would become aware of it if he were to consider the question even very briefly, there is reason to think that the naïve person is guilty of a certain kind of negligence. For, surely, it is not too much to expect an inquirer to reflect upon such questions as whether the experience he has had is sufficient for the judgments he is making, what additional experiences are available, and whether having these experiences would improve the epistemological status of his beliefs, and to seek additional experience as required by the results of this reflection. After the discussions in the last chapter, it will be obvious that there is a problem about saying exactly how much reflection one must devote to such questions before one proceeds rationally. Fortunately, as I argued there, it is not necessary for us to settle this question.

The concept of misleading evidence might be taken to supply a model for understanding corruption. The approach we are examining begins with the ideal of a person forming beliefs on the basis of all the evidence. But it is not ordinarily possible to acquire all the evidence, so the evidence that must be acquired before a conclusion may rationally be drawn must somehow be identified. Since the conception of rationality is internalist, with rationality understood in terms of a person doing all he can, *as determined from his own point of view*, to insure the truth of his beliefs, it is up to the inquirer to reflect upon the matter and decide for himself just how much evidence he needs. If this reflection leads an inquirer to the conclusion that a certain body of evidence that he might set about acquiring is, as a matter of fact, misleading, he would presumably be under no obligation to acquire it, and it might even be irrational for him to seek to acquire it. But, surely, just as a person can regard evidence he is aware of but does not possess as misleading, it is possible for a person to think, indeed, to have a deep, settled conviction, that some experiences are misleading – that they will influence his beliefs in a way that takes him farther from the truth.[39] If such a judgment about the nature of certain formative experiences would stand up to the appropriate sort of reflection, then, surely, the inquirer would be under no obligation to set about exposing himself to the formative experiences in question. Moreover, given that formative experiences have the potential to be more "corrosive" than misleading evidence, in the sense that the mere acquisition of additional evidence may not counteract the negative effects of the misleading, or better, *corrupting*, experience, it would seem that it would be irrational for the person to set about acquiring an experience he believes to be corrupting.[40]

While this way of understanding corruption will be adequate for certain cases, in particular, for cases like those of Janet and the Amishman, where we intuitively think a person is rational in avoiding experiences he *considers* corrupting, it is by no means clear that it is adequate for all examples of corrupting experience. In fact, it is reasonably clear that it does not even apply to the example of Billy I gave in the last section. For Billy had no reason to suspect the experience of reading the novel would corrupt his judgment, and, perhaps, he even had reason to think it would improve the status of his judgment. For example, he may have felt that since romantic novels are so popular with women, they must accurately represent what many women consider to be ideal in a relationship. And, although it is not strictly relevant to the present issue, we might note that Billy certainly would not have considered the experience corrupting after he enjoyed it; indeed, he would be likely to think the experience finally put his judgments on the right track.

The fact that we cannot understand all cases of corruption solely in terms of the rationality of belief suggests that similar problems arise with respect to naïveté. We might suspect that, just as the internalist character of irrationality limits it to cases where an experience appears to be corrupting *from the inquirer's own point of view*, a naïve person's beliefs will be irrational only when either the person realizes that these beliefs are grounded upon an inadequate experience base, or the person is negligent in virtue of his failure to consider whether his experience base is adequate. Unfortunately, not all cases of naïveté are like this. In some cases where we would intuitively regard a person as naïve, the person believes, and upon reflection would continue to believe, that he has had an adequate range of experience. In such cases, the person might have worked out an elaborate view regarding how much experience an inquirer should have, and why the experiences he has not had are unnecessary, but we would regard this view as a rationalization in the pejorative sense of the term. Notice that certain of the modifications we made to the example of Jay, while considering whether the method of reflective equilibrium could be counted upon to drive him to acquire additional experience, were of exactly this character. We imagined, for example, that Jay might, upon reflection, come to hold that his experience base is not at all narrow, or that the experiences he lacks would not markedly affect his views. In such cases, even though we would want to say that the person is naïve, and that his moral judgments are somehow deficient, we would have to grant that these judgments are rational, since by the person's own lights, his formative experience is not deficient. My comment on this outcome should, by now, be familiar: To say a belief is rational is to make a comparatively weak claim. There is a temptation to think of every sort of epistemic deficiency as irrationality, but this is a temptation that ought to be resisted. There are many ways for rational beliefs to fall short of knowledge, e.g., by not being warranted. So, granting that a belief is rational in no way precludes criticizing the belief on other epistemological grounds.

I might say, therefore, that I have got what I needed, but not all I might have wanted. It is fairly clear that one aspect of the epistemic deficiency of the naïve inquirer's moral judgments does have to do with rationality. And we have seen that we cannot expect inquirers to be guided by an ideal of exposure to all formative experiences, for it would not be rational for them to seek to enjoy formative experiences that their reflections lead them to regard as potentially corrupting. This is what I needed. For, in order to sustain my objection to the method of radical reflective equilibrium, and the attempt to extend this method by requiring exposure to all available formative experience, I needed to discover not just epistemic deficiencies that these methods could not insure against, but types of irrational belief, or revision of belief, from which they cannot protect us. And I have discovered these types of irrationality. The radical method will lead to irrational beliefs in cases where a person would come to believe that he has had insufficient relevant formative experience if he were to reflect sufficiently on the adequacy of his formative experience, but has failed to reflect on the issue of formative experience. And the extended version of reflective equilibrium would lead to irrational revision of belief in cases where it would direct an inquirer to enjoy formative experiences that the person would believe to be corrupting upon adequate reflection. It would, perhaps, have been nice if all there were to naïveté and corruption were irrationality, particularly if the method of reflective equilibrium could be modified so that it could guarantee protection from irrationality. But it seems that any hope we might have had for such a simple outcome has been in vain. There are aspects of the epistemic deficiency of naïve and corrupt inquirers that are not a matter of mere irrationality. It would seem, then, that methods that can insure only the rationality of inquiry will not be able to protect inquirers completely from naïveté and corruption. But, rather than dwelling upon what merely rational methods cannot do, let's move on to consider whether, and how, the method of reflective equilibrium might be amended, so that it can protect us against the sort of naïveté and corruption that are irrational.

4.7 CORRECTING THE METHOD OF REFLECTIVE EQUILIBRIUM: BALANCE AND REFINEMENT

There are two ways in which one might try to amend the radical method of reflective equilibrium to obtain a method that will lead naïve inquirers to broaden their formative experience without forcing inquirers to have experiences that would corrupt their moral judgment. One might try to draw a distinction between enriching and corrupting formative experiences on the basis of the inquirer's own system of beliefs, or one might identify them absolutely, in some way that does not depend upon the inquirer's beliefs.

We might take Aristotle as a representative of the latter approach. For Aristotle held not only that the young are unfit for moral inquiry, but also that only those who have been brought up well are fit for such inquiry:

> Hence any one who is to listen intelligently to lectures about what is noble and just and, generally, about the subjects of political science must have been brought up in good habits.[41]

Particularly in combination with his views regarding the young, this passage suggests that there are certain specific kinds of formative experience that one must have if one is profitably to engage in moral theorizing. Apparently, Aristotle would hold these to be the experiences one would have as a result of the activities required to form good habits. One could agree with the general Aristotelian approach while differing with respect to the specific formative experiences that are required, and also with respect to the occurrences, activities, or experiences that are apt to give rise to these formative experiences, and the firmness of the connection between these occurrences, activities, or experiences, and the formative experiences. But one who holds this general Aristotelian conception of moral methodology will agree that the way to amend the method of reflective equilibrium is to supplement it by identifying the formative experiences that one needs to have, and those that one needs to avoid, and then drawing a more or less firm and objective distinction between the occurrences, activities, or experiences that are apt to cause the enriching formative experiences, and those that are apt to give rise to the corrupting formative experiences.

This Aristotelian approach is externalist in the sense that the necessary experiences are identified objectively. Instead of being identified with reference to the inquirer's own system of moral judgments and epistemic standards, they are identified independently, according to some standard that the inquirer may or may not find compelling. As a result, any attempt to revise reflective equilibrium along Aristotelian lines will face obvious difficulties. The most serious is that such a method would lead certain persons to behave irrationally. Because the Aristotelian approach identifies specific occurrences, activities, or experiences, or types of occurrences, activities, or experiences, as necessary for any moral inquirer, and makes this identification without appealing to the inquirer's own system of beliefs, it is possible that such a method will require an inquirer to do things, or enjoy experiences, that are apt to be corrupting, according to the inquirer's most deeply held moral and epistemic standards. Recalling the examples I presented above, we might say that there is a danger that an Aristotelian version of reflective equilibrium would force either Janet or the Amishman to seek out the experiences, or engage in the activities, these individuals consider corrupting. This is because the Aristotelian method is not based upon an adequate understanding of these examples, or at least, it is not based upon the understanding I intended. These examples were supposed to call upon *epistemic*, not moral, intuitions. The lesson was supposed to be that there is something *epistemically* amiss with a method of moral inquiry that requires a person to enjoy experiences or engage in activities that he considers corrupting after due consideration. I did not intend to appeal to any feeling that the experiences, or activities, either Janet or the Amishman considers corrupting are, in fact, either immoral or morally corrupting. My intention was to remain neutral on this issue.[42] The Aristotelian cannot accept this interpretation of these examples. He can only understand them as cases where the activities, and experiences, in question are *in fact* corrupting, or more precisely, that these activities and experiences give rise to formative experiences that are not among those a person should have in the course of moral inquiry. This, according to the Aristotelian, will be the reason Janet and the Amishman need neither engage in these activities nor have these experiences. The fact that they consider them corrupting, after seriously reflecting upon the matter, really has nothing to do with their having no obligation to engage in the activities or seek out the experiences. For it seems as though it would be possible for a person to consider the activities and experiences corrupting that the Aristotelian takes to be necessary, in which case, the Aristotelian method would direct the person to do the things, or have the experiences, anyway. The Aristotelian could avoid this consequence if neither the formative experiences he requires inquirers to have nor the activities or experiences that are apt to give rise to them could be considered corrupting by anyone. But this is highly unlikely. The Aristotelian approach is therefore at odds with the intuitions I took to determine my appraisal of Janet and the Amishman.[43]

Before moving on to the other approach to amending the method of reflective equilibrium, it is worth noting that the Aristotelian approach is, in a sense, conservative, while, in the main, recent philosophy has been decidedly liberal in its approach to moral inquiry.[44] A liberal approach to moral inquiry is committed to the idea that an adequate method of moral inquiry must be neutral between substantive moral conceptions. Conversely, a conservative approach will hold either that there is no such neutral method of moral inquiry or that no neutral method can be adequate. An Aristotelian revision of reflective equilibrium might be more or less conservative, depending upon the formative experiences that it takes to be necessary. If persons tend to react differently as a result of the required formative experiences, with some making one moral judgment, and others tending to disagree, the Aristotelian approach will not seem seriously to violate the liberal ideal of a neutral method. However, the formative experiences the Aristotelian approach is likely to require could involve much more.

The experiences might be considered enriching, rather than corrupting, only by those who are already committed to a certain substantive moral theory. Or they might, as a matter of fact, lead all, or nearly all, persons to make the same moral judgments, judgments that militate in favor of a certain moral theory. Or the required formative experiences might be such that a person will need certain kinds of help, or guidance, for them to influence his moral judgments. If the Aristotelian has formative experiences of any of these kinds in mind, and I suspect that Aristotle himself thought the requisite experiences would be of at least the third type, then the Aristotelian approach will be conservative indeed, entirely abandoning the ideal of a moral methodology that is neutral between substantive moral theories.

The other approach to amending the radical method of reflective equilibrium, the approach I prefer, is more in sympathy with broadly coherentist methods of moral inquiry. These methods are opposed to the Aristotelian approach we have just considered, in being both liberal and internalist. Coherence methods maintain the neutrality characteristic of a liberal approach by being internalist, in the sense that they allow each person to begin with the considered moral judgments he happens to hold, and to proceed by revising conflicts inherent in his belief system according to which of the propositions involved he considers most likely to be true, usually after a certain amount of reflection, and by considering alternatives to his moral conception, again deciding what to do on the basis of how likely to be true he considers the alternatives themselves, and the philosophical propositions that might serve as premises for arguments about the alternative moral theories. Such an approach will favor no particular moral theory, unless there is something about every moral inquirer, e.g., shared fundamental moral judgments, that in practice leads them to accept the same substantive theory. But, of course, if something like this should prove to be the case, we would not have a non-neutral method, but the happy result of a neutral method leading all inquirers to the same moral theory.

Building upon the broad coherentist framework, one might take our discussion of the rationality of acquiring evidence to suggest a way of introducing a mechanism for enriching a person's moral experience. According to our discussion, a person should not believe a proposition on certain evidence unless it is rational for him to believe that the total evidence would support that proposition. Whether it is rational for the person to believe that the total evidence would continue to support his conclusion will be determined by what the person would believe about this matter after reflecting fully upon it. Full reflection is obviously an ideal that we cannot expect a person to reach, so, in practice, we can only require that the person give some amount of consideration to the matter before forging ahead. As I have already admitted in similar contexts, it is difficult to say exactly how much consideration a person must give to such matters for his beliefs to be rational. But I think we can be excused for not addressing this problem here. For one thing, providing an answer to this sort of question is not a special problem for moral methodology. If a precise, systematic answer is forthcoming, we can surely incorporate it into our methodology. And in the mean time, we seem to have a pretty good intuitive sense of how much consideration is too little, and how much is about right.

Applying this view of the rationality of believing on less than complete evidence to the problems of naïveté and corruption, I propose the following additions to the method of radical reflective equilibrium: First, as the inquirer seeks to fashion his moral and philosophical beliefs into a coherent system, he must consider the matter of formative experience. Just as in the standard method of reflective equilibrium, the inquirer is required to consider alternative moral conceptions, and the arguments that might be offered for or against these conceptions, I require the inquirer to consider the formative experiences he may have had, bearing in mind the difficulties involved in identifying such experiences, and then to consider which of the experiences that he might seek out, and activities that he might engage in, are apt to broaden his range of formative experience. The inquirer must also consider both what might be said for and against each experience, and activity, with regard to whether it would produce enriching or corrupting formative experiences, and what might be said about the total array of formative experience he has enjoyed, with specific attention to such questions as whether it is minimally broad, whether it is skewed in any way, and how it might be enhanced. Given the cultural setting in which any contemporary inquirer is likely to be operating, I maintain that a great deal of the inquirer's reflection on these questions will have to involve consideration of literature, film, theater, and even music and art, with an eye to determining, most importantly, what is likely to refine further his capacity for making sensitive moral judgments, but also whether experience with any of this might corrupt his judgment.

Secondly, the inquirer obviously cannot rest content with merely considering these questions regarding formative experience. He must seek out experiences and engage in activities accordingly, attempting to expose himself to those experiences, and engage in those activities, that he considers likely to give rise to the formative experiences he considers minimally necessary, while avoiding those he considers corrupting, and then engaging in activities, and seeking additional experiences, particularly, as I have said, with literature, film, art, and music, that he considers likely to refine his moral judgment further. I call this the method of balance and refinement: *balance*, in order to indicate the strong coherentist component that is carried over from radical reflective equilibrium, and *refinement*, because the method deviates from earlier versions of coherentism in seeking to improve or develop the inquirer's faculty for making moral judgments, rather than simply systematizing the output of this faculty.

A naïve person, such as Jay, will begin without beliefs about formative experiences. The method of balance and refinement will require the naïve inquirer to think about how much formative experience one needs to be competent to make moral judgments, and then to seek to acquire additional formative experience where appropriate. We would hope that this consideration will lead the naïve inquirer to believe that his formative experience is inadequate in various ways, and then to seek, in a reasonable way, to acquire the sorts of formative experience he needs. However, an inquirer in Janet's or the Amishman's position will not be under any obligation to acquire additional formative experience, since he will be aware of the formative experience he lacks and will have reasons for thinking that this experience would be corrupting rather than enriching; and since he will have already given considerable thought to the matter, these reasons will hold up upon reflection.

There is, obviously, a cost associated with the method of balance and refinement. For while it is clear that it would not force persons to have formative experiences they consider corrupting, and we can hope that it will drive naïve inquirers to broaden their formative experience, it may not do enough in the way of driving such inquirers to acquire additional formative experience. In particular, it seems that it would allow a person who accepts rather weak epistemic standards, and who would continue to accept such standards upon reflection, to hold the belief that additional formative experience is unnecessary on the basis of what we would consider a sham of an argument, or a rationalization in the pejorative sense of the term. Indeed, to be perfectly honest, I must point out that this method will not deal with some of the variations on the example of Jay that I described while considering whether reflective equilibrium can be counted upon to force naïve inquirers out of their naïveté, nor will it deal with persons who might fall into corruption unwittingly, so to speak, i.e., without any prior hint of the corruption. If we bear in mind the distinction between formative experiences and what gives rise to them, we will realize that the inquirer must work at one remove from formative experience. Because the inquirer must work in this way, it becomes even more likely that his best efforts to improve his situation with respect to formative experience, by engaging in certain activities or seeking out various experiences, will not enhance his formative experience. Thus, for example, it is possible that an inquirer come to believe that there is a problem with his range of formative experience, but then form a rational, but inept, plan for acquiring the additional formative experience.

These facts might strike some as the ground for a decisive objection to my proposal, with some thinking that I have not even managed to do better with respect to the objections I pressed against reflective equilibrium than reflective equilibrium can do in the face of those same objections. I do not agree. Let's recall the specific example of Jay. Throughout my initial consideration of that example, and the problem it poses for reflective equilibrium, I described Jay's beliefs as epistemically deficient. At the same time, I made it quite clear that our concern is with rationality in particular. It later emerged that while a part of the epistemic deficiency of the naïve inquirer's beliefs constitutes irrationality, irrationality does not exhaust this epistemic deficiency. We need to be clear that the first requirement of an adequate method of moral inquiry concerns its *rationality*. Thus, it is most important that a method of inquiry guarantee rational inquiry. Precisely formulated, my objection to the method of reflective equilibrium was that it cannot guarantee rational inquiry, and the example of Jay suffices to establish this point. Turning to the method of balance and refinement, we find that although it is not adequate to deal with *all* the epistemic deficiencies that plague Jay's moral beliefs, it can obviously be counted upon to insure that he will proceed rationally. Indeed, the method of balance and refinement was so obviously constructed precisely to insure that the inquirer would, in effect, formulate his own standards governing formative experience, and then live up to those standards, that I do not think I even need to argue explicitly for the claim that this method can guarantee rational inquiry. Now, it might be nice if the method could be counted upon to do more than this, e.g., to lead all inquirers to moral truth or knowledge, but that does not diminish the fact that this method stands alone in being able to guarantee that it will not lead inquirers into irrational revisions of belief. So, while I would agree that something is epistemically amiss with the beliefs of a naïve person who avoids acquiring additional formative experience on the basis of what we would consider a rationalization, or who comes to hold bizarre ideas about how to acquire enriching formative experiences, I would simply stress that the problem is not that the person is irrational, and hence, that it is not a problem that a method of moral inquiry must be able to deal with in order to be adequate.

Let me try to come at this issue from a somewhat different angle. One remarkable thing about the Aristotelian and coherentist approaches to the problem of naïveté and corruption is that each of them seems to have a very strong intuitive appeal for a significant number of philosophers, even after they understand the deficiencies of each solution. Indeed, there seems to be no middle ground. Upon hearing the examples I have described, most philosophers find one or the other of the two solutions to be perfectly obvious. This indicates to me that they are understanding the examples, and the problems they pose, in different ways. I suspect that their understandings diverge in something like the following way. It is quite clear that there is something epistemically deficient about the beliefs of the naïve person, but it isn't entirely clear just what the deficiency is.

On the one hand, we might think about the examples as follows. One thing we would like to see is inquirers doing all they can to insure the truth of their beliefs. In the case of a naïve inquirer, when the enriching experiences the inquirer lacks are available to him, and when the inquirer is aware of them, or would become aware of them upon reflection, we surely cannot say that the inquirer has done all he can to insure the truth of his judgments. We need to direct the inquirer to consider the narrowness of his experience, what sorts of experiences are out there that he might seek, whether having these experiences might not bring his judgments closer to the truth, and so on. We will hope that reflection upon such questions will lead the inquirer to believe that he should seek out additional experience, and then to seek out experience accordingly. But we must recognize that reflection may not have this effect upon the inquirer. It may lead the inquirer to believe that he is already sufficiently experienced, or that the experiences he lacks would be corrupting, or that he needs experience, but experience we would consider extremely bizarre, and unlikely to alter his naïve moral views. If the inquirer's reflection should yield any such result, we may not be happy about it, but we cannot say that the inquirer has not done all he can to insure the truth of his belief, so there really is nothing we can do about him, at least by way of engaging in rational inquiry. The approach I have adopted to the problem of naïveté is based upon this way of looking at the epistemic deficiency of the naïve person. But it is not the only way of looking at this deficiency. Indeed, not even the only correct way of looking at it.

The Aristotelian, I believe, is more concerned with whether the person's faculty of moral judgment has been properly trained, or with whether it is reliable. If you are out to train someone to do something, you do not ordinarily let them decide what sort of experience they need. You set the curriculum for them. This is how the Aristotelian looks at moral inquiry. He will focus on the role moral experience can play in refining a person's capacity for moral discrimination, aiming at the development of one's discriminative abilities. The point to make about this Aristotelian view is not that it is mistaken or illegitimate. We should say, rather, that it is more appropriately thought of as having to do with whether a person's moral beliefs are warranted than with whether they are rational. It would, of course, be a good thing if these two epistemic goods, rationality and warrant, necessarily came together. Perhaps they do come together for certain individuals, whose reflective understanding of which formative experiences are enhancing, and which are corrupting, turns out to be correct. But the sorry fact is that rationality and warrant can come apart. I have already made it clear that I put rationality first. I simply do not believe that we can accept a method of moral inquiry that might drive inquirers either to believe things that, all things considered, they do not regard as likely to be true, or to seek out experiences that they believe to be corrupting.

It might be objected, at this point, that I have not fully appreciated the Aristotelian's intention. It might be claimed that he is out to describe a rational approach to moral inquiry as well, but that he is using a different conception of rationality than the one I have adopted. However, the Aristotelian's conception is not *fundamentally* different from mine, as my previous remarks might have suggested. Moreover, it might be objected that the approach I have advocated is on all fours with the Aristotelian approach in another, more crucial respect – it cannot guarantee rational beliefs, and revisions of belief, to all inquirers, any more than the Aristotelian approach can. I shall begin with the second of these charges, and attempt to work my way back to the first.

Suppose that some inquirer reflectively believes, after he has had some experience, that the experience corrupted his moral judgment. If a person believes that he is corrupted, upon reflection, in this way, all the moral beliefs he takes the corruption to have affected will be irrational. There may be a rational path out of corruption for the person, if he believes that something will relieve his corruption, and believes that this belief is not a result of the corruption. But certain individuals may come to believe that they are corrupted, that their corruption infects all their believings, and that there is no escape from their corruption. Such individuals will have irrational beliefs, and it would seem that the method of balance and refinement would be unable to guarantee them a rational means of escaping their irrational beliefs. Hence, it is not the case that the method of balance and refinement can guarantee rational inquiry to all inquirers. There are circumstances in which this method cannot protect the inquirer from irrational revisions of belief, just as there are circumstances in which an Aristotelian approach cannot protect the inquirer.

I would admit that such rationally inescapable corruption is possible. And hence, I confess to having exaggerated my claims for the method of balance and refinement. But, I would plead, I have only exaggerated a little. For there is no rational path for the victim of the kind of corruption we are considering, so it can hardly be held against the method of balance and refinement that it cannot lead rationally such victims to rational beliefs. So we can say that balance and refinement can guarantee rational inquiry to every inquirer for whom this is possible. Balance and refinement is, therefore, different from the Aristotelian approach, after all. For while both approaches will let inquirers fall into irrationality in certain circumstances, balance and refinement does this only where there is no alternative. And I might, I think fairly, add that while balance and refinement is unable to get certain persons out of trouble, it does not guide them into it as the Aristotelian approach does.

, At this point, however, the Aristotelian is liable to complain that the preceding discussion is conducted in terms of my conception of rationality, a conception he does not share. As I made clear when I introduced the notion, rationality, in my sense, is not entirely subjective. Certain things are not determined from the inquirer's own point of view: Specifically, logical relations and what constitutes reflection are not determined from the inquirer's own point of view. Moreover, it might be charged, when I uncovered the possibility of naïveté and corruption, I built more into the concept of reflection, by requiring inquirers to consider the nature of their formative experience, how they might enrich their experience, and what might corrupt them. To the Aristotelian, this will seem to be no different, in principle, from what he directs. According to his conception, to be rational a person must have had certain experiences, and cannot have had certain others, regardless of what the person might think about this. According to mine, the person must have reflected upon certain matters, and proceeded according to the results of these reflections, again, regardless of what the person might think about all this. According to my conception of rationality, balance and refinement is rational, and the Aristotelian approach is not. According to an Aristotelian conception of rationality, the Aristotelian approach is rational, and balance and refinement is not. Neither conception of rationality is determined entirely from the inquirer's own point of view, so I have no complaint against the Aristotelian. The Aristotelian, however, along with everyone else, has a complaint against me. For, as I have myself shown, according to my conception of rationality, no rational inquiry can guarantee warranted beliefs, while according to his conception of rationality, his own rational approach to moral inquiry can guarantee warranted beliefs.

My response to this powerful line of criticism is rather simple, but not, I hope, unconvincing. I have tried to deviate as little as possible from a purely subjective conception of rationality. This is because I was out to answer a question that is raised from an egocentric point of view. I wanted to tell the inquirer how to proceed, but I wanted the directions to be ones that the inquirer could accept. An inquirer may not accept my directions immediately, but it will always be true that, if an inquirer reflects on the matter, he will come to accept my directives. The method of balance and refinement is rational in precisely this sense. It leads the inquirer to the system of beliefs that he considers most likely to be true, by steps that he would think he should take, or that he would take to be best after reflecting upon the matter. The Aristotelian approach is not like this. It directs the inquirer to proceed in a certain way, just as I do. But the inquirer may not agree to the Aristotelian's directions, even after thinking the matter through. At this point, where I would say, "You must trust yourself," the Aristotelian will say, "You must trust me." Here we have reached what I take to be the most fundamental level. If I am asked why we should not trust the Aristotelian, I will simply say that each person must think about it, and proceed as seems best to him. I do not respond only to the Aristotelian in this way. For it should be clear that the criticism of alternatives to reflective equilibrium as irrational that I offered in the last chapter comes down to exactly the same thing. All such alternatives are liable, at some point, to direct an inquirer to trust something other than his own judgment. Again, I simply say that each person must think about it, and proceed as seems best to him. If it is asked why we should prefer our own reflective judgment, or why this is what rationality ultimately consists in, I have nothing more to say. If this means that we will have no guarantee of true beliefs, reliable beliefs, warranted beliefs, consensus, or what have you, I will still say the same thing. You must reflect, and believe accordingly, and this is the essence of rationality. Perhaps this is what lies behind my efforts to retain a deontological element in my concept of rationality – when we believe irrationally, we somehow deny ourselves. And this I take to be wrong.

Given that I have abandoned the hope that there is a rational, and hence acceptable, method of moral inquiry that can be counted upon to lead inquirers to warranted moral beliefs, the question that I face regarding warrant is not whether there is any guarantee that we will attain it. Rather, I fear that given the perspective I have adopted, I will face a challenge to provide some sort of reason for thinking that warranted moral beliefs are so much as conceivable on my approach. The next chapter is devoted to addressing this challenge. But before I turn my attention towards this challenge, I would like to make one last point about the method of balance and refinement before closing this chapter. I am concerned this method will be taken to be no more than a small wrinkle on reflective equilibrium, a wrinkle that has no claim to be regarded as a distinct method of moral inquiry. For, as I have pointed out, balance and refinement shares a great deal with more familiar, coherentist methods. In addition, the idea that the inquirer should expose himself to literature, film, etc. seems to be a very natural extension of the familiar injunction to consider alternative moral conceptions and relevant philosophical arguments. I would like to offer two reasons for thinking that, in spite of its similarity to reflective equilibrium, the method of balance and refinement ought to be regarded as a new and distinct method of inquiry. The first reason is more practical, and the second more theoretical.

We can get at the practical reason most directly by asking what moral philosophy conducted according to the method of balance and refinement would look like, and comparing this with moral philosophy as it is standardly practiced.[45] The most immediately apparent difference would be that many more articles would be devoted to providing philosophical discussions of literature, film, art, and the like. To be specific, articles like those by Stanley Cavell,[46] Martha Nussbaum,[47] and Philip Quinn[48] would be vastly more common than they are today. This is not, of course, to say that there would be no place for the more familiar sort of philosophical ethics. Indeed, given the large overlap between reflective equilibrium and balance and refinement, there would be a large place for moral philosophy as we have known it. But there would also be much more philosophical attention paid to life experience, literature, etc., and more importantly, such discussions would play a much more significant role in our philosophical inquiry into morality. A second difference would not be apparent quite so immediately. Many of the discussions, particularly the discussions of life experience, literature, etc., would be much more psychological or epistemological than we now expect philosophical ethics to be. Specifically, a certain amount of attention would need to be paid to the precise way in which exposure to various things, that is to say, various experiences, affects our moral judgment. This type of discussion is not now common in the philosophical literature. As I said above, we seem to proceed on the assumption that all of us have had experience that sufficiently prepares us to engage in moral inquiry. My inclination is to believe that this assumption is false, and in addition, that even those who have what we might call a sufficient experience base can continually improve, or refine, their moral judgment by continued experience, most significantly with literature, film, and so on. For this reason, I consider serious discussion of the role of experience in the development of moral judgment a significant, and necessary, addition to moral inquiry.

This second difference between how moral philosophy as we know it looks and what moral philosophy would look like under the method of balance and refinement leads nicely into what I called the more theoretical reason for taking balance and refinement to be distinct from reflective equilibrium. As it is ordinarily described, reflective equilibrium fits with what might be called an intellectualist, or scientistic, picture of what moral philosophy is all about. There is a body of "data," i.e., considered moral judgments. These might be the judgments of a particular person, or a group of persons. It does not much matter. The idea is to come up with a theory that accounts for the data. Philosophical ethics is a sort of complex question of curve fitting. Of course, the defenders of reflective equilibrium would object to the foundationalist sound of the description I have just offered, and stress the many ways in which the so-called "data" can be revised for theoretical reasons. But, while I would not quibble with their claim, I do find it interesting to note that they are always careful to point out that this treatment of considered moral judgments is not significantly different from the treatment the data receive in science. For we all now know that even scientific data are theory-laden. And so I say, reflective equilibrium yields a scientistic picture of philosophical ethics.

The method of balance and refinement marks a break with this sort of scientism. While balance and refinement allows a place for a kind of curve fitting, it grants an equal place to the refinement of the faculty which yields the moral judgments I have been referring to, rather loosely, as "data." There is no denying the fact that refining the capacity for making moral judgments is vastly more an art than a science. Returning to the familiar comparison with science that I generally oppose, I might put my point by saying that the philosopher who employs the method of balance and refinement cannot view himself solely as a theorist, but must also see himself as the extremely complex, touchy, perhaps even quirky, measuring instrument that must be used to secure the "data." Thus, we might say to those who are fond of comparisons with science that according to balance and refinement the practice of philosophical ethics will look vastly more like the *actual* practice of science – a huge amount of time must be spent tinkering with instruments in order to get them to function optimally. The enormous difference in the case of ethics is, of course, that according to the method of balance and refinement, *the inquirer* is the instrument in question. The inquirer is an instrument that must proceed by its own lights, to tinker with itself, in an effort to get itself to operate optimally. We cannot ignore this fact and proceed to consider methodological questions about moral inquiry as if it involved only theorizing.

4.8 CONCLUSION

In this chapter, we have uncovered two phenomena: naïveté and corruption. I maintain that the possibility of naïveté and corruption must have a profound impact upon our thinking about moral methodology. In the first place, if naïveté and corruption are real possibilities, then the method of wide reflective equilibrium, whether it is understood in the more ordinary way or in the radical way which I have elaborated and defended through the first three chapters, cannot guarantee rational moral inquiry. Secondly, although it is not difficult to amend reflective equilibrium to obtain a method that can guarantee rational inquiry, the method that we thereby attain, the method of balance and refinement, turns the philosophical inquiry into morality into something markedly different from what we have known. In particular, the method of balance and refinement lacks the look of science that has held such a strong fascination for philosophers, particularly in recent years. Finally, although the method of balance and refinement can guarantee us a rational inquiry into morality, it cannot guarantee that it will lead us to moral knowledge, or warranted moral beliefs. For no matter how careful we are in our efforts to refine our moral judgment, there is always a real possibility that we are either naïve or corrupt. The discouraging fact is that there is no absolute protection against all the epistemic deficiencies of naïveté and corruption to be found in proceeding rationally. This opens the way to asking,

"Is it so much as possible to attain warranted moral beliefs by following the method of balance and refinement?" I will address this question in the next chapter. A positive answer to this question, which is the answer I shall defend, constitutes the second prong of the strategy for defending the method of balance and refinement that I described in Chapter 2. I have, in this chapter, executed the first prong of that strategy by showing that the method of balance and refinement constitutes the only rational approach to moral inquiry.

Part III
Warrant

5   A perceptual model for the warrant of moral beliefs

5.1 INTRODUCTION

Let us take stock of exactly where we stand in the overall course of the argument. In the first two chapters, I tried to show that most discussions of moral methodology are hampered by an incorrect, overly simplified understanding of the epistemic goal of moral inquiry. Often, the goal is simply taken to be true moral beliefs, with methods being criticized if they cannot guarantee that they will lead every inquirer to the correct moral theory. Nonetheless, everyone recognizes that moral inquiry is aimed at more than mere true belief. We do not want to believe the truth by lucky guess, or by accident, or, as J. S. Mill put it, as a mere superstition. What we want is moral knowledge, and this requires that our true moral beliefs have a certain high positive epistemic status, i.e., warrant. Warrant is usually understood in terms of some sort of truth-conduciveness, as often as not, in terms of simple reliability. This understanding leads many to consider a moral method's inability to guarantee true belief to any inquirer to be a fatal flaw. I have argued that our epistemic goals are actually more complicated, and diverse, than such discussions of moral methodology suppose. We do indeed seek true moral belief, and we do seek moral knowledge. But we also wish to proceed rationally, and rationality is not resolvable into actual truth, or actual truth-conduciveness. Judgments of rationality evaluate how well the believer has done in terms of her own epistemic standards, given what she has to go on. Moreover, even when we turn to the more external, and objective, concept of warrant, it is not clear that warrant is resolvable into some sort of truth-conduciveness. Hence, the familiar criticism that reflective equilibrium can offer no guarantee that it will lead the inquirer to the truth is at best incomplete. It would be good for this method to guarantee us the truth, but even if it cannot, it does not necessarily follow that the method is unacceptable. Since no other method of moral inquiry can guarantee that it will lead inquirers to the truth, we need to know how reflective equilibrium does with respect to our other epistemic aims before we cast it aside. Specifically, we need to know how reflective equilibrium fares in our rational quest for *warranted* beliefs.

In the last two chapters, I have been concerned with the rationality of moral inquiry. I argued that, although reflective equilibrium is better at rationally leading inquirers towards a moral theory than any of the alternative methods, it still falls short. The method of reflective equilibrium cannot adequately protect us from the sort of irrationality involved in naïveté. There is, however, a successor to reflective equilibrium, the method of balance and refinement, that can guarantee the rationality of moral inquiry, even for naïve inquirers. However, the sort of rationality at issue here is relatively weak. So, it remains possible that, even after employing this method, the inquirer's moral beliefs will have merely the sort of rationality that comes from having an orderly, coherent structure to one's beliefs. But a sophisticated madman's beliefs might have such an orderly structure! Unless one following the method can hope for a bigger epistemic payoff, the method of balance and refinement deserves a lukewarm recommendation at best. And so we come to warrant. Can the method of balance and refinement guarantee that it will lead us to warranted moral beliefs? If it can, then if we fall short of moral knowledge, it will be because, even though we have proceeded rationally and ended up with warranted beliefs, for all that, we will have had a streak of bad epistemic luck that has left us with false beliefs.

My aim, in the present chapter, is to address this issue regarding warrant. But the formulation of the question just above is misleading. In Chapter 1, I criticized Norman Daniels' attempt to defend the method of reflective equilibrium based on the contention that we cannot expect all inquirers employing the method of reflective equilibrium to converge on a single moral theory. In the last chapter, I argued for the possibilities of naïve and corrupted inquirers who may be unaware of their epistemic predicaments, and unable to discover their predicaments, even by the most meticulous reflection. Therefore, the method of balance and refinement seems to be in a more precarious position than my formulation of the question regarding warrant suggests. There is no prospect of arguing that this method will lead all inquirers to warranted beliefs. The real issue, then, is whether it makes sense to speak of moral beliefs being warranted at all, given that irresolvable rational disagreements and rational, but naïve or corrupt, inquirers are real possibilities. A more felicitous formulation of the question follows: Are warranted beliefs a possibility for inquirers employing the method of balance and refinement? Even if I answered, "Yes," I would not have a powerful conclusion in hand. It is one thing to give up Cartesian longings for a method that will lead us from premises that are certain, by steps that certainly preserve truth, to beliefs we can be certain are true. But can we really be satisfied with a method of moral inquiry if all we can say for it is that it is possible that the method will yield warranted beliefs?

To answer this question we need to recall the overall structure of the argument I am offering for the method of balance and refinement. I have already argued that balance and refinement is the *only* rational approach to moral inquiry. Moreover, the goal of moral inquiry, i.e., a correct view of how best to live, is of the first importance. Finally, as I argued in Chapter 2, the inquiry is, in a sense, forced upon us. With this as the background, the discussion of warrant takes on a different character than one might have expected. It is not as though I am trying to convince someone to employ, for example, a new system I have devised for predicting the winners of horse races. In this case, I should expect to be asked to prove the reliability of my system. But I am not out to *entice* philosophers into employing the method of balance and refinement, so I need not offer strong assurances that their efforts will be rewarded with moral knowledge, or at least, warranted moral beliefs. Such an effort might be necessary if moral inquiry, like placing bets at the race track, were not vitally important, or were an optional matter, or there were a choice as to the method one might employ. In any of these cases, the inquirer would need some fairly strong reason to engage in the inquiry at all, or to approach it in the particular way I advocate, rather than doing something else. But given the reality – the importance of moral inquiry, the lack of alternative rational methods, and the necessity of proceeding – I need not offer any *enticement* to the inquirer either to take up the task or to approach it in the way I've advocated. I am not out to lure the inquirer into an activity, but to offer some protection against pessimism, some reason for hoping that her efforts might not prove vain, some reason for thinking she just might, in the end, win warranted moral beliefs, and maybe even moral knowledge.

This description of my view, in terms of warding off pessimism, is, perhaps, overly dark. So let me try to put it in a different, and I hope a brighter, light. While I do not hold that a method of moral inquiry *must* yield warranted beliefs in order to be adequate, I think that, to be adequate, a method of inquiry should do everything that can rationally be done for those who follow it. Specifically, a method of inquiry should put inquirers in the best possible position with respect to attaining knowledge. I do not believe that any rational method of inquiry can guarantee true, or even warranted, moral beliefs. But it does not follow that methods of moral inquiry are off the hook with respect to warrant. If there were a number of rational methods of inquiry, the adequate one would be the one that brought inquirers, so to speak, closer to knowledge than the others. Since, as I have argued, balance and refinement is the only rational method of moral inquiry, we need not compare its performance with other methods. But we cannot rest content with this method just yet. For we should rule out entirely any method, even the only rational method, if it leaves the inquirer in no position to know at all, that is, if it is not possible for a person who follows the method to come to have warranted beliefs. Accordingly, to show that the method of balance and refinement is not ruled out on this score, I need to show that it is possible for inquirers employing it to attain warranted moral beliefs.

Notice that I am supposing there to be a middle ground between a method guaranteeing, at least, a high likelihood of truth, and so, also, warranted belief and knowledge, and the method's making no contribution at all to the epistemic status of the inquirer's beliefs. This supposition is likely to be greeted with some skepticism, skepticism that arises from placing too much emphasis on methods. We are inclined to think that a method must take care of every significant feature of inquiry, and should be a mechanical thing that will take nearly any person,[1] no matter what her beliefs, the epistemic status of these beliefs, or the person's intellectual capacities and the degree to which these capacities have been developed, to a true system of beliefs, and that features of the method, not the person, will play the preeminent role in accounting for the epistemological status of the theory the person ends up accepting. Coherentist methods obviously deviate from this impersonal, mechanical conception of method, since the individual inquirer's degrees of commitment play a significant role in theory construction. But I think we must move farther still from the mechanical conception. We must give up the idea that we can account for the epistemic status, specifically the warrant, of the beliefs an inquirer is led to by a method of inquiry primarily in terms of features of the method. It is this notion that leads to the demand for guarantees, and the inability to see a middle ground between bringing everyone, and bringing no one, to knowledge, or warranted belief. For, since it is the *method's* responsibility to bring persons to the truth, warranted beliefs, or knowledge, we are left with the idea that an adequate method must be able to guarantee, to everyone who follows it, beliefs that are true, warranted, or known. We tend to think that, if the method cannot offer such a guarantee, it does nothing at all, that there is no middle ground. However, if we shift the emphasis from the method to the individual inquirer, and hold that various features of the inquirer play the most significant role in accounting for the epistemic status of the beliefs accepted, a middle ground begins to emerge. We will tend to think that an adequate method should *aid* the inquirer in her quest for knowledge. When we ask what a minimal necessary condition is for the adequacy of a method, rather than requiring guarantees, we will simply require that it be possible for some persons to come to have warranted beliefs as a result of following the method, viz., those who come to the process in the right frame of mind, or make the right contribution to the process. We would then want to show that the method does *more* for those who employ it than meet this minimal requirement. But my goal in this chapter is the modest one of showing that the method of balance and refinement can meet this minimum requirement.

5.2 ESTABLISHING THE POSSIBILITY OF ATTAINING WARRANT

There is no consensus among philosophers regarding the nature of warrant, or the criteria for warranted beliefs. Moreover, in Chapter 2, where I tried to clarify the concepts of epistemic evaluation I was going to employ, I challenged one of the few things regarding warrant about which there is a consensus, i.e., that it is to be understood in terms of some sort of truth-conduciveness. I then claimed warrant to be a matter of believing what is appropriate in the face of one's experience. Realizing this claim to be controversial, I drew back from it, but continued to insist that so believing is at least a distinct positive epistemic value that we want our beliefs, including our moral beliefs, to possess. I proposed to call this positive status "experiential warrant." But all of that was a while ago, so let us briefly review what we said about the concept of warrant.

Warrant is the positive epistemic status that a true belief must have to be knowledge. Having warranted beliefs is a matter of meeting standards that identify what would be epistemically good, excellent, or best. The relevant standards are objective and external. The received view regarding the sense in which believing in conformance with these standards is best is that it is best with respect to the epistemic aim of believing truths and not believing falsehoods. If one accepts this view, to have warranted beliefs is to believe in such a way that it is objectively likely that one's beliefs are true.[2] In Chapter 2, I challenged the received view by describing non-deceiving demon cases. These are cases where a demon has disconnected the person's experiences, e.g., her visual experiences, from reality, while maintaining the usual connection between the person's beliefs and reality, and hence, the usual level of truth-conduciveness, or reliability. A victim of such a demon might have a visual experience exactly like the experience I have when watching one of my cats playing with a string, and experience the same forceful inclination to believe that there is a cat before her, as a result of having this experience, but nonetheless spontaneously, truly, and reliably believe that she is driving home from work, and that the steering wheel, dashboard, and windshield of her car are immediately before her.[3] I do not think that such a person's beliefs would be warranted, but setting that aside, I would insist that such a person would not be in an epistemically ideal state. She would be better off, epistemically, if her beliefs and her experiences were not at odds with one another, i.e., if her beliefs were experientially warranted, as well as truth-conducive.

Given that I have said so little about warrant, it might seem that I should provide a detailed account of warrant, and then demonstrate that it is indeed possible for inquirers employing the method of balance and refinement to end up with moral beliefs that satisfy the account. Unfortunately, any attempt to develop and defend an account of warrant would require a book of its own, and therefore take us much too far afield. I have, then, a good practical excuse for not arguing for the possibility of balance and refinement leading inquirers to warranted beliefs on the basis of a complete account of warrant. There are also strategic reasons for not arguing in this way. It is not clear that an argument based on such an account of warrant would best serve our purposes. First, any such account would be extremely controversial. As a result, if I were to rely upon such an account in defending the method of balance and refinement, my defense would be convincing only to those who happen to accept my controversial account of warrant. I would like to offer a more broadly convincing defense, a defense that does not depend on the outcome of debates regarding the correct analysis of warrant.

Secondly, even if I could produce an account of warrant that was not controversial, it is not clear that an argument based on such an account would serve my purpose. I am afraid that such an argument would just seem too easy. To see what I mean, consider two of the contending accounts of warrant: reliabilism and Plantinga's account in terms of proper function. Beginning with either account, the argument for the *possibility* of warranted moral beliefs follows rather trivially, provided we suppose that there is such a thing as moral truth. For, if there are such truths, there is no reason why either some individuals might not reliably come to believe these truths, or there might be some component of our cognitive architecture designed to produce belief in these truths. And so the arguments would go according to any plausible account of warrant. However, arguments of this sort do not help my case. They do not allow me to offer the inquirer any real hope that she might win warranted moral beliefs by employing the method of balance and refinement.

There are a number of ways of responding. One might claim that the problem arises from the supposition that there is such a thing as moral truth. If I had not begun with this supposition, I would have had to provide an account of moral truth, and then show that we are reliably connected with such truths, or how we might have been designed to form beliefs in these truths. Neither sort of argument would be trivial, and an argument of either sort would seem to have a good chance of providing what I need for my overall argument. Nonetheless, I am not inclined to become embroiled in the debates regarding moral truth. I shall, instead, admit that I made a mistake in saying simply that I need to show that it is *possible* for a person employing the method of balance and refinement to end up with warranted moral beliefs. A demonstration of the kind of abstract possibility this statement suggests clearly does me no good. What I really need to show is that it is possible, for inquirers like all of us, to end up with warranted moral beliefs, even though they must pursue their inquiry via a method that is unlikely to bring them to a consensus, and that offers only limited protection against the dangers of naïveté and corruption. I need to provide a way of thinking about moral inquiry, pursued in accord with the method of balance and refinement, conducted under these circumstances, that enables us to conceive of how moral inquiry could result in warranted moral beliefs. Preferably, this way of thinking about moral inquiry will not make it ridiculously implausible to suppose that inquirers have a real chance of attaining warranted moral beliefs. I will approach this task indirectly, by first examining, in the next section, a perfectly natural way of thinking about the epistemology of moral inquiry conducted in accord with the method of balance and refinement. In Section 5.4, I shall first explain why the natural account, described in Section 5.3, is inadequate, and then describe a more adequate account, which is based upon a perceptual model. My intention is that this perceptual account will indicate how we might begin to conceive of our moral beliefs being warranted, and the role of balance and refinement in warranting these beliefs.

5.3 AN INTELLECTUALIST ACCOUNT OF MORAL INQUIRY

Let's begin by thinking about reflective equilibrium, as it is ordinarily conceived. We will assume that the method leads the inquirer to warranted beliefs, and ask how we might account for these beliefs being warranted. According to the more traditional conception, reflective equilibrium constitutes a familiar view of theory construction. A person begins with a large body of beliefs, moral, philosophical, and factual. She tidies them up by eliminating obvious epistemic messes, such as inconsistencies. She then extends this body of beliefs by generalizing to a moral theory. Given that the inquirer's initial beliefs and degrees of commitment play a foundational role in the method of theory construction, it seems natural to assume that the epistemic status of the outcome of the process will depend upon the status of the inputs. This assumption provides just the framework within which the discussion of reflective equilibrium has ordinarily been conducted. As we saw in Chapter 1, critics such as R. M. Hare and Peter Singer charge that the method is nothing more than a modern version of intuitionism. They contend that it can therefore lead to little more than a polishing up of the prejudices ossified in a person's considered judgments. Since these judgments determine the outcome, the method cannot be legitimate, unless the credentials of these starting points can be demonstrated. Again, as we have already seen, Norman Daniels has responded to this line of criticism. He reminds us of the distinction between wide and narrow equilibrium, stressing both that considered moral judgments do not play a simple foundational role in theorizing, because of the broad range of conditions under which reflective equilibrium allows for their revision, and that background theories play a significant role in the process. But in the end, he grants that considered moral judgments need to be defended, although he does urge that this defence can only be provided within reflective equilibrium, not prior to the construction of a moral theory.

This entire debate seems to presuppose (sometimes explicitly, sometimes implicitly) a kind of foundationalist, "garbage in–garbage out" view of the epistemology of moral theory construction. This is certainly more true of the critics of reflective equilibrium. For they not only criticize reflective equilibrium, because our considered moral judgments have not been shown to be credible, but, when they turn to offer a positive view, they argue that we must construct a substantive moral theory on the basis of some such things as facts, analysis of the meaning of moral terms, or logic, all of which smacks of a rather strong, old-fashioned, foundationalism.[4] But it is true of the defenders of reflective equilibrium as well, for they seem to agree with the critics in holding that any very serious epistemological deficiency infecting the inquirer's considered moral judgments will be transmitted to the theory as a whole. And they admit, after all, that some defense of the credibility of our considered moral judgments must be forthcoming.

Not all defenders of reflective equilibrium will be led to the foundationalist camp without a fight.[5] They will claim that accepting the demand to offer an argument for the credibility of our considered moral judgments does not indicate any sort of closet foundationalism, but a sophisticated form of coherentism. They will claim that the argument is not offered to secure the foundations. The point of the argument is rather to complete the construction of the sort of coherent system of beliefs that gives rise to warrant. Coherentists have recognized, for a long time, that coherence involves more than mere logical consistency, so they have argued that, in order to be coherent, a system of beliefs must also be probabilisticly consistent, have elements that are interconnected by logical, evidential, and explanatory relations, and so on.[6] The latest twist is to require of coherent systems that they contain arguments for the reliability of observational beliefs that are spontaneously formed as a result of perceptual experiences, and not as a result of explicit inference.[7] It seems open to coherentists to offer a similar account of the argument for the credibility of our considered moral judgments, thereby avoiding any appearance of foundationalism.

If a coherence account of warrant were acceptable, my task in this chapter would be a simple one. Indeed, it might then seem that I was too quick to claim that no guarantees regarding warrant could be offered. For surely, if one managed to bring one's beliefs into a state of reflective equilibrium, one's beliefs would have the sort of coherent structure that gives rise to warrant. And the method of balance and refinement inherits enough from reflective equilibrium that inquirers employing it would end up with coherent systems of belief as well. Of course, the end points imagined by these methods are ideal states that no one can seriously hope to attain, but they are ideals we can continuously approach. So, if we assumed that degree of warrant is proportional to the degree of coherence within our system of beliefs, we could be sure that our inquiry would lead to an ever greater level of warrant for our moral beliefs.

Unfortunately, coherentism does not cohere with the picture of moral inquiry that emerged in the last chapter. Specifically, if coherentism provides the correct account of warrant, then either it should not be possible for naïve or corrupt inquirers to hold coherent beliefs, or the beliefs of naïve and corrupt inquirers who have coherent systems of belief are, as a matter of fact, warranted. I have already argued that the method of reflective equilibrium cannot be counted on to remedy all cases of naïveté and corruption, and, since this method aims at such an involved and comprehensive coherence, it seems that no matter how we might tinker with the requirements for coherence, it will remain possible for naïve and corrupt inquirers to hold coherent beliefs. When discussing naïveté and corruption in the last chapter, I did not look into warrant in detail, but it is perfectly clear that, in many of the examples of naïveté and corruption I presented, the person's moral beliefs fall short of knowledge, and these beliefs would continue to fall short of knowledge even if they were a part of a coherent system and they turned out to be true. So it is not the case that the beliefs of all naïve and corrupt persons who also have coherent beliefs are warranted.

So we have ended up in the foundationalist's camp after all.[8] How, then, are we to account for the warrant of the moral beliefs produced by reflective equilibrium, in particular, the moral theory the person is led to adopt? As it is ordinarily understood, the method of reflective equilibrium construes moral inquiry as primarily concerned with arguments, i.e., with examining the logical and evidential relations among believed propositions. Beliefs are then revised accordingly, and more general propositions that subsume particular judgments and less general beliefs are accepted. As a result, the inquirer comes to accept an ever more coherent system of beliefs. Since we have rejected coherentism, we cannot say that this process can, all by itself, bring these beliefs to be warranted, no matter what the epistemological status of the initial beliefs might have been. The most obvious thing to say is that the arguments constructed in the process of seeking reflective equilibrium serve to *transfer* epistemological status from belief to belief to belief, and eventually, to the moral theory.[9] Of course, even foundationalists need not claim that this is the only thing going on here. If it were, the theory that we eventually arrived at would be unlikely to have sufficient positive epistemic status to be warranted. For not all the arguments involved will be deductive, and hence, some of the arguments might be thought to "leak" a little epistemic status as they transfer it. It is open to foundationalists to claim that, by bringing one's beliefs together into the kind of complex logical, evidential, and explanatory structure sought in reflective equilibrium, one *augments* the epistemological status of the beliefs involved, provided, of course, that these beliefs were not deficient to begin with.[10] The inquirer begins with considered moral judgments, and extends her beliefs out towards a moral theory. Ideally, this process will serve to bring the inquirer's considered moral judgments and moral theory into contact with equally firm considered judgments and theories of other sorts, e.g., epistemological and metaphysical beliefs and theories. This process may lead to some, and perhaps considerable, revision of considered moral judgments, and it cannot be denied that the defenders of reflective equilibrium conceive of the whole process as augmenting the epistemic credentials of the beliefs involved. But the basic conception here is of the theorizing transferring the epistemic status of certain beliefs, perhaps including the inquirer's background philosophical beliefs, as well as her most securely held considered moral judgments, out to the theory as a whole. Since the significant features of moral inquiry, according to this account, are arguments and systemization, and the epistemic significance of these features is understood in terms of the transfer and augmentation of epistemic status, respectively, this is an *intellectualist* moral epistemology.

The method of balance and refinement is less neat than reflective equilibrium, as it is ordinarily understood, and the conditions under which I have argued we must conduct our inquiry are perhaps less favorable than they are ordinarily thought to be. We might, nonetheless, try to extend the intellectualist account that I've just sketched to such a moral inquiry. If we think of our moral beliefs as being warranted in virtue of (i) the transfer of epistemological status by argument, and (ii) the augmentation of epistemological status by systematization, how should we account for naïveté, corruption, and the role of literature in moral inquiry? Discerning the general shape of this account takes no great exercise of imagination. The account will assume that moral experience is epistemologically interesting, primarily because it is a source of information or evidence. A naïve person's beliefs cannot be warranted, because they are based on insufficient information. Since the naïve person begins with too few data, not enough epistemic status is transferred to the theory for it to be warranted. The problem here is not, as in the case of rationality, that the naïve person's beliefs are not based on an amount of experience, and hence evidence, that the believer *considers* to be sufficient. The problem is that the information is *objectively* insufficient, whether the believer realizes this or not. It might seem that we do not need to think of experience in any more complicated way to account for corruption. As we noted in the last chapter, misleading evidence might be taken to provide a nice model for corruption. We concluded there that we could not understand all cases of corruption in the way we were exploring, but this was not because we tried to model corruption on misleading evidence. It was because we were concerned with the possible irrationality of corruption, and so had to limit ourselves to experiences the inquirer *took* to be misleading. But there is no rationale for such a limitation when we are focusing on warrant. Regardless of whether a person considers evidence to be misleading, conclusions based on misleading evidence will not be warranted. This fact seems to allow for a more adequate explanation of corruption.

So much for the basic ideas of naïveté and corruption. What kind of account can we give of the role in moral inquiry that the method of balance and refinement assigns to the consideration of material, apart from what has traditionally been considered philosophical, i.e., literature, theater, film, music, art, and so on?[11] Specifically, what are we to say about how literature can serve to relieve naïveté and cause corruption? According to the account we are considering, the problems of naïveté and corruption revolve around information or evidence. So the solution to these problems would seem to be more information. One would generally think that the relevant information could be conveyed by such things as reports of observations, experimental results, and so on, but the example of the naïve inquirer, Jay, that I presented in the last chapter apparently indicates this is not so. Perhaps there is some information that must be acquired either through direct experience with certain things or activities, or through imagination guided by literature. It is not difficult to see how literature could play an important, although not essential, role in relieving naïveté. First, it is perfectly obvious that a novel can convey new information to a person. Secondly, the experience of reading a novel might lead a person to take account of information in a different way. For example, we often "know" something without the knowledge really "sinking in" and affecting the rest of our system of beliefs as it should. In trying to understand how religious mystics take their experiences to influence the epistemic status of their beliefs, Nelson Pike has proposed a similar idea. He proposes that the mystical experience does not provide the person with new knowledge, or even new and stronger evidence for old knowledge. Rather, the mystical experience provides a sort of "cognitive wallop," which Pike describes as follows:

> There is a distinction between just knowing something and really getting it, that is, between correctly believing with evidence and grasping something at the base of the mind as something more than just correct information. That which was only known before now resonates more as a kind of cognitive feeling than as an ordinary thought. The new understanding – the depth grasp – that is what I want here to suppose has been added in this case.[12]

It does not seem unreasonable to suppose that the experience of reading a novel could provide a similar sort of "cognitive wallop" in the moral realm.

While the account we are constructing will see the most clear-cut epistemological contributions of literature as involving information, there is no need for us to ignore other potential epistemological contributions. For example, we need not deny that novels can function in the same way as the more familiar, abbreviated, and stylized examples philosophers usually employ. We might even add that the moral judgments a person makes about a novel are more reliable, either because the case is more true to life, and described in more detail, or because one thinks that the proper object of moral judgment is a larger slice of life than philosophical examples can portray. Regarding the latter, recall Aristotle's remark about what it is proper to call happy:

> But we must add "in a complete life." For one swallow does not make a summer, nor does one day; and so too one day, or a short time, does not make a man blessed and happy.[13]

If we accept this view of what it is proper to call happy, it would be natural to say that our judgments regarding the happiness of more nearly complete lives, i.e., lives as they are described in many novels, are likely to be more accurate than similar judgments regarding philosophical examples.

Finally, as I noted in the last chapter, Martha Nussbaum has suggested that there are certain philosophical views that cannot be presented accurately in the form, or prose style, that is common for philosophical treatises.[14] She argues that the Greek tragedies should be taken to represent such a conception of the good life: a conception that is fundamentally different from that defended by Plato, at least in the early and middle dialogs, and a conception that Plato took seriously, and took himself to be arguing against. She makes similar claims for the novels of Henry James and Charles Dickens, among others, vis-à-vis more contemporary moral theorizing.[15] However, as striking as this view is as a position regarding philosophical theories and the connection between a theory and the form and style of its presentation, it does not require any new epistemological thinking to account for the beneficial effects of literature on naïve inquirers, or for that matter, mature inquirers. For it has long been held that a person should not jump to conclusions, that ideally, a person should hear out all the relevant alternatives to her position before making a final judgment. For this reason, such methods as Rawlsian reflective equilibrium require that a person consider relevant alternative moral conceptions, as well as philosophical arguments designed to decide among them. One might not have thought this would include reading Aeschylus and Sophocles, James and Dickens, in addition to such authors as Plato, Kant, and Hume, but if Nussbaum is right, it does.

5.4   A PERCEPTUAL ACCOUNT

It might, therefore, appear that we can offer a familiar, intellectualist explanation of how moral inquiry, conducted according to the method of balance and refinement, might yield warranted moral beliefs, even in the face of the possibilities of naïveté and corruption. However, this appearance is not accurate. The picture I have sketched cannot render the epistemology of the kind of moral inquiry I have envisioned aright. First, if we think of the naïve person's problem primarily as a lack of information or evidence, it is difficult to see how experiences with other types of art, e.g., viewing an abstract painting or listening to music, could possibly contribute to relieving moral naïveté. Secondly, if the transition from being morally naïve to being a mature moral judge were solely a matter of acquiring information, what could we possibly make of the problem of corrupting experience? There is the analogy with misleading evidence, but it is rough. For there is one significant feature of corruption that it does not mirror. As Aristotle recognized, corruption can be permanent. But there is always an antidote to misleading evidence, and a relatively painless antidote at that, viz., more information.

Thirdly, and most importantly, the above account of the role of literature in moral inquiry is just too simple. It is obvious that a novel, play, or movie can provide a person with new information. And I would not wish to deny that they can both present alternative philosophical conceptions, and function in the same way as the more simple examples that are common in the philosophical literature. Maybe they can even provide some sort of "cognitive wallop." But these functions do not *exhaust* the roles literature can appropriately play in moral inquiry. If they did, and we do not agree with Nussbaum that there are moral conceptions that can *only* be presented in such "non-philosophical" styles as Greek tragedies, then the role of literature in moral inquiry would be purely heuristic. For consideration of literary works would not do anything that could not be done, perhaps more cumbersomely, within the confines of a traditional philosophical approach. The interesting case of naïveté, however, is one where the person is well informed, and philosophical argument does not have the power to alter the person's naïve moral judgments. In this case, the person has a coherent and comprehensive system of moral, philosophical, and empirical beliefs that support her moral judgments. So there is no belief in her system that one could "latch onto" and use to convince her to alter her other beliefs. In order to disrupt such a person's settled convictions, and force her out of her naïveté, the person must be brought to have additional significant moral experiences. This kind of experience can be rather difficult to live through, but fortunately, it comes infrequently in actual life. I maintain that literature provides a remedy for both features. But if exposure to literature can, in this way, bring a person who has led a rather dull, morally colorless life to a high level of moral sophistication, it seems a gross distortion to think of literature as serving simply an heuristic function. For literature would be doing something that the familiar sort of philosophical inquiry could not do.

We should not be surprised at the failure of the intellectualist account. For that sort of account fits most closely the mechanical type of inquiry represented by reflective equilibrium, as it has *ordinarily* been understood. But the radical interpretation of reflective equilibrium I defended in Chapter 1 marks a significant departure from the mechanical conception of moral methodology, and the method of balance and refinement moves even farther away from such a conception. The method of balance and refinement does not look anything like a mechanism for transferring epistemic status. It is not a method of inquiry in the familiar sense that exclusively involves performing certain operations upon a set of propositions or beliefs, e.g., deductive inference or inference to the best explanation. For like the radical method of reflective equilibrium, the method of balance and refinement allows that, in certain circumstances, a person will alter the beliefs and degrees of belief that served as the inputs to the method discontinuously, i.e., in a way that is not dictated by elements of her initial system of beliefs. In addition, the method of balance and refinement is so sensitive to the fact that such revisions might be provoked by experiences or activities, e.g., the consideration of material not ordinarily classified as philosophical, that it directs inquirers to consider which such experiences and activities might be enriching, and to pursue them accordingly. As a result, the method of balance and refinement, like the radical method of reflective equilibrium before it, seems to open up the possibility of a person beginning with a set of beliefs that are utter epistemic trash, and ending up with beliefs that have some significant positive epistemic status.

If we are going to tell a story that is adequate to the method of balance and refinement, and that has a person following the method end up with warranted moral beliefs, then we need to think about the epistemology of moral theory construction differently. There are two distinctive features of balance and refinement: first, the acquisition and revision of moral beliefs, where the alteration in the inquirer's system of beliefs is not a response to the recognition of some quasi-logical deficiency in her original system of beliefs, or the consideration of philosophical arguments or positions, and secondly, the inquirer's reflection on whether her capacity for making moral judgments has been adequately developed, and how it might be developed by further experience, and the seeking out of appropriate experience, particularly with literature, according to the result of this reflection. As a result of both features, the method of balance and refinement is not accurately represented as a function from the person's old beliefs onto the new beliefs. We should not, therefore, expect that its epistemology would resemble that of processes that are accurately represented by such functions. We should instead suspect that, if a person following this method is led to beliefs that are warranted, the explanation of the epistemic status of these beliefs would be similar to that of warranted beliefs that result from other more familiar belief-producing processes that do not take beliefs as inputs, and that are developed and enhanced by experience. We might, therefore, expect a significant part of the epistemology of a balanced and refined person's beliefs to look more like the epistemology of perception than the epistemology of deduction or induction. Thinking of our moral beliefs as produced by a faculty roughly analogous to perception is nothing new. However, authors have tended to think in terms of the wrong sort of perception, i.e., in terms of the perception of simple qualities, such as seeing that a book is red or tasting the saltiness of a pretzel.[16] When I talk of perception, I am thinking of our capacity to make fine perceptual discriminations on the basis of a sort of complicated gestalt, where typically a person can acquire the ability to make the relevant discriminations only after a considerable amount of experience, and sometimes even training. Think, then, of the ability of connoisseurs to make fine discriminations between wines, the ability of an experienced biologist to "see" through a microscope, or, to use an example with which I am more familiar, the ability of a riding master to "see" various things about a moving horse. My claim is that, if we think of our faculty of moral judgment as analogous to our faculty for making such complex perceptual discriminations, we begin to see how the method of balance and refinement might lead to warranted moral beliefs. More particularly, this analogy will yield an account of moral naïveté, the role of literature in correcting naïveté, and the possibility of corruption.

Before I attempt to defend this claim, it will be helpful to have an example of the kind of perception I wish to use as an analog clearly in mind. Growing up in a suburban setting, and doing graduate work in cities, I managed to spend most of my life without becoming acquainted with horses. But, after marrying an equestrienne, and moving to the country, over the past few years I have spent a great deal of time with equines. Among many other things, this has provided me with a recent first-hand experience with perceptual training. Here is a specific example of the kind of thing I have in mind. Having four legs rather than two, a horse has more options for moving forward than a human being. While ordinarily we are stuck with walking or running, and there isn't a whole lot of difference between these, a horse can walk, trot, canter, and gallop.[17] Cantering is a bounding three-beat gait. The horse first moves forward a back leg, then the other back leg along with the diagonal front leg, then the remaining front leg, followed by a moment of suspension. As a result, a horse can canter in two different ways, depending upon which hind leg begins the sequence. A horse can canter on the left or the right lead.[18] Now the interesting thing about cantering, in the present context, is that even after I got the basic idea down, I could not "see" on which lead a horse was cantering. All I could see was a thundering beast, legs going every which way, and I could not sort it all out. I can vividly remember my wife explaining again and again the idea of a lead, and being exasperated because I could not tell which lead the horse was on. But the problem was not that I did not understand the concept of a lead, nor did I lack any information. My eyes were functioning perfectly well, and I suppose that they were creating a representation that had all the detail I needed to apply the concept of a lead. But I just could not do it. I could not sort out all those legs. So, although in one sense I was seeing everything I needed to, in a more important sense I was unable to "see" what I had to in order to apply the concept. After some experience watching horses, I started to get the knack – I could sort things out well enough to apply the concept explicitly to what I was seeing. Still more experience, and I got to the point where I could immediately "see" a horse's lead, in just about the same way I could all along see whether a horse was walking, trotting, or cantering. So even though, in a certain sense, I was seeing the same thing throughout this process, in another perfectly ordinary sense, I somehow acquired the ability to "see" something that I had been unable to "see" before.

In a sophisticated style of riding, such as dressage, there is a great deal more to see than a cantering horse's lead. Not all of the things one can learn to discriminate are as purely "objective" as a horse's lead. One learns to discriminate and evaluate together: to see, e.g., whether a horse's back is soft, whether it is straight, "through," engaged, "on the bit," collected, and also to see the quality of a horse's gaits, and whether this quality is enhanced or inhibited, as the horse performs various movements. It takes a great deal of time and experience to develop the relevant perceptual capacities, and perhaps no amount of experience, or even training, could bring the perceptual capacities of some up to the level of a really good trainer. I am continually amazed at the ability certain trainers have to see things about a horse and rider combination to which I am completely blind. But I have noticed a steady development of my own discriminative faculties, and I can now see things to which I was once completely insensitive.

There is a natural way to think about my little story. I have a faculty of visual perception, but this faculty did not come to me fully developed, able to make all the perceptual discriminations that there are to make. Perceptual experience is required for this faculty to come to be able to make these discriminations. While it is unclear exactly how such experience functions, it is quite clear that it does not simply supply information. The experience does not serve merely as additional input to the perceptual faculty that processes this input and yields a belief as output that is added to the store of beliefs a person has already accumulated. While also serving as such an input, the experience must somehow alter the nature of the perceptual faculty itself, so that it functions differently, yielding output for a given input that is different from the output that same input would have previously evoked. It is not just that the perceptual faculty functions differently. With experience, it functions *better*, producing beliefs with more warrant or producing warranted beliefs where previously it produced either no beliefs at all or unwarranted beliefs.

What I now want to suggest is that the kind of perception I have just described provides a natural model for thinking about naïveté and moral experience. The problem with a naïve moral judge is not that there is any information she lacks, or that the system of theories and concepts that she has built up is somehow inconsistent, or even that there is some alternative theory that she has failed to consider. The problem is that a significant number of the beliefs she is using to develop her moral theory are the products of a faculty of moral judgment that has not been used enough, or been used on a sufficient number of different types of situations, or objects, or perhaps, been used on the right kinds of situations, or objects, for it to have developed to the point where it is competent to make the sorts of discriminations it is being used to make. The result is that the person's moral judgments are not warranted.

I would go on to say that one, and I do mean *only* one, significant function of literature is to supply the kind of experience that is needed to develop a person's faculty of moral judgment. It is easy to see several ways in which novels can serve this function. First, the kinds of complex situations that require careful moral judgment fortunately do not arise all that often in a person's life. Therefore, a person's personal experience is unlikely to provide the sheer number of cases that it is likely to take to develop the person's faculty of moral judgment fully. Literature is ideally suited for supplying additional cases on which a person can exercise her moral faculties. Secondly, when we do encounter situations that require moral discernment in real life, we are often emotionally involved to such a great extent that it is difficult to determine whether our moral faculty is operating freely in generating judgments or is clouded by intense emotion and overwhelmed by biases. Literature supplies cases that are sufficiently distant to minimize the effects of personal bias and the clouding of judgment by excessive emotion while still providing a realistic enough case to engage our emotions to the degree that seems necessary for the proper functioning of our capacity for moral judgment. Thirdly, while the situations described in novels are far more complex than the kinds of examples common in the philosophical literature, they are far less complex than real situations.[19] Framing devices in novels, plays, and films serve to simplify, by forcing the reader to attend to certain matters and ignore certain others. More importantly, situations are interpreted for us to a certain degree in a novel. The author is able to provide some guidance to us as we attempt to understand the situation she describes. The most obvious and mundane way in which the author provides such guidance is by deciding what to include, and what to leave out. By providing a less complex, partially interpreted, scenario, a novel not only provides an example that might help a person to see how to sort out the salient features of a real-life situation for herself, but provides a manageable task on which to exercise a less than completely developed moral faculty.[20]

In connection with this last point about the role of literature in moral development, it is interesting to note the similarity with certain cases of perceptual discrimination. We can learn to make some perceptual discriminations on our own, with nothing more than repeated experience. But, except for prodigies, we seem to need training, or the guidance of a knowledgeable person, to learn to make other discriminations, e.g., regarding music, fine wines, and even the movements of horses. Perhaps it is not true that we literally *need* such training. It may just be that training vastly accelerates learning, so that it seems we need it. Or it may be that we do not need training, in principle, but need it only because acquiring the discriminative ability would take more experience than we could get in a lifetime. But in either case, the point still holds. Practically speaking, we need training to learn to make these discriminations. What about moral discrimination? It might at first seem that the role of training or guidance here is absolutely straightforward, since we all had such training as children. However, the kinds of morally significant situations children encounter and are taught to make judgments about seem to differ by orders of magnitude from what adults frequently encounter and must judge. Thinking that the moral training we received as children is all that we require to make judgments about such situations is a little like thinking that I have had sufficient training to judge an Olympic dressage competition. But if our childhood training was not sufficient, where do we get the required training as adults? We certainly do not continue to receive the kind of moral instruction, directly from another person, we had as children. And such instruction would ordinarily be offensive to adults, and absurdly unlikely to have any good effect.[21] I suggest that literature, theater, film, and for religious people, sacred texts, etc., do much of the work in providing the additional training.[22]

I would not want to underestimate the importance novels can have, simply as a result of offering us the opportunity to practice thinking about difficult, and interesting, situations, and complex personalities, and providing us with examples of how to discriminate carefully salient features of such situations and characters. It is possible to improve our ability to make fine perceptual discriminations simply by practicing, and, as I have just indicated, guidance can be useful, and may be necessary. I do not see any reason to expect our faculty for making moral judgments to be any different. Nonetheless, I recognize that I have taken only the smallest step towards understanding how literature can serve to enhance our ability to make moral judgments; however, it is an important step. We can make no progress in understanding either the epistemology of our moral beliefs or the role of literature in moral inquiry until we stop trying to force things into the mold supplied by the intellectualist conception. And I am confident that the perceptual model I have suggested is true at least to this extent: We have a faculty for making moral judgments, but this faculty does not come to us in its final form. It must be developed. And an important part of moral inquiry should be concerned with the development of this faculty. I am also confident that by thinking about perception, about how our perceptual capacities are developed, and about how perception serves to warrant beliefs, we will get some guidance in answering the related questions about moral inquiry and moral epistemology. In particular, we will begin to see that experience, and literature, and perhaps even more, standard philosophical argumentation and theorizing, can function in two importantly different ways. They can provide inputs to our faculty of moral judgment, and they can systematize and extend the outputs of this faculty by argument and the construction of explanations and theories. But experience, literature, and even philosophy can also serve to alter the functioning of our faculty of moral judgment, for better or for worse, and it is this function that philosophers have neglected in thinking about moral methodology and moral epistemology.

As a sort of confirmation for looking at our faculty for moral judgment on the model of perception, we might note that it provides a natural way for us to make sense of the corruption of a person's faculty of moral judgment. In other areas, where we recognize a faculty for making fine perceptual discriminations that has been developed through training or extensive experience, we recognize the possibility of this faculty losing its high degree of attunement. Thus, for example, an expert wine taster can become jaded, or, through exposure to inferior wines, lose his faculty for making fine discriminations. This kind of corruption was nicely described by J. S. Mill, as it can affect a person's ability to enjoy refined pleasures:

> Capacity for the nobler feelings is in most natures a tender plant, easily killed, not only by hostile influences, but by mere want of sustenance; and in the majority of young persons it speedily dies away if the occupations to which their position in life has devoted them, and the society into which it has thrown them, are not favorable to keeping that higher capacity in exercise. Men lose their high aspirations as they lose their intellectual tastes, because they have not time or opportunity for indulging them; and they addict themselves to inferior pleasures, not because they deliberately prefer them, but because they are . . . the only ones which they are any longer capable of enjoying.[23]

Some might think that literature does not have the potential to corrupt – to damage or incapacitate a person's faculty of moral judgment somehow – and that we therefore cannot understand moral judgment by using a perceptual model. My initial inclination is to deny that literature lacks the potential to corrupt, and I hope the examples I presented in the last chapter were sufficiently plausible to justify my inclination. But even if I am wrong, and literature does not have the power to corrupt, I do not think that this constitutes a serious challenge to my position. For surely not every sort of experience that has the potential to enhance or to develop a perceptual faculty must also have the potential to corrupt it. And just as surely there are experiences with this capacity – life experiences can have the invasive, corrosive power or subtle, seductive power it takes to corrupt. Think, for example, of Sue Bridehead's reaction to the death of her children in Thomas Hardy's *Jude the Obscure* or of the concerns the Amish have about their children attending "English" schools beyond the eighth grade.[24] The proper way of understanding this kind of corruption is in terms of the disruption or incapacitation of a quasi-perceptual faculty of moral judgment. The corrupting experience alters the functioning of the faculty, so that the evaluative judgments it produces are no longer warranted.

I have taken only a small step towards developing the analogy between perception and moral judgment with the sort of precision that would be required to really cinch my argument. But carefully developing this analogy is surely a project of its own, and a very large project at that.[25] Moreover, the analogy between moral judgment and perceptual judgment is imperfect. Nonetheless, I think that the analogy is close enough, and that I have said enough about how it might be developed, for the purposes of the argument I am trying to construct. My aim has been the very modest one of describing a way of thinking about the epistemology of moral judgment and theorizing that allows us to see how it might be possible for inquirers employing the method of balance and refinement to attain warranted moral beliefs. All I wish to claim for the perceptual model I have described is that it provides such a way of thinking about moral epistemology. More particularly, I think it allows us to see that moral inquiry, as I have described it – where reflection on literature is given a very significant role in moral inquiry, where beliefs are revised or accepted even though no argument requires their revision or acceptance, and where moral naïveté and corruption are taken as serious possibilities – is not at all bizarre or unexpected. As I have tried to show, there are rather close analogs of each of these features in perception, so, if we approach moral inquiry with a perceptual model of its epistemology in mind, we should be expecting to find these things in the moral realm. We will not be shocked or dismayed when they turn up.

Now, of course, those who hold onto certain epistemological theories will think that I have stopped short, that I have not demonstrated that moral judgment and theorizing share the most epistemically significant feature with perception. The theorists might differ with respect to what that feature is, with, for example, some saying I need to show that moral judgment is as reliable as perceptual judgment is, or that moral judgment constitutes an element of our cognitive architecture that aims at the production of true beliefs, as our sensory systems do. But I would need to show such things only if I were out to demonstrate that moral inquiry conducted via the method of balance and refinement does *in fact* yield warranted moral beliefs. I have made it quite clear that my aim has been to show how it might be *possible* for moral inquiry to yield warranted beliefs, and as I argued above, it is ridiculously easy to show that it is possible that our moral beliefs have the additional features required by the familiar alternative accounts of warrant. So I have not stopped short after all.

Before I close, I would like to address two additional concerns. The one has to do with experiential warrant, and the other with the role the method of balance and refinement plays in warranting our moral beliefs. The latter concern can be put in the form of an objection. It might be said that, while I have described a way in which a person's moral beliefs might be warranted, I have said nothing about the role of balance and refinement in the warranting of a person's moral beliefs. One might well wonder why the fact that it is possible for a person's moral beliefs to be warranted should serve to support a certain method of moral inquiry, if that method has nothing to do with those beliefs being warranted. There are two points to make in response to this concern.

First, even if the method of balance and refinement did not play any direct role in the warranting of the beliefs of a person following that method, this would not, in my opinion, provide a ground for objecting to the method. According to my view, we should not expect a method of inquiry, moral or otherwise, to do *all* the epistemological work. As I see it, the method makes a contribution, and the person employing the method makes a contribution. Each has a proper role to play as we pursue our inquiry towards whatever goals we may have. In the case of moral inquiry, our goal is complex, as I have said many times, including both rational and warranted belief. The method of balance and refinement has a great deal to do with insuring that the inquirer's beliefs will be rational, relatively less to do with those beliefs being warranted. But this is no fault of the method. I take it that we employ something very close to the method of balance and refinement in forming a common-sense/scientific conception of the world around us. Surely if this method were to be employed by Mr Magoo, his picture of the world would be very odd. I'm inclined to say that this odd picture would be rational, in spite of its oddity, but not warranted. The important thing to see, however, is that this latter fact counts against Magoo, not the method. The method would have done its job, in spite of Magoo's failing. Moreover, while one might maintain that rational belief is not in general a necessary condition for knowledge, or warrant, rationality is necessary for the kind of systematic, theoretical knowledge that is the goal of the moral theorist. In this case, the method of balance and refinement would not be serving as an idle wheel. It would contribute to our obtaining systematic, rational moral knowledge even though it was not directly involved in the relevant beliefs coming to be warranted.

Secondly, the method of balance and refinement has a more direct role to play in our moral beliefs being warranted, indeed, several roles. For one thing, it is the method that sends us out to seek experiences that will serve to refine our faculty for moral judgment. Moreover, even if we have a faculty that is functioning well, and, therefore, producing warranted beliefs, these beliefs will have to be fitted together into a coherent moral system, and the method of balance and refinement plays a role not only in the construction of this system, but in accounting for the warrant of some of the beliefs in the system. Just because I deny that we can think of the whole epistemology of moral theory construction in terms of the transfer and augmentation of epistemic status, by argument and systematization, it does not follow that I hold arguments, and efforts to systematize, to be absolutely irrelevant to moral inquiry. I do not hold that all warranted moral beliefs are the direct products of a faculty analogous to certain kinds of perception. Some moral beliefs arise, and are warranted, in this way, but others are constructed on the basis of such beliefs, and their status as warranted is derivative. Finally, and in a certain sense most significantly, the sort of experience a person has when thinking in a straightforward, old-fashioned, philosophical way can function in the way I have suggested various life experiences, and experiences attained through literature, music, and art, can function. Philosophical argumentation, system building, and the consideration of alternative philosophical theories can function in two very different ways. They can lead one along the path they seem to take directly, from beliefs one has by argument to new beliefs, or from a system of beliefs to a philosophical theory that provides a good account of these beliefs. But philosophy can also work, so to speak, beneath the surface, causing changes in a person's judgmental faculties, so that these faculties no longer function in the same way, yielding the same beliefs and theories, as they previously did. It seems to be a plausible supposition that such authors as Wittgenstein and Nietzsche intended their philosophical arguments to operate in this "subterranean" way.

Turning now to the matter of experiential warrant, it should be obvious what I will have to say. The concept of experiential warrant that I tried to identify in Chapter 2, Section 4 is obviously most at home with sense perception. Perhaps, it is most at home with visual perception, since the experiences that accompany visual judgments are so vivid and highly articulated. Still, I think that there is something similar to be found in the moral realm. Consider a case where we have an especially forceful impression of wrongdoing or evil. For example, on the evening news I recently saw footage of the aftermath of an Iraqi gas attack on a Kurdish village. Millions of quite ordinary, informed, and thoughtful people saw this same footage. They recognized that it was being shown, in part, because it was sensational, and, in part, for its propaganda value. Still, the vast majority of these people surely judged that the attack was morally wrong, more, that it was an immense moral outrage. I feel quite certain that the vast majority of persons who made this judgment made it in the face of a particularly powerful experience. The experience that goes along with making this judgment is not like the experience that accompanies remembering what I had for breakfast, or the judgment that five times five is twenty-five. For one thing, part of the experience that prompts me to judge the gas attack to be morally evil involves my emotions being engaged in a certain way. One component of this experience is a certain peculiar, and particular, feeling of outrage and revulsion, and if it is not as highly articulated as perceptual experience can be, this element of my moral experience is every bit as vivid and forceful as perceptual experience can be. Moreover, it seems to me that this aspect of the moral experience is epistemically relevant. Were I to have seen the films of the village and spontaneously judged the act to be evil, even though my emotions were not engaged in the way I have so poorly described, I would not be able to place the same sort of confidence in my judgment. Finally, to get to the point about experiential warrant, just as we think it epistemically desirable that our perceptual beliefs correspond with our perceptual experiences in a natural, straightforward fashion, we would clearly want our moral judgments to correspond with our moral experiences. Think, for example, of the mental life of a person within the power of a non-deceiving demon who disrupted the connection between this aspect of her moral experience and her moral judgment.

212 Balance and Refinement

The person would feel this deep sense of outrage and revulsion at the most ordinary things, at things that she firmly judged to be morally acceptable. Such a person would certainly not be in an epistemically ideal state.

Hence, it seems that we can speak of experiential warrant in the moral realm as well as in the perceptual realm, and even say that this is an epistemic good that we would wish for our moral beliefs. What, then, about the connection between the method of balance and refinement and experiential warrant? I need to provide an answer to this question only because nothing goes without saying among philosophers. It is clear that literature, film, music, art, and the like have the power to give rise to the sorts of moral experiences I have tried to describe, and this is particularly true of the emotional element of these experiences. It is, therefore, to be expected that because reflection upon all this is given a more prominent role in moral inquiry, the moral judgments inquirers come to form will be aligned quite closely with these experiences. In addition, since the method of balance and refinement mandates that inquirers reflect upon whether their faculty for making moral judgments has been sufficiently developed, and how it might be enhanced, inquirers will have to pay considerable attention to the nature and character of the moral experiences produced by this faculty. We can only expect that this attention will result in a high level of attunement of moral experience, and hence, moral judgment, to what are believed to be the morally significant features of situations. This is not, of course, to deny that the more traditional sort of moral inquiry, involving reflection upon facts, construction of arguments, development of theories, and so on, is incapable of influencing our moral experiences, including even the emotional element of these experiences. But given that even such inquiry has some capacity to bring our moral experiences, and our moral judgments, into harmony, there is no doubting that the method of balance and refinement will be quite effective in producing such harmony, and this harmony just *is* experiential warrant.

5.5 CONCLUSION

Thus ends my attempt to explain how it might be that the moral beliefs of inquirers employing the method of balance and refinement are warranted. I have not, of course, shown that these beliefs are warranted. I have, in effect, shown only that a significant part of moral inquiry as I conceive of it might resemble, as seen *from the inside*, the development and refinement of a quasi-perceptual faculty of judgment. If I am right, a part of moral inquiry might be taken to resemble the training and then improvement, through experience, of perceptual abilities as, e.g., in the case of an expert horse trainer. But not everything that looks this way, from the inside, actually produces warranted judgments. On the one hand, we have cases like that of an expert tracker who through training and experience comes to be able to "read" the signs in the forest, to be able to "see" that a bear slept here two nights ago, or that a hawk frequently perches in this tree; on the other hand, we have cases like that of a shaman being trained to "see" spirits through the use of psycho-active herbs. I imagine that both activities have a similar appearance from the inside, that both would be taken by the practitioners to be the development of a judgmental faculty that human beings possess. But, of course, only the former actually is; only the former sort of training and experience gives rise to an ability to form warranted judgments. I have done nothing to show that we have a faculty of moral judgment that can be developed so that it will produce warranted moral beliefs. As I said at the beginning of this chapter, that was not my aim. I am not out to convince someone who stands apart from moral inquiry to become engaged in it, by offering strong assurances of its ability to yield knowledge. I merely wish to offer some ray of hope to all of us who are already engaged in this activity, some reason for thinking that what we are doing, and have no choice but to be doing, might actually lead us to knowledge. I think that the sort of argument I have offered succeeds in doing this. A similar argument would offer a ray of hope to, for example, the shaman, but that is no deficiency in my argument. Having even good reason to hope that you are tapped into some sort of truth does not entail that you are.

My defense of the method of balance and refinement is now complete. I think it is fair to describe the dominant conception of moral inquiry as intellectualist and mechanical. The idea is to perform certain quasi-logical operations on believed propositions, operations that will yield a comprehensive moral theory, and allow evaluations of particular actions, where the operations in question are as close to algorithmic as possible. Even so liberal-minded a methodology as Rawlsian wide reflective equilibrium seems to adopt this picture of moral inquiry. My aim has been to oppose any such mechanical conception. While arguments surely have an important place in any philosophical inquiry into morality, they are not the whole story. A significant part of moral inquiry is concerned with refining our ability to make sensitive moral judgments. We must both seek to improve our judgment, and to fit our judgments together into a systematic moral outlook. Contemporary writers concerned with moral methodology have almost exclusively focused on the latter element of inquiry. I wish to correct their vision. I have sought to show that methods that do not pay serious attention to the origin of our moral judgments, and the development of our capacities for making such judgments, cannot guarantee inquirers so much as rational, let alone warranted, moral beliefs. Once our vision is corrected, certain things stand out, things that previously we were unable to see: moral conversions, the possibility of naïveté and corruption, and the significant, nearly essential, role of life experience and experience with literature, film, theater, music, and art in moral inquiry. Although I move away from the predominant conception of moral inquiry by small steps, I end up with a totally different perspective. And if I really have rendered moral inquiry aright, our practice must change. We should no longer even want ethics to look like mathematics or science, as so many contemporary moral theorists seem to want. Instead, we will think of moral inquiry as involving a roughly equal blend of the individual inquirer developing and improving her moral sensibility, and the individual seeking to examine and revise the various judgments her refined sensibility produces and to construct a theoretical account that systematizes these judgments. The latter will allow much of moral inquiry to be continuous with past practice. But the former suggests that philosophical inquiries into morality, and also, then, philosophical writing about morality, must include, for example, detailed reflection on specific novels, films, and real-life experiences, where the intention is not to provide some argument, but quite literally to bring oneself and others to perceive what we have as yet been unable to see.

Notes

INTRODUCTION

1 There are, it seems, other moral attitudes, e.g., repugnance, revulsion, outrage, which we would not be tempted to describe primarily in terms of thinking something.

2 I do not mean to deny that, at least ordinarily, when one accepts a moral proposition, one's motivations are activated in ways in which they characteristically are not activated when one accepts a non-moral proposition. I mean to be focusing on the attitude one takes towards the statement or proposition. This attitude seems to me to be the same in the two cases. I would say that the difference lies in what happens when one adopts this attitude towards different types of propositions.

3 While it is undeniable that we accept our beliefs to various degrees, this is a problematic idea. For there are various ways in which we might explain what it is for belief to come in degrees, and it is not clear either whether these explanations ultimately get at the same feature of belief, whether there are a number of different ways in which our beliefs come in degrees, but the degrees must always match, or whether there are fundamentally different ways in which beliefs come in degrees, so that a single proposition can be believed to different degrees in different senses. When I spoke of our degree of acceptance above, I was thinking of something felt, of something we can determine just by introspecting. But one might also think of degree of belief in terms of a judgment or a higher order belief rather than in terms of feeling, i.e., as how likely we consider, or judge, the proposition to be true. It seems to me that these are not the same thing. Consider, for example, what an obsessive compulsive person who is aware of her disorder might say about her belief that she latched the paddock gate, "I do not feel at all sure that I latched the gate. In fact, I doubt that I latched the gate. But this is just the sort of thing I get stuck on, and it is, in fact, very likely that I latched the gate after all." Then there is the notion of degree of belief at work in probability theory, as something measured by the bets a person would be willing to make. This is supposed to be a more precise notion than either of the rough and ready notions I introduced above, but it is not clear to me how it can be. For how is it that a person decides what bets to take? Specifically, will she be guided by her felt commitment to the relevant propositions, or will she be guided by her cool judgments of the likelihood that these propositions will be true, or is it some combination of these, or is

it something else entirely? I don't know. I must confess that I have not successfully sorted out the various notions of degree of belief. So in the discussions of reflective equilibrium that follow, I am not always careful to distinguish among them, perhaps in the vain hope that my own degrees of belief all match up. If I had to choose, however, I would take the relevant notion of degree of belief to be defined in terms of what seems to one more likely to be true, where this is more like a judgment about the belief than a felt commitment. I am not, however, entirely comfortable thinking of this seeming as a judgment or a second-order belief.

4 I mean to include under "systematic moral view" either substantive normative theories, meta-ethical theories, or a combination of the two.

5 See Rawls (1971) and (1974-5).

6 We will encounter Mr Magoo at various points. I believe Magoo made his first appearance in the contemporary epistemological literature in Sosa (1974). Sosa uses Magoo to illustrate that a rationally justified true belief might fail to be knowledge in a case where the believer has defective cognitive equipment.

1 THE METHOD OF REFLECTIVE EQUILIBRIUM AND THE NO CONTACT WITH REALITY OBJECTION

1 Rawls (1971): 19-21, 48-51, and (1974-5): 5-22. To be exact, Rawls was first to apply the method in the moral realm, and to describe and advocate wide reflective equilibrium in particular. Prior to that, Nelson Goodman described the method that has come to be known as narrow reflective equilibrium and claimed it should be used to construct or justify theories of deductive and inductive inference. Goodman (1955).

2 Daniels (1979): 256-82, and (1980): 83-103.

3 A moral theory is said to explicate a set of considered judgments when a person conscientiously applying the principles to the cases covered by the considered judgments would make the particular judgments which are either elements of the set of considered moral judgments or entailed by the general principles which are elements of this set. Cf. Rawls (1951): 184-6.

4 By a type of belief I have in mind types that can be identified with reference to such factors as the form or content of the proposition believed. It may be possible to identify types of beliefs that are immune to revision in other ways, e.g., by appeal to a person's degree of commitment to them.

5 Since this statement of the objection assumes moral statements to bear truth values, it is likely to strike a sour note with advocates of non-cognitivism. However, the objection can be raised in a way that harmonizes with most versions of non-cognitivism. All the objection requires is that there be a suitable gap between moral "truth" and the individual's beliefs. Versions of non-cognitivism which do not support the objection hold moral "truth" for an individual to be whatever the person happens to believe it to be, or would believe it to be after due consideration, or perhaps even would believe it to be in reflective equilibrium. Rawls seems to defend something like this last position in Rawls (1980). Nonetheless, the objection can be understood most easily, and seems to be most telling, when brought against the conjunction of a coherence method in ethics with the view that moral statements are objectively true or false. For this reason, and also because I find this conjunction of methodological and meta-ethical positions attrac-

tive, I shall assume for the remainder of the discussion that moral statements are objectively true or false.

6 BonJour (1985), and (1976).
7 Daniels (1979).
8 ibid., 258.
9 Rawls (1971): 47.
10 ibid., 47–8.
11 ibid., 47.
12 The approach I take here is not trouble free. Basically, I require a person's initial moral judgments to be filtered through her own epistemic principles. But there are, quite obviously, obstacles in the way of saying just which principles these are. They will presumably have to be something more than the epistemic principles the person happens to accept prior to any reflection, but they can't very well be the principles the person would accept after completing some ideal process of reflection, such as that involved in reflective equilibrium. In addition, the approach I take regarding epistemic principles leads to similar considerations regarding logical principles. Should logical principles be granted special status, and imposed externally on the inquirer? In practice, such an imposition may not pose much of a problem, since we find substantial, although certainly not universal, agreement regarding logical principles. But the theoretical problem remains. For if logical principles are determined internally, the nature of conflicts and support relations will be determined internally as well. This will mean that, at best, it will only be possible to say whether a set of propositions is coherent, if it contains a sufficiently well-developed set of logical principles, which can then be used to determine the logical relations among the other propositions in the set. And, since most people do not have such well-developed logical views, it will not be possible to say whether most actually believed sets of propositions are coherent, where the conflicts within them lie, or even what follows from what. To determine any of these matters, we would need to know, for example, what logical principles the person would accept upon a certain sort of reflection. From this, it would follow that sets of propositions that are not sufficiently comprehensive, i.e., that do not contain a sufficiently developed set of logical principles, will not be coherent, or incoherent, in any absolute sense, but will only be so relative to a certain inquirer. Similar considerations led BonJour to combine his coherentist view regarding empirical justification with a foundationalist position regarding *a priori* justification. BonJour (1985): 193. I am not really happy with this approach, but working through the alternative, thoroughly coherentist, and internal approach would vastly complicate my project. I shall, therefore, assume that logical relations need not be decided from the inquirer's own point of view. But, unlike BonJour's, my heart is not really in this assumption, and I make it solely to simplify the discussion.
13 Why should we think this? Rawls would have to be thinking that the excluded initial moral judgments were either formed by some faculty other than that of moral judgment, or at least, that they are somehow tainted by some other faculty. Otherwise, it would seem that although the excluded judgment is in error, it might still accurately reflect the functioning of the person's faculty of moral judgment. Consider, for example, an analogous claim made about our faculty of visual perception. A perceptual judgment made regarding an array of objects designed to produce an illusion does not

accurately reflect the nature of the objects, e.g., their relative sizes. But it should not be ignored in our efforts to understand our visual faculty, for it does accurately reflect the functioning of this faculty. Similarly, it would seem that if our aim is to characterize the functioning of our faculty of moral judgment, we should not rule out those judgments that fail to meet some external epistemic standard. Indeed, it may not even be appropriate to rule out judgments that fail to satisfy the person's own epistemic standards. Consider, for example, a person whose moral judgments reflect racial bias, but who also recognizes that these judgments are the result of having been brought up in a conservative southern family. It is possible that in spite of this realization, the person cannot help but go on making racist judgments. It seems to me that in such a case, we might want to say that these judgments do accurately reflect the person's sense of justice, but that the person's moral sense has been warped. Of course, if our task is to say something about justice, rather than this person's sense of justice, we would do well to exclude the judgments in question.

14 Daniels (1979): 265.

15 Notice that there is no good reason to grant epistemic principles this sort of special treatment, except that we think some such principles are so firmly held, and so tied up with other things we firmly believe, that we think it nearly inconceivable that we ever revise these principles. But of course, if there are other, non-epistemic, beliefs like this, it may well be convenient to eliminate initial moral judgments that conflict with these beliefs at the outset as well. The resulting notion of a considered moral judgment, which is the notion I favor, is admittedly quite weak. Indeed, the only reason for retaining it, rather than thinking of reflective equilibrium as involving simply moral judgments, a moral theory, and background beliefs, is to maintain continuity with previous discussions of reflective equilibrium.

16 I am assuming that the inquirer will end up at the same equilibrium point, whether these beliefs are dropped early or late.

17 Just as the epistemic principles against which a person's considered moral judgments must pass muster are the person's own, and not some external standard, the standards of simplicity and elegance relevant at this point are those accepted by the person.

18 Notice an infelicity of this notation: I do not mean the subscripts "n" to indicate that the same number of revisions have been made to {CMJ} and {MT}. The "n" rather stands for "narrow" here. Similarly, the subscript "w" used below indicates "wide" rather than a number of revisions.

19 Daniels (1979): 258. I shall offer some reasons for doubting this characterization in Chapter 4, Section 4, but until then, I shall simply follow Daniels.

20 I would be willing to say that the same thing is true when the conflict is between background psychological or sociological beliefs and a moral judgment. However, this consequence need not be accepted to avoid the coercion of moral judgments. For presumably, philosophical beliefs will always be necessary to bring psychological, sociological, biological, or other sorts of empirical background beliefs into conflict with moral judgments or theories. Hence, these philosophical beliefs are open to revision, if the inquirer is firmly enough convinced of her moral beliefs.

21 The temporal separation of narrow from wide reflective equilibrium is inaccurate. These are more accurately viewed as two distinct methods, where narrow reflective equilibrium is not a point on the way towards wide

reflective equilibrium. A person attempting to reach a point of wide reflective equilibrium would probably bring her background theories, as well as her considered moral judgments and moral theory, into play virtually from the start.

22 Hare (1973).

23 Singer (1974).

24 Nielsen (1979).

25 Daniels (1979): 264–7.

26 Lyons (1975): 146.

27 Brandt (1979): 18–19.

28 ibid., 20.

29 It would be unfair to criticize Brandt for not saying more about credibility. He was trying to raise the criticism of reflective equilibrium in the most general way possible. For this reason, he could not even assume, for example, that the proponents of the method agree that moral statements are true or false, or that an acceptable method should yield true beliefs, or at least, increase our chances of believing truths. I shall be able to simplify the discussion, since I am taking it for granted that moral statements are true or false.

30 I should admit that I am not really confident that this is the best way to understand credibility. However, it seems to be what Brandt has in mind when he raises the no credibility objection, even though he has claimed, in correspondence, not to understand how a reliabilist account of moral justification would go. In addition, this understanding of credibility allows me nicely to present the portion of Daniels' response to Brandt I wish to discuss, and to make the connection between this response and BonJour's coherentist conception of observation.

31 There is a considerable literature on reliability in connection with knowledge and justification. For a general introduction, see Alvin Goldman (1979).

32 Brandt (1979): 21.

33 Singer (1974): 516.

34 BonJour (1985): 108.

35 The position would be externalist in so far as factors to which the person does not have access, i.e., the reliability of her beliefs, determine the epistemic status of these beliefs.

36 Daniels (1979): 268–73.

37 Although, even in these cases, the explanation of our failure might have to do with the object of inquiry, i.e., morality, rather than the method.

38 I'm not sure how seriously we should take this analogy, to which, it should be admitted, Daniels devotes no more than a few sentences. For it seems initially to suggest that ordinary perceptual beliefs were not justified (assuming that something like BonJour's coherence account of observation is correct, but must be fleshed out with a considerable amount of science) until very recently. But if we try to avoid this unlikely consequence by allowing for a common-sense (BonJour style) argument for the reliability of ordinary observations, we will lose our excuse for not already having an argument for the credibility of moral judgments in hand.

39 Daniels (1979): 272.

40 Taking credibility to be a matter of reliability, (I) requires that the percentage of true considered moral judgments exceeds some threshold,

and (II) requires that the degree of credence a person initially places in a moral judgment provides a good indication of how reliable the judgment is.

41 This was not the case with Rawls' earliest formulation of the method of reflective equilibrium in Rawls (1951). He there required that considered moral judgments must be agreed to by all competent moral judges.

42 Daniels argues convincingly for the extreme revisability of considered moral judgments in response to critics who have charged that reflective equilibrium is a version of intuitionism. Daniels (1979): 264–7.

43 One way in which it could happen that {CMJ$_w$} contains mostly false beliefs while {MT$_w$} contains mostly true beliefs is if many of those background beliefs which are necessary to apply the moral theory to the cases the considered moral judgments cover are false.

44 While inappropriate as a response to the no credibility objection, the suggestion that the beliefs in {CMJ$_w$} might be shown to be reliable would constitute an appropriate response to the no contact objection. I shall, therefore, return to consider this suggestion below.

45 I would say that, if he actually ends up with a coherent system of moral and philosophical beliefs, R. M. Hare could be construed as providing an example of such a person. Presumably, he made all kinds of moral judgments before he ever thought about philosophical ethics or the meaning of moral language. But once he did start thinking about the philosophical questions, these moral judgments "lost out" to various beliefs about the meaning and use of moral terms which took over the role of determining his moral principles, and in turn, his considered moral judgments. I will discuss this issue in more detail in Chapter 3, Section 4.

46 The argument of the last few paragraphs may lead some to question whether, in so greatly de-emphasizing the role of considered moral judgments, I have abandoned the method of reflective equilibrium entirely. I suspect that this reaction results from an identification of reflective equilibrium with what has come to be known as narrow reflective equilibrium. Other authors who have appreciated the distinction between wide and narrow reflective equilibrium, e.g., Rawls and especially Daniels, have emphasized the extreme revisability of considered moral judgments. What I have been saying follows directly from this extreme revisability. More positively, we might say that the core notion behind the method of wide reflective equilibrium is that no type of belief or judgment, and certainly not considered moral judgments, has a privileged status in theory construction. Theory construction is to be guided by the inquirer's degree of commitment to the relevant propositions. In the scenarios I have described, where considered moral judgments do not play a significant role in determining the moral theory the person accepts in reflective equilibrium, this core idea still applies. Revisions, and ultimately the moral theory accepted, are determined by the inquirer's degree of commitment to the relevant propositions.

47 By "comparatively high degree of confidence," I do not mean something like "very sure." Rather, I mean "high, compared to beliefs with which it conflicts." Thus, the beliefs with a "comparatively high degree of confidence" in my sense will be precisely those beliefs that play a significant role in guiding the inquirer towards a state of reflective equilibrium.

48 At a more fundamental level the defender should attack the idea that a method must reliably lead to true beliefs if it is to be acceptable. I will be developing such a more fundamental attack beginning in Chapter 2.

49 I originally drew this distinction in DePaul (1987).

50 I intend "conflict" to be understood broadly. Thus, for example, a set of logically inconsistent propositions is in conflict. Another example is provided by a set of propositions where all the members save one together provide strong evidence against that member. (In cases of the latter sort, a person is under no obligation to resolve the conflict unless the conflict remains in the total set of her beliefs, since it is possible for a subset of a person's beliefs to provide evidence against a proposition when the total set of the person's beliefs provides strong evidence in its favor.) It is even possible for a set of particular moral judgments, no two of which concern the same case, to be in conflict. This occurs when there is no non-arbitrary way of distinguishing the cases along the lines indicated by the judgments.

51 If two inquirers began believing the same things to the same degrees, but they proceed to consider and resolve conflicts in different orders, they would, as a matter of fact, almost certainly end up at different equilibrium points. But that is not why this characterization of the conservative conception is inaccurate. For recall that one of the idealizations or simplifying assumptions involved in my characterization of reflective equilibrium is that order does not matter. So I am saved from saying something false, here by a previous simplification/falsification.

52 Had I not already simplified the discussion by assuming that all inquirers would agree to the same standard view of logical relations, a similar point would apply to the logical element of conflicts. See note 15 above.

53 Recall that conflicts can develop between moral and philosophical propositions. For example, a person who highly values theoretical simplicity might find certain of her moral judgments conflicting with this value, if she were to realize that, by altering these moral judgments, she could accept a more simple moral theory.

54 Given that I have been stressing the conservative aspect of the conservative conception of reflective equilibrium, it is important to remember that, even conceived conservatively, reflective equilibrium may lead a person to a moral view that is very different from her initial moral view. However, the person would have to be moved to such a different moral view by steps that were required to resolve conflicts inherent in her initial moral and philosophical viewpoint, and dictated by elements of her initial viewpoint to which she was more strongly committed than the revised elements. I discuss an example of such an apparently radical, but truly conservative, change of belief in the next section.

55 I do not, however, stand alone. Henry Richardson (1991) argues "that reflective equilibrium cannot be understood solely in terms of the relations among judgments," and for a more "psychological" conception in which emotions play a significant role.

56 There is some reason to think the method would not even look like conservative reflective equilibrium. For even the conservative method allows for *extensive* revisions of considered judgments, e.g., in cases where a few very strongly held beliefs conflict with the bulk of the inquirer's pre-philosophical system of beliefs. And such extensive revision would seem to

be, practically speaking, incompatible with the person's initial beliefs and degrees of commitment being reliable.

57 I first suggested the distinction between the radical and conservative conceptions of reflective equilibrium in DePaul (1986). When I read that paper at the Central Division APA meeting, Norman Daniels, who was the commentator, maintained that all conversions could be explained in terms of the conservative conception. When I read an early version of the present chapter at the Pacific Division APA meeting in March, 1987, my commentator, Bernard Baumrin, made the same point.

58 To cite only one example, Bertrand Russell offers the following description of what is arguably a radical conversion. "When we came home we found Mrs Whitehead undergoing an unusually severe bout of pain. She seemed cut off from everyone and everything by walls of agony, and the sense of the solitude of each human soul suddenly overwhelmed me. Ever since my marriage, my emotional life had been calm and superficial. I had forgotten all the deeper issues, and I had been content with flippant cleverness. Suddenly the ground seemed to give way beneath me, and I found myself in quite another region. Within five minutes I went through some such reflections as the following: the loneliness of the human soul is unendurable; nothing can penetrate it except the highest intensity of the sort of love that religious teachers have preached; whatever does not spring from this motive is harmful, or at best useless; it follows that war is wrong, that public school education is abominable, that the use of force is to be deprecated, and that in human relations one should penetrate to the core of loneliness in each person and speak to that . . . . At the end of those five minutes, I had become a completely different person. For a time, a sort of mystic illumination possessed me. I felt that I knew the inmost thoughts of everybody that I met in the street, and though this was, no doubt, a delusion, I did in actual fact find myself in far closer touch than previously with all my friends, and many of my acquaintances. Having been an Imperialist, I became during those five minutes a pro-Boer and a Pacifist. Having for years cared only for exactness and analysis, I found myself filled with semi-mystical feelings about beauty, with an intense interest in children, and with a desire almost as profound as that of the Buddha to find some philosophy that should make human life endurable." Russell (1978): 149.

59 I am obviously presupposing a kind of realist attitude towards beliefs. If one tends towards an anti-realist view of beliefs, which freely attributes beliefs *wherever* they are necessary to explain behavior as "rational" (in a certain specific sense of rational), the kind of fact at issue in conversions constitutes *the* respectable reason for attributing beliefs. See, for example, Dennett (1971).

60 In addition, in succeeding chapters, where I shall consider the significant role of literature, theater, film, music, and art in moral inquiry, I hope it will become clear that moral conversions can occur.

61 An analogous issue arises in debates about conditionalization. The position I take corresponds to those who hold, in opposition to Bayesians, that rational revision of belief does not have to proceed via conditionalization. Bas van Fraassen has argued that if you are willing to add enough beliefs, you can maintain any revision to have proceeded via conditionalization.

But what does this show? Is there any reason to suppose the person had these beliefs? See van Fraassen (1993).

62 To do this, one need not defend the credibility of our *considered* moral judgments. Some other class of propositions might provide the basis for the epistemic status of the propositions accepted in wide reflective equilibrium. Cf. DePaul (1986).

63 This form of the no contact objection could also be raised against conservative reflective equilibrium, as could the version of the Wimpy response described below. The issues I raise in the next section, regarding convergence, apply whether a Wimpy defense of radical or conservative reflective equilibrium is intended.

64 I shall henceforth speak as though there is just one mechanism, assuming that the same overall conclusions can be drawn if there are many mechanisms, not all of which are reliable.

65 Williams (1985).

66 MacIntyre (1981).

67 As I mentioned above, this criticism could be avoided if, for example, there were one mechanism that is reliable only in certain circumstances. The human visual system is a mechanism of this type: It is not reliable in the dark or under water, but it is in air and sunlight. For this rejoinder to work, it would have to be shown that the circumstances of persons who come to different moral theories in reflective equilibrium are sufficiently different. However, it does not seem that persons who differ with regard to their considered moral outlooks are always, or even usually, from different backgrounds, although it is perhaps likely that persons with different backgrounds will come to different moral views.

68 Daniels (1979): 272.

2 A STRATEGY FOR DEFENDING A METHOD OF MORAL INQUIRY

1 Although in the end, I will seek to argue for the method of balance and refinement, since I have not yet described that method, in this chapter I shall speak as if I will be defending the radical version of reflective equilibrium, which is the sire of balance and refinement. In Chapter 4, we will find that the radical method of reflective equilibrium falls short of being a rational method. I will then develop the method of balance and refinement to overcome the difficulty upon which radical reflective equilibrium founders.

2 Laurence BonJour does think he can argue that long-run coherence is truth-conducive, but I am not convinced. See BonJour (1985), Chapter 8.

3 *Nicomachean Ethics* 1094a. Irwin (1985): 2.

4 Being analyzed "as some sort of connection with truth" does not necessarily guarantee reliability. For example, Chisholm seeks to explicate terms of epistemic appraisal in terms of an intellectual requirement for a person to try "his best to bring it about that, for every proposition h that he considers, he accepts h if and only if h is true" (Chisholm (1977): 14). Since the requirement is to *try* to believe all and only the truths one considers, and one does not always accomplish even what one tries very hard to do, this explication yields no sort of reliability.

5 Goldman (1986): 3.

6 I do not here mean to suggest that reliabilism and foundationalism are necessarily at odds. If all versions of foundationalism are supposed to be internalist, they clearly would be, but there does not seem to be any good reason for making this supposition. As an illustration of the point, notice that Goldman's theory can be seen as a version of externalist foundationalism: Certain beliefs are justified independently of their relations with other beliefs, in virtue of being produced by a reliable cognitive mechanism, and other beliefs are justified by standing in the right kind of relation to other justified beliefs, i.e., by being produced by a reliable belief-dependent mechanism that took those other beliefs as inputs. On the other hand, reliabilism is apparently inconsistent with coherentism, since according to coherentism, beliefs are always justified in virtue of their relations with other beliefs.

7 Alston (1988): 269.

8 BonJour (1985): 7–8. It is not surprising that a coherentist would endorse these *words*. But usually they would be endorsed because *both* justification and truth are accounted for in terms of coherence. What is interesting about BonJour is that he accepts a correspondence account of truth.

9 One might say that, in these cases, the goal of the activity is survival, rather than a successful crop or a kill respectively, and that the methods of farming and hunting in question are reliable, in the sense that they are likely to enable survival. While I wouldn't want to deny that the ultimate goal of these activities is, in some sense, survival, I still believe that, in a straightforward sense, the goals are as I originally described them. And in any case, I can still make my point even if we take the goal of the activities to be survival. For if conditions were bad enough, say during a drought, it might be that these methods are not very reliable even at insuring survival. Yet, given that engaging in them affords the best chance for survival, we might nonetheless regard the methods as adequate.

10 Mill (1859), Chapter 2.

11 I say "at least" because some "fourth" condition designed to handle Gettier-style problems will almost certainly be required. For the original formulation of the "Gettier" problem, see Gettier (1963), and for an absolutely thorough discussion of Gettier-style examples and the analysis of knowledge, see Shope (1983). I shall, however, henceforth ignore this possibility, and speak as if knowledge is simply justified or warranted true belief. I do this in the belief (perhaps more accurately: hope) that Gettier-type problems are not *significant* within the domain of moral beliefs. It is, of course, easy to construct a Gettier problem involving a moral proposition. One could, for example, disjoin a true moral belief with a false, but apparently justified, belief to produce a Gettier example. What it is more difficult to see is how Gettier-style problems might arise, if we confine ourselves to the sorts of moral beliefs, and compounds of moral beliefs, and the sorts of justificatory arguments that standardly figure in moral philosophy. The view that holds knowledge to be something other than true belief, no matter what or how much is added, since *knowledge* is not a species of belief, is perhaps held by a sufficiently large, or vocal, minority to deserve some mention. But I shall fulfill any such obligation to mention the view only by offering this confession: I do not find this view sufficiently plausible to bother having anything to say against it.

12 I have chosen "warrant" rather than "justification," because this usage avoids two confusions: first, confusion between the practice of justifying and the state of being justified, where I am concerned with the latter; secondly, any possible confusion between being epistemically justified in believing a moral proposition and justifying morality by somehow showing that moral action is always in our own best interest. Some, e.g., Plantinga, maintain that the term "justification" is more deeply misleading, because it suggests an unacceptable "deontological" conception of justification. Regarding the deontological conception of justification, see Plantinga (1990) and also Alston (1985). Personally, I do not hear "warranted" as being any less deontological than "justified."

13 In saying that we would not be satisfied with testimonial knowledge, I certainly do not mean that there is no role for testimony in moral inquiry. We might, for example, come to know something only because an authority has produced a convincing argument for it that we can follow. In such a case, the expert gives us not only his assurance that the proposition is true, but also his reasons for believing it is true. When I speak of testimonial knowledge here, I am thinking of the case where we believe something solely because it is asserted by someone we recognize as an authority, without any inkling of what other, more fundamental, reasons there might be for believing it.

14 There might be some reason for thinking that I have not drawn the distinction in quite the right way here. For example, suppose careful philosophical inquiry leads a person to a divine-command ethic. All of such a person's knowledge might appear to be derivative, as a result, perhaps being based upon scriptures, and in any case, ultimately being dependent upon God's moral knowledge. (A similar story could be told about a moral theory that had, e.g., the views of a society somehow determining morality.) In such a case, one might argue, the inquirer would not attain primary or fundamental knowledge, although he would have attained a kind of *reflective* knowledge, which would be opposed both to the kind of derivative knowledge we gain from authorities, and also snap, intuitive knowledge, of the sort I discuss just below. I have no very strong reason for opposing this suggestion. It isn't clear to me that it makes all that much difference for what I wish to go on to argue. But I am hesitant to back away from what I've said. For, I do not think that in the example of a divine-command ethic, the inquirer's knowledge is really derivative. Presumably it would not be quite accurate to speak of knowing on the basis of God's authority, at least, not if we think of this as the sort of authority an expert has. Rather, since it would be God's command that *makes* actions right or wrong, when one knows what God has commanded, one would not have knowledge based on testimony, but knowledge based upon recognition of the fundamental ground of morality. Even if the inquirer knew what God had commanded on the basis of the testimony of some scripture, we should not consider his moral knowledge less than fundamental. For the case is exactly parallel to, e.g., that of a utilitarian, who accepts the moral theory on the basis of philosophical argument, but makes use of sociological research reported in journals to determine some of the facts needed to apply his theory to a particular case.

15 Plantinga offers similar examples against coherence theories of warrant. Plantinga (1992).

16 I'll have more to say about the precise sense of rationality involved here below.

17 I mean, by this, to indicate that I do not wish to rule out the sort of intuitionism that sees morality as lacking a sort of easily defined structure.

18 The practical aim I mention here is more general than the practical aim I mentioned in the first paragraph of this section.

19 Here, and elsewhere, I claim that moral inquiry is, in a certain sense, forced upon us. One might admit that some sort of moral inquiry is forced upon us, while doubting that the sort of involved philosophical inquiry with the specific aims I am in the process of setting out is forced upon us. To give a particular example, one might think that, having noticed an apparent inconsistency in his moral views, a young boy might seek the advice of a trusted elder, and simply believe what he is told. An inquiry into morality would have been forced upon the boy, but apparently an inquiry that properly ends with mere testimonial knowledge. Perhaps I should back off a little, and merely claim that we are forced to set out upon some sort of moral inquiry, an inquiry that for many develops into the kind of inquiry I have described. But I also want to suggest that what I am here calling a philosophical inquiry into morality is not something startlingly different from the kind of moral thinking that people ordinarily do. I believe ordinary thinking about morality imperceptibly shades into philosophical inquiry. In addition, I believe that most normal adults, in fact, most normal adolescents and even children, are inevitably drawn, to a greater or lesser degree, into some kind of full-blown philosophical thinking about morality. So I do not really think that, for example, the boy described above can ultimately rest content with the testimonial knowledge he obtained.

20 R. M. Chisholm occasionally identifies "positive epistemic status" in terms of its role in the concept of knowledge. Such a specification of the concept of warrant, in particular, can be found in Plantinga (1990).

21 I say that such a failure is "characteristically" culpable, since a person can sometimes be excused from blame. In fact, if we accept the distinction commonly drawn between "objective" and "subjective" duty, we might want to say that we never blame someone simply for failing to live up to the standards defining *objective* duty. When it appears in some instance that we do, this is because subjective and objective duty coincide in that case, and what is in fact being blamed is failure to satisfy subjective duty.

22 I say that failure to satisfy such standards is not *characteristically* blamed, because there are cases where a person is blamed for not satisfying such a standard. For example, we might blame a person for his high blood pressure, in a case where he is not taking prescribed medication or following dietary recommendations. However, in such cases, the person's failure to meet the standard results in an appropriate way from a violation of some duty, and strictly speaking, any blame arises from the violation of this duty.

23 This is why I was careful when discussing examples above to speak of beliefs being irrational *in a certain sense*.

24 Think, for example, of the more vituperative atheists criticizing belief in God as irrational.

25 I say only that we are likely to hold the beliefs to be irrational, because in at least some cases, say where the person is working in some particularly demanding, highly technical area, we do not regard even self-contradictory

beliefs as irrational. Think, for example, of Frege believing that for every property, there is a class of things having that property, before Russell uncovered the paradoxes this entails. I do not think we would want to label this belief of Frege's irrational.

26 I will return to this point below, in Section 2.4.

27 I intend this claim to be interpreted so that it is compatible with the major options for accounts of warrant, i.e., coherentist, foundational, and reliabilist accounts. I do not mean to imply that the received view is some version of reliabilism.

28 More must obviously be said about the sense of reflection involved in this formulation. I assume that a complete account would proceed along something like the lines developed by Richard Foley. See Foley (1987). Since Foley defines rationality in terms of ideal reflection, there is a danger of losing the deontological component I wish to be involved in rationality. However, as will become apparent in Chapter 3, Section 3, the sort of rationality that does the real work in my argument is defined in terms of considerably less than ideal reflection. I should also note that a simplifying assumption, made while characterizing the method of reflective equilibrium, will apply here as well. This is the assumption that all inquirers will, perhaps after a little reflection, settle on standard logical principles. See Chapter 1, note 12. Without this assumption, the discussion would have to be complicated, since such matters as, for example, whether a belief satisfies an epistemic standard would have to be determined relative to the logical standards the inquirer would accept upon reflection, where it is an open question what these standards might be.

29 There are other ways of drawing the distinction between internalism and externalism. For some, the distinction concerns the location of the properties, or characteristics, that determine a belief's epistemic status. On this reading, warrant is an external concept, since objective likelihood of truth is "outside" the believer, while rationality is internal, since what the person would think is likely to be true upon reflection is presumably determined by various things that are "inside" the person.

30 To my way of thinking, David Brink's discussion of moral epistemology, and therefore his defense of realism, is flawed in just this way. For it is tied too closely to a dubious coherentist account of epistemic justification. See Brink (1989), Chapter 5.

31 In this section, I have relied very heavily on the work of three people in ways I have not always bothered to document. They are: Richard Foley, Alvin Plantinga, and William Alston. See especially Alston (1988) and (1985), Foley (1987), and Plantinga (1992), (1990), and (1988). I have also benefitted from many discussions with Plantinga and Foley.

32 BonJour (1985): 7–8.

33 I use the term "ground" rather than "reason" to include both other beliefs (to which reasons are limited) and experiences (e.g., perceptual experiences). I would even like to keep open the possibility that some grounds are psychological states or processes that are neither beliefs nor experiences.

34 I do not mean here that the horse would not have some additional monetary value as a result of his bloodlines, for because of the gullibility of many people, it may as a matter of fact have some additional monetary value!

35 In fact, I'm oversimplifying here. As my discussion of our epistemic aims in moral inquiry should have indicated, I would want to include rather more than knowledge in a complete specification of our general epistemic aims.

36 Think, here, of Kierkegaard's Johannes the Seducer. See "Diary of a Seducer" in Kierkegaard (1843).

37 Alston (1985): 70.

38 ibid., 71.

39 I am taking a liberty with Alston here, for he stops short of identifying warrant with J_e, claiming only that J_e is the important concept of justification for epistemology. His more complex, final position does not, however, avoid the criticism I mean to be making here, since he identifies warrant, even more closely than J_e, with truth-conduciveness.

40 Alston (1985): 71.

41 I should qualify this claim. The beings would not have immediate perceptual knowledge of their world. They might come to have knowledge, and hence warranted beliefs, via some other route. For example, over time they might construct some sort of abductive argument, grounded in the long-term success of their system of beliefs about their world, and come to know on this basis.

42 As I have described this example, it invites us to think of the beings having a rich and varied experiential life, but a life where there is not even any complicated, indirect connection between what is experienced and either reality or the beings' beliefs. We might instead imagine a kind of total experiential "inversion," where there is a regular, or lawlike, relation between the beings' experiences and beliefs, but a bizarre relation, unlike the straightforward connection that exists between our experiences and beliefs. I discuss an example of this sort below. Or again, one might instead think of the demon making the lives of his beings very dull and colorless, as well as causing them epistemological problems. The demon might simply deprive his beings of all perceptual experience, or allow them some constant, unchanging experience, while at the same time constructing them so that their beliefs about their world reliably match the nature of that world. The demon's victims in this example might be similar to actual victims of "blind sight." This sort of case differs from the previous cases in that the beings would not, as a result of their experience, feel any inclination to believe in accord with experience drawing them in a direction that conflicts with what they come to believe.

43 Perhaps, it is even inaccurate to think of beliefs held at an instant, as well.

44 This claim is subject to the proviso I mentioned earlier, concerning the possibility of the person's attaining knowledge via some other route.

45 I should note that I take R. M. Chisholm to have worked more diligently than any other philosopher at developing a precise characterization of just the epistemic concept I here propose to call experiential warrant.

46 I should point out that this type of case is difficult for some internalist accounts of warrant, e.g., BonJour's coherentism, to handle. Indeed, the case is modelled after examples used by Plantinga and Alston against such versions of internalism. Chisholm's account is exceptional among versions of internalism in that it is well equipped to deal with this type of case.

47 One might propose that scientific realists provide an actual counter-example to what I have been saying. For, if they are thoroughgoing and consistent, they will not form many ordinary beliefs, e.g., that the surfaces

of things are colored, that the things are solid, etc., but will, instead, believe that the thing reflects a certain wavelength of light, is composed mostly of empty space, and so on, and they will form these commonsensically "odd" beliefs on the basis of the very sensory experiences that ground more ordinary beliefs for the rest of us. I would not admit that such thoroughgoing scientific realists provide a counter-example to my view, since they are not in an ideal situation. They would be in an epistemically superior position, if they did not, first, have to resist forming ordinary beliefs on the basis of their experience, and then take complicated detours to get from experience to their beliefs about the world. They may, after all, have knowledge. But I would still maintain that they are not in an ideal epistemic situation.

48 See Gilbert Harman's discussion of observation and moral judgment in Harman (1977), Chapter 1.

49 It might be objected that, while there is some sense to be made of my notion of experiential warrant in the case of perception and, perhaps, some other sorts of belief, no sense can be made of this notion in the case of moral beliefs. More specifically, it might be objected that, in the case of moral judgments, no distinction can be drawn between degree of belief and what I have called experiential warrant. But it seems to me that such a distinction can be drawn. For one thing, in many cases, we believe propositions very strongly, perhaps even with maximum strength, but only because we have deduced them from other propositions that we believe with equal strength. The result of our deduction may have come as a complete surprise to us, precisely because the conclusion did not have the aura of intuitive obviousness that is one source of experiential warrant, in the case of moral propositions. Moreover, it is not the case that experiential warrant necessarily follows degree of belief. A person may come to doubt moral propositions he once made, quite spontaneously, and with a high degree of conviction, say, on general theoretical grounds, without this doubt washing away the felt obviousness that still attaches to the proposition, even though it is no longer even believed. Thus, for example, we can imagine a person raised in a conservative southern town having spontaneously judged that interracial marriage is immoral, having come to doubt, and eventually disbelieve, on the ground that skin color cannot be a morally significant factor, but still find that the proposition that interracial marriages are wrong excites the same sense of intuitive obviousness.

50 If we suppose, instead, that Magoo's experience is like what we would have if we were seeing what he believes himself to be seeing, perhaps we would say that his beliefs are experientially warranted, and if we were Chisholmians, or convinced by my arguments from Section 2.4, warranted.

3 THE CASE FOR THE RATIONALITY OF RADICAL REFLECTIVE EQUILIBRIUM

1 See Chapter 1, note 50, for more on what I mean by a conflict.

2 I would also claim that belief in both members of a *pair* of conflicting beliefs might be rational, in conditions similar to those I have just described, even though the believer could not reassure herself by thinking that each belief has a better than 0.5 chance of being true.

3 I have described this case very abstractly, but I think that it may be a very common sort of case. For although not all writers on moral dilemmas would agree (e.g., Walter Sinnott-Armstrong (1988)), moral dilemmas arguably fit my abstract characterization of contradictory beliefs that might nonetheless be rationally retained. In such cases, moral principles that may have been arrived at for diverse reasons turn out to be in conflict, in that they yield incompatible directives in a certain class of particular situations. If what I've said here is correct, it might often be rational to decide what to do in the dilemma situation as best as one can, while continuing to accept the principles that gave different directives regarding the dilemma situation.

4 Regarding the treatment of logical principles, see Chapter 1, note 12, and Chapter 2, note 28.

5 I do not mean to indicate that some full-blown form of coherentism is implied. This conception of rationality is also compatible with certain sorts of foundationalism, i.e., weak or subjective versions. The conception rules out the existence of some class of foundations that must be accepted by everyone, regardless of their own epistemic standards. But it allows that each person's beliefs might have a foundational structure, and that the epistemic standards certain, most, or even all persons accept might constitute a form of foundationalism.

6 Curiously, it might be that some people have beliefs that are rational quite by accident. But a little reflection will convince most of us that our chances of winning a state lottery are vastly better than our chances of being the beneficiary of such a happy epistemic accident!

7 There may be certain degenerate cases where it might be rational to follow even these bizarre methods. In such cases, the inquirer becomes convinced that what seems true to her, upon reflection, is not to be trusted, and that either the oracle or brainwashers are to be trusted, or that her own "intuitions" provide a sort of negative guide to the truth. As I say, it might be that for such persons, it would be rational to adopt one of the methods I said were clearly unacceptable, but this is not entirely clear. For presumably, if the person formed such belief without reflection, we are not committed to saying that it is rational, while if the belief were to be held upon reflection, it would be self-defeating. In cases of the latter sort, we might have to say that there simply is no rational method for the person to follow.

8 I am thinking in particular of Foley (1987).

9 Conditionalization is a principle governing change in degree of belief over time, or, more specifically, when new data are acquired. If C_0 and C_1 are a person's credence functions at t_0 and t_1 respectively, and the person learns something, B, at t_0, then conditionalization requires $C_1(A) = C_0(A/B)$.

10 See Chapter 2, Section 3.

11 I wish to note two things. (1) This, of course, supposes that we are dealing with the sort of case where reflection yields a clear answer, where one of the propositions comes to seem quite likely to be true, and the other comes to seem quite likely to be false. In a case where the difference between the two propositions does not seem terribly great, it may be that the believer comes to doubt both. As I noted above, it might also be that in spite of reflection upon the conflict, both beliefs continue to seem correct to the believer, in such a way that she considers it worth accepting the certainty of holding at least one false belief to have a chance of holding a true belief. In this type of

case, given appropriate firmly held epistemic principles, I am willing to say that it might be rational to retain both members of a conflicting pair of beliefs. (2) This might offer a way of determining how much reflection is needed for a belief to be rational – reflect until it results in a settling of belief. The natural response to uncovering a conflict is to reflect. Do so until the conflict is resolved!

12 These beliefs need not be terribly sophisticated or even specific. Thus, we might have the belief that one should not jump to hasty conclusions, or that one should keep an open mind, or avoid being dogmatic, by listening to all sides before making up one's own mind. Presumably, if a person has such beliefs, they will have to be refined during the course of reflection, and thus come to play a more active role in governing beliefs. So it need not be the case that a person has anything like a well-worked-out epistemological theory for epistemological beliefs to play an important role in attaining reflective equilibrium.

13 I suppose this remark indicates that I am thinking of professional philosophers, or perhaps academics more broadly. For it would probably be excessive to require this of ordinary people engaged in moral thinking. However, I think that something like this will be required of ordinary persons. There are various identifiable moral, political, and religious views debated in the public arena, and I should think that rational revision of belief by ordinary persons requires reflection upon these alternatives. Thus, my grandfather, a really very radical union coal miner, need not have reflected upon Robert Nozick's libertarian arguments to hold his moral/political views rationally. But, I should think, he would have had to reflect upon what ordinary Republican politicians and free-market economists, writing and speaking for the public, had to say on behalf of their views. And, as a matter of fact, he did, although not perhaps in an ideally cool-headed fashion.

14 It might be objected that I have drawn the contrast unfairly, comparing something like analytic epistemology, on the one hand, to the moral life of a real community of people, on the other. To get a fair comparison, the objection might continue, I should, instead, consider the epistemic life of some real community, e.g., the workings of an appropriate research group within the scientific community. Presumably, I would then find a richness comparable with what we find in the moral realm. Now, the fact is that I was not consciously thinking of analytic epistemology when I drew the comparison here, but, of course, that does not insure that I got things right. For I am not really all that familiar with the workings of the relevant sorts of research communities. However, while I suppose I can grant that a careful study of the workings of such communities would reveal more than I have suggested, I still do not think that we will find anything to compare with ethics. In particular, I do not see where anything comparable to the various moral emotions might be found even in the epistemic life of a real scientific community.

15 What I recall being a "Far Side" cartoon comes to mind. The cartoon pictured a man with a normal-sized meal before him but a very small head. The caption read, "Never eat anything bigger than your head."

4 NAïVETÉ, CORRUPTION, AND THE METHOD OF BALANCE AND REFINEMENT

1 *Nicomachean Ethics* 1095a. Ross (1925): 3.
2 Of course, Aristotle's main concern here is not epistemological at all. It is practical. He was clearly worried that the young do not have their passions under sufficient control for any knowledge of ethics or politics to have the proper effect on their behavior.
3 I should probably say that I intend to be using "experience" in a very broad sense here, equivalent to something like psychological state, process, or occurrence. Thus, in particular, I do not wish to use "experience" in a way that implies even that one is necessarily conscious of an experience.
4 Dostoyevsky (1866).
5 Magarshack (1951): 552.
6 In using the term "theory" here, I follow Svidrigaylov, who, having overheard Raskolnikov's confession to Sonia, characterizes Raskolnikov's motive as a theory, when he tries to blackmail Raskolnikov's sister. See Magarshack (1951): 502.
7 Magarshack (1951): 558.
8 ibid., 555.
9 ibid., 556.
10 Notice that all of these potential causes are operating in Raskolnikov's case. For the novel begins with him performing an action he believes to be right, and he subsequently comes into close contact both with Sonia, who is virtuous, and Svidrigaylov, who is vicious and amoral, both of whom also have markedly different values from Raskolnikov.
11 In Chapter 5, Section 4, I will argue, in some detail, that changes in moral belief resulting from the kinds of experience I have just indicated cannot be interpreted as being produced by anything like an argument.
12 There is, obviously, a close connection between what I am here calling a formative experience and the sort of discontinuous moral conversion I discussed in Chapter 1, Section 7. Indeed, one might, with a fair degree of accuracy, say that formative experiences and moral conversions are, at bottom, pretty much the same kind of thing, except that the latter are provoked by reflection on a philosophical argument or theory, while the former are provoked by something else, e.g., reading a novel.
13 Having pointed out these various problems associated with my notion of formative experience, in order to simplify the discussion, I am, in general, going to ignore them. This will quite often be true, in particular, of the distinction between the occurrences, activities, and experiences that can give rise to formative experiences. So, having been warned, please read what follows charitably, realizing that in certain places, where it may look as though I have become confused, I am really trying to simplify my presentation. For it really would be tiresome of me constantly to be speaking first about occurrences, activities, and experiences that are apt to give rise to formative experiences, and then of the formative experiences themselves. I shall occasionally remind you where I am simplifying by blurring this important distinction, and where I think it might be specially significant, I shall try to tighten up my presentation.
14 Allow me to stress something that should be obvious. I am using the term "reasoning experience" in my own way. When I contrast reasoning experi-

ences with formative experiences, I do not mean to suggest that the latter must be experiences with no reasoning elements (here used in the more ordinary sense). I mean to claim only that there are experiences which can affect a person's moral judgments which do not, in any obvious or important sense, fit either of the paradigms of reasoning experience.

15 Presumably one of the formative experiences that, as a matter of fact, played a major role in leading Raskolnikov to abandon his moral views was actually putting them into action, by killing the elderly pawnbroker. One can hope that this act was not necessary to correct Raskolnikov's moral thinking. But it is interesting to contemplate the possibility that some corrupt persons who hold perverse moral outlooks, indeed, who rationally hold these outlooks, could not correct their thinking without acting upon their views. Such persons would be doomed to persist in their perverted moral thinking unless they undertook to put this thinking into action, thereby performing evil deeds.

16 Jay would probably be considered naïve in the ordinary sense of the term, but in calling him naïve, I mean to indicate something more particular, i.e., an epistemological deficiency resulting from his limited experience. Just as, according to Aristotle, the inadequacy of the young for the study of ethics involved their emotional immaturity, as well as an epistemological deficiency, so too naïveté, in the ordinary sense, involves an emotional shortcoming, as well as an epistemological deficiency. I am concerned only with the epistemological side of naïveté here. But, I should acknowledge that there is a certain danger in attempting to separate the two, since this will tend to mask any possible epistemological significance that the emotional side of naïveté might have.

17 Rawls (1971): 47–8.

18 In the first chapter, I questioned this conception of considered moral judgments, because it has the potential to hold inquirers to epistemic standards they may not accept. The difference between my understanding of considered moral judgments and the more standard Rawlsian conception is relevant to the point at issue here. However, since on my understanding it is even less likely that the filtering needed to obtain considered moral judgments can be counted upon to improve Jay's epistemic position, I shall present the argument here in terms of the more familiar understanding of considered moral judgments. And, in any case, the kinds of considerations that might arise at this point in the discussion, on my understanding of considered moral judgments, i.e., those involving Jay's acceptance of bizarre epistemic standards, simply arise later if we adopt the more familiar conception of considered judgments, viz., at the point of transition to wide equilibrium.

19 Rawls does place this restriction on considered moral judgments in earlier treatments of moral methodology. See Rawls (1951).

20 Recall that I am willing to grant that a person might hold Jay's view of war in reflective equilibrium in a way that is rationally unobjectionable and hence poses no problem. For example, if Jay were to acquire enough of the sorts of experience regarding war that he lacks, and hold onto his evaluation of war in spite of his exposure to these additional experiences, I am prepared to grant that he might *rationally* maintain his moral view regarding war. After all, rationality is a matter of doing all one should, as seen from one's own point of view, and what more could we ask of Jay?

21 Because we are supposing that the inquirer has already attained a state of narrow equilibrium, we can be sure there are no conflicts among moral principles and considered moral judgments.

22 Rawls says the notion of reflective equilibrium "varies depending upon whether one is to be presented with only those descriptions which more or less match one's existing judgments except for minor discrepancies, or whether one is to be presented with all possible descriptions to which one might plausibly conform one's judgments together with all relevant philosophical arguments for them." Rawls (1971): 49. And he goes on to suggest that we deal with the impossibly large task of considering all possible conceptions and philosophical arguments by restricting ourselves to studying "the conceptions of justice known to us through the tradition of moral philosophy."

23 It is, of course, possible for consideration of a philosophical argument to occasion a formative experience in someone, but this would not be a characteristic effect of such consideration.

24 Martha Nussbaum would deny that there is an alternative moral conception that can be *extracted* from certain morally significant novels, not because these novels do not present alternative moral conceptions, but because the content of these conceptions cannot be separated from the literary forms in which they are presented. See Nussbaum (1990). If she is right, the injunction to consider alternative moral conceptions will force Jay to expose himself to the relevant literature, thereby relieving his naïveté. However, her suggestion is controversial, and more importantly, it goes beyond the common understanding of reflective equilibrium in precisely the way in which I wish to press beyond this conception, viz., by requiring exposure to literature in the first instance, and on similar grounds, film, theater, art, and music, in addition to philosophy, as traditionally understood. I shall, therefore, not treat her position at this point in the argument.

25 This point is even more obvious if we consider formative experiences that are not even (clearly) linguistic, e.g., listening to music or viewing paintings. I did not wish to rest the point on the existence of such experiences, since their existence may be controversial.

26 I hope I will be excused for not citing any examples of philosophers I take to be naïve!

27 Note the similarity of this approach to the approach Richard Brandt takes to identifying rational desires. He holds them to be desires that would survive repeated reflection on *all* the relevant facts. See his discussion of "cognitive psychotherapy" in Brandt (1979), Chapter VI. I think that his method faces objections analogous to those I raise against reflective equilibrium immediately below, particularly the second of these objections.

28 I am granting that a distinction can be drawn between formative experiences and experiences of emotional and physical trauma so that the discussion can move along. However, I suspect that any attempt to draw the distinction would encounter a number of serious and theoretically interesting difficulties.

29 It is, of course, doubtful that *one* such experience would have much effect upon Janet. My thought is more that an extended series of such experiences

would affect her. I do, however, believe that it is possible for one experience to have an effect.

30 I am indebted to Philip L. Quinn for suggesting the possibility of examples of this type, which led me to begin thinking about the problem corrupting experiences might pose for moral inquiry.

31 Given the discussion of Jay, I obviously do not wish to imply that Janet's beliefs are epistemically acceptable solely because she has brought them into reflective equilibrium. I mentioned that her beliefs are in reflective equilibrium only to suggest that she has examined the various connections among her beliefs, eliminated any incoherences, and settled upon the overall moral view that she considers most plausible, all things considered. I have argued that attaining such coherence is not enough for a method of moral inquiry, but I do think that attaining it is an important virtue in a method.

32 Indeed, I wonder whether it is *really* possible to experience *both* life-styles.

33 As we saw, when I introduced the radical conception of reflective equilibrium, some philosophers are uncomfortable with the idea that a person can just change some moral judgment, or acquire a new judgment "out of the blue." They think that change of belief, or acquisition of new belief, must always, somehow, be tied to existing beliefs. One with this mind-set will find the example I have described difficult to understand without supposing that Billy had beliefs consistent with his final view regarding women right from the start. These beliefs may not have been explicitly formed in his mind, but they must have been present for the romantic novel to have the effect it did. The novel did not suggest a new view of appropriate relations between men and women to Billy; rather it served to confirm in his mind the view he held all along, but for some reason had tried to suppress. I would not want to say that there could not be examples that conform to this interpretation. There surely are. But I would argue against any assertion that all examples of change in belief *must* be so understood, and in particular, that this example *must* be understood in this way. Another word of caution is appropriate. Any example of corruption, or even simple change in belief, which is bound up, as this example is, with the sorts of images a person associates with sex is likely to be complicated. And, there is a danger that precisely because of the power such images exert over persons, and consequently their moral judgments, corruption might be easy to imagine in this area, even though it is next to impossible to imagine in other areas. (Those who doubt that such images exert a powerful influence upon moral judgments might consider whether it is plausible to suppose that images of homosexual relations, particularly between men, powerfully influence the moral judgments certain people make about gays and lesbians.) I certainly would wish to deny any such suggestion. I think that our moral views regarding a wide range of topics are subject to corruption. But I admit that corruption of the sort I here tried to describe is particularly easy to comprehend. That is exactly why I chose this example, thinking that my main problem would be to demonstrate the possibility of *any* sort of corruption.

34 It is interesting to note that the Amish probably view all of us as we view Billy, i.e., as having corrupted our capacity for making judgments regarding how best to live, with this corruption sustained by our continued involvement in our modern life-style.

35 See Harman (1971) and (1980), and Foley and Fumerton (1982).

36 For example, when I walk into the barn on a perfectly normal morning and have a very quick visual impression of a dark bay horse with a big star standing in her usual stall, just before I start to climb up to the hay loft, it will be rational for me to believe the horse to be there, without acquiring any additional evidence.

37 A person may know that Lyin' Jack witnessed the crime, and has made a statement to the press, and still not need to read Lyin' Jack's statement, since the person knows of Jack's well-established record of asserting falsehoods.

38 Notice that I have simplified the discussion here by, once again, ignoring the distinction between formative experiences and the occurrences, activities, and experiences that cause, or are likely to cause, formative experiences. One thing that would emerge if we complicated my discussion to attain greater accuracy would be that the inquirer must work at one remove from formative experiences, considering what he might do or experience that might give rise to the appropriate sorts of formative experiences. I will keep the discussion simple through the remainder of this section, but in the next, where I set about describing the method of balance and refinement, I will tighten things up.

39 I should emphasize that in saying that these formative experiences are misleading, all I mean to commit myself to is that they lead the inquirer away from truth. It should by now be clear that I do not think that the mechanism by which such experiences lead the inquirer away from truth is importantly similar to the mechanism by which misleading evidence leads inquirers away from truth.

40 Throughout this discussion of corruption, and the previous discussion of naïveté, I have been assuming that experience includes both "first-hand" experience with something and imaginary access to the thing, e.g., by way of vivid, detailed "visualization." Thus, for example, a person might upon reflection decide that such "visualization" of a certain activity will be sufficient for forming judgments about it. Other things being equal, it would be rational for a person who believes this to proceed without actually engaging in the activity. In other cases, however, the person might decide that he needed actual experience. Vivid imagination is likely to be particularly important in determining what might be corrupting, since such imaginary access is likely to be what convinces the person that some experience is likely to be corrupting. It is possible, however, for a person to consider even imaginary access to a thing potentially corrupting. I suppose such imaginary access might actually be corrupting, although I suspect this would usually require repeated, perhaps obsessive, imaginings.

41 *Nicomachean Ethics* 1095b. Ross (1925): 5.

42 My intention was the same in the case of Jay. I did not wish to evoke any feeling that Jay had got things wrong morally, but to make the point that his view of war was epistemically unacceptable in virtue of the formative experience on which it was based, regardless of his view's moral acceptability.

43 It is, however, difficult to determine why one views examples as one does. So I should perhaps allow that an Aristotelian might be able to articulate a compelling analysis of the examples I have described, which shows that our judgments regarding the examples are, in fact, based on ideas that certain

types of activity or experience really enhance our capacity for making moral judgments, while other activities or experiences serve to corrupt this capacity.

44 My use of "liberal" and "conservative" is analogous to their use in political philosophy, where liberals hold that the government should be neutral with respect to conceptions of the good life, while conservatives think that the government's actions must flow from a particular moral conception.

45 Recall that, in the last chapter, I argued that even those moral philosophers who most strongly object to reflective equilibrium as a matter of fact employ this method. I therefore regard moral philosophy, as we actually see it, to be a good indication of what it would look like if we all used reflective equilibrium – for nearly everyone does use reflective equilibrium.

46 See, for example, Cavell (1987) and (1981).

47 See, for example, Nussbaum (1990).

48 See, for example, Quinn (1991) and (1989).

5 A PERCEPTUAL MODEL FOR THE WARRANT OF MORAL BELIEFS

1 I say nearly any person because certain very minimal requirements will have to be met, e.g., that the person not be deranged, brain damaged, or mentally retarded.

2 I do not mean by this statement to endorse some sort of simple, or even complicated, reliabilism. I am merely saying that believing in a way that is objectively likely to be true is a major component of the concept of warrant. I leave open how this component is to be fitted into a complete account of the concept of warrant.

3 It is significant that there is no regular relationship between the visual experiences the person is having, and the beliefs she forms. This is not a case where the experience that ordinarily indicates the presence of a cat to us has come to serve as evidence, to this person, that she is in the driver's seat of her car.

4 The clearest example of the sort of view I have in mind is provided by R. M. Hare (1952) and (1981).

5 See Brink (1989), Chapter 5.

6 See BonJour (1985), Chapter 5.

7 See ibid., Chapter 6.

8 When I say that we have ended up in the foundationalist camp, I do not, of course, mean that balance and refinement is a foundationalist method. It is much closer to a coherence method. What I mean is that some sort of foundationalist account will have to be given for the warrant of the moral beliefs inquirers are led to accept by following this method. For a detailed explanation of how a foundationalist epistemology can be "laid over" a coherence method, specifically reflective equilibrium, see DePaul (1986). In saying that balance and refinement is "closer to a coherence method," I do not mean to indicate that it is a coherence method. Just as coherence theories of epistemic concepts accept a doxastic assumption, coherence methods of inquiry must accept an appropriately modified doxastic assumption. A version of the doxastic assumption applying to methods of inquiry might read as follows: The only things relevant to the outcome of a method of inquiry are the inquirer's beliefs and degrees of belief. The method of balance and refinement obviously makes no such assumption.

For a nice discussion of the doxastic assumption as it applies to theories of justification, see Pollock (1986): 19.

9 Pure coherentists would not be sympathetic to this view, since they hold that warrant attaches, in the first instance, to systems of beliefs that have an appropriate sort of internal structure, and only derivatively, to the individual beliefs. See BonJour (1985) and (1976). Note, however, that even on such a view, there is a place for the transfer of warrant. For most coherentists would hold that some sub-systems of beliefs within a coherent system, e.g., religious beliefs, and, I think, moral beliefs as well, will be warranted only if they stand in the right logical and evidential relations to beliefs in the main system of belief, i.e., the system less the relevant sub-system. And, while beliefs in the main system will be warranted in virtue of their coherence, that coherence will in no way be dependent upon the presence, or absence, of the beliefs in the sub-system. Thus, such sub-systems do not contribute to coherence and hence to the warrant of the beliefs in the main system, so the warrant of the beliefs in such sub-systems can be seen as deriving from that of the main system. These beliefs will be warranted only if they are entailed, or supported in some other way, by the beliefs in the main system.

10 Consider, e.g., Roderick Chisholm, who has long held that the coherence (his term is *concurrence*) of a body of beliefs will serve to increase the epistemological status of the beliefs. See Chisholm (1977): 82–4.

11 For convenience, I shall henceforth simply speak of literature, and novels in particular, although I would stress that the points I wish to make apply to plays, films, poems, and, perhaps with some tinkering, visual arts and music.

12 Pike (1986): 32.

13 *Nicomachean Ethics* 1098a. Ross (1925): 14.

14 Nussbaum (1986): 12–18.

15 Nussbaum (1990).

16 This is not quite fair, even to contemporary authors. John McDowell has pressed an analogy between morals and secondary qualities, but his account of secondary qualities is not at all the simple sort I suggest here. See McDowell (1985). David Wiggins has offered an even more complex account of moral judgment, which sees it as similar in important respects to our sense of such things as what is funny. See Wiggins (1987).

17 These are the horse's natural gaits. A horse can be trained to move forward in other ways, e.g., by pacing. Some trained gaits are even more bizarre, and farther from what is natural for the horse, e.g., the "rack," a gait taught to saddlebred horses.

18 Cantering, then, is a little like skipping with four legs. A little thought (or perhaps trial and error) will reveal that when you skip you take a stride with one leg forward, and the other trailing behind, then switch and take the next stride with the other front leg forward. If you skip along without changing the forward leg, you can get a picture of what cantering is like. What we call skipping is the two-legged equivalent of a horse doing flying changes of lead every stride, which is a complicated movement for a creature with four legs.

19 An analogous point holds for sensory perception, visual and otherwise. It is often more effective to train a person to make a discrimination using simple and less than wholly accurate representations, rather than actual examples.

Consider, for example, how we teach certain bird songs, by saying they sound like "bob white, bob white," or "kill deer," rather than by playing tape recordings of the songs. A similar point holds in the visual realm. Consider, for example, the way birding manuals almost always use drawings of the various species, rather than photographs, and even more stylized silhouettes to teach readers to discriminate birds in flight, perching and so forth. I am told that spotters were similarly taught to recognize incoming German planes in Britain during the Blitz, and that such training was shown to be more effective than training with photographs.

20 Martha Nussbaum has explored in some detail the ways in which the novels of Henry James can perform this function. See especially her article on *The Golden Bowl* in Nussbaum (1990).

21 You might consider, in this regard, a rather old-fashioned example: the biblical story of David and Bathsheba, and the prophet Nathan. After an adulterous affair with Bathsheba, which leaves her pregnant, and arranging to have her husband killed in battle, David is approached by Nathan. But Nathan does not simply tell David that he has done wrong in such and such ways. He tells him a story about a rich man who takes a poor man's only possession, a ewe lamb.

22 My talk of training and guidance here does not contradict what I said in the last chapter about the individual ultimately having to trust her own judgment. I was speaking there of rationality, which is a subjective, internalist concept, while we are here concerned with warrant, which is an objective, external concept. What I have said here is, therefore, consistent with what I said in the last chapter. For while one must trust her own judgments to proceed rationally, one must get the right training to be warranted. It may be the case that one has no reason to trust, and plenty of reasons to doubt, the only person who can provide the training necessary to acquire some discriminative ability. In such a case, it would be irrational to trust the person, but trusting her would be the only way of acquiring the discriminative knowledge in question. In addition, the sort of advanced training I have been talking about does not proceed by anything like blind faith. To become involved in such training, one must have reached a certain level of competence. One employs this competence, one considers and discusses, as one is trained. Notice that the same thing characteristically happens when one reads a morally significant novel.

23 Mill (1861), reprinted in Warnock (1974): 261.

24 For a discussion of the Amish stand on education, see Keim (1975).

25 For some indication of the magnitude of this project, compare William Alston's attempts to develop, with his characteristic precision, a perceptual account of religious experience. Alston (1991).

Bibliography

Alston, William (1991) *Perceiving God*, Ithaca: Cornell University Press.
—— (1988) "An Internalist Externalism," *Synthese*, 74.
—— (1985) "Concepts of Epistemic Justification," *The Monist*, 68.
Audi, Robert and Wainwright, William J. (eds), (1986) *Rationality, Religious Belief, and Moral Commitment*, Ithaca: Cornell University Press.
BonJour, Laurence (1985) *The Structure of Empirical Knowledge*, Cambridge: Harvard University Press.
—— (1976) "The Coherence Theory of Empirical Knowledge," *Philosophical Studies*, 30.
Brandt, Richard (1979) *A Theory of the Good and the Right*, Oxford: Clarendon Press.
Brink, David (1989) *Moral Realism and the Foundations of Ethics*, Cambridge: University Press.
Cavell, Stanley (1987) *Disowning Knowledge*, Cambridge: University Press.
—— (1981) *Pursuits of Happiness*, Cambridge: Harvard University Press.
Chisholm, Roderick (1977) *Theory of Knowledge*, 2nd edition, Englewood Cliffs: Prentice Hall.
Daniels, Norman (1980) "Reflective Equilibrium and Archimedean Points," *Canadian Journal of Philosophy*, 10.
—— (1979) "Wide Reflective Equilibrium and Theory Acceptance in Ethics," *Journal of Philosophy*, 76.
—— (ed.) (1975) *Reading Rawls*, New York: Basic Books.
Dennett, Daniel C. (1971) "Intentional Systems," *Journal of Philosophy*, 68.
DePaul, Michael R. (1987) "Two Conceptions of Coherence Methods in Ethics," *Mind*, 96.
—— (1986a) "Coherence Methods in Ethics and the No Contact with Reality Objection," presented to the Central Division Meetings of the American Philosophical Association.
—— (1986b) "Reflective Equilibrium and Foundationalism," *American Philosophical Quarterly*, 23.
Dostoyevsky, Fyodor (1866) *Crime and Punishment*.
Foley, Richard (1987) *The Theory of Epistemic Rationality*, Cambridge: Harvard University Press.
Foley, Richard and Fumerton, Richard (1982) "Epistemic Indolence," *Mind*, 91.

Fraassen, Bas C. van (1993) "Rationality does not Require Conditionalization," in E. Ulman-Margalit (ed.), *The Israel Colloquium: Studies in the History, Philosophy and Sociology of Science*, 5, Dordrecht, Kluwer.

Gettier, Edmund (1963) "Is Justified True Belief Knowledge?" *Analysis*, 23.

Goldman, Alvin (1986) *Epistemology and Cognition*, Cambridge: Harvard University Press.

—— (1979) "What is Justified Belief?" in Pappas (1979).

Goodman, Nelson (1955) *Fact, Fiction and Forecast*, Cambridge: Harvard University Press.

Hare, R. M. (1981) *Moral Thinking*, New York: Oxford University Press.

—— (1973) "Rawls' Theory of Justice – I," *Philosophical Quarterly*, 23.

—— (1952) *The Language of Morals*, Oxford: Clarendon Press.

Harman, Gilbert (1980) "Reasoning and Evidence one does not Possess," *Midwest Studies in Philosophy*, 5.

—— (1977) *The Nature of Morality*, New York: Oxford University Press.

—— (1971) *Thought*, Princeton: University Press.

Honderich, Ted (ed.) (1985) *Morality and Objectivity*, London: Routledge & Kegan Paul.

Irwin, Terence (trans.) (1985) Aristotle, *Nicomachean Ethics*, Indianapolis: Hackett.

Keim, Albert N. (ed.) (1975) *Compulsory Education and the Amish: The Right Not to be Modern*, Boston: Beacon Press.

Kierkegaard, Søren (1843) *Either/Or*.

Lyons, David (1975) "Nature and Soundness of Contract and Coherence Arguments," in Daniels (1975).

McDowell, John (1985) "Values and Secondary Qualities," in Honderich.

MacIntyre, Alasdair (1981) *After Virtue*, Notre Dame: University of Notre Dame Press.

Magarshack, David (trans.) (1951) Fyodor Dostoyevsky, *Crime and Punishment*, London: Penguin Books.

Mill, John Stuart (1861) *Utilitarianism*.

—— (1859) *On Liberty*.

Nielsen, Kai (1979) "Our Considered Judgements," *Ratio*, 19.

Nussbaum, Martha (1990) *Love's Knowledge*, Oxford: University Press.

—— (1986) *The Fragility of Goodness*, Cambridge: University Press.

Pappas, George (ed.) (1979) *Justification and Knowledge*, Dordrecht: D. Reidel.

Pike, Nelson (1986) "John of the Cross on the Epistemic Value of Mystic Visions," in Audi and Wainwright (1986).

Plantinga, Alvin (1992) *Warrant*, Oxford: University Press.

—— (1990) "Justification in the 20th Century," *Philosophy and Phenomenological Research*, 50, Supplement.

—— (1988) "Positive Epistemic Status and Proper Function," *Philosophical Perspectives 2, Epistemology*, ed. James Tomberlin, Atascadero: Ridgeview Publishing Co.

Pollock, John (1986) *Contemporary Theories of Knowledge*, Savage, Maryland: Rowman and Littlefield Publishing Co.

Quinn, Philip (1991) "Hell in Amsterdam: Reflections on Camus's *The Fall*," *Midwest Studies in Philosophy*, 16.

—— (1989) "Tragic Dilemmas, Suffering Love, and Christian Life," *Journal of Religious Ethics*, 17.

Rawls, John (1980) "Kantian Constructivism in Moral Theory: The Dewey Lectures, 1980," *Journal of Philosophy*, 77 (Sept.).
—— (1974–5) "The Independence of Moral Theory," *Proceedings and Addresses of the American Philosophical Association*, 48.
—— (1971) *A Theory of Justice*, Cambridge: Harvard University Press.
—— (1951) "Outline of a Decision Procedure for Ethics," *Philosophical Review*, 60.
Richardson, Henry (1991) "The Emotions in Reflective Equilibrium," unpublished.
Ross, W. D. (trans.) (1925) Aristotle, *The Nicomachean Ethics*, Oxford: University Press.
Russell, Bertrand (1978) *Autobiography*, London: Unwin Paperbacks.
Shope, Robert (1983) *The Analysis of Knowing*, Princeton: University Press.
Singer, Peter (1974) "Sidgwick and Reflective Equilibrium," *Monist*, 58.
Sinnott-Armstrong, Walter (1988) *Moral Dilemmas*, Oxford: Basil Blackwell.
Sosa, Ernest (1974) "How do you Know?" *American Philosophical Quarterly*, 11. Reprinted in Ernest Sosa, *Knowledge in Perspective*, Cambridge: University Press, 1991.
Warnock, Mary (ed.) (1974) *John Stuart Mill: Utilitarianism and Other Writings*, New York: New American Library.
Wiggins, David (1987) *Needs, Values, Truth: Essays in the Philosophy of Value*, Aristotelian Society Series, 6, Oxford: Basil Blackwell.
Williams, Bernard (1985) *Ethics and the Limits of Philosophy*, Cambridge: Harvard University Press.

Index